SKYSCRAPER RIVALS

Skyscraper Rivals

The AIG Building and the Architecture of Wall Street

DANIEL M. ABRAMSON

PRINCETON ARCHITECTURAL PRESS

NEW YORK

PUBLISHED BY

Princeton Architectural Press

37 East 7th Street

New York, New York 10003

212.995.9620

For a free catalog of books, call 1.800.722.6657.

Visit our web site at www.papress.com.

©2001 American International Group, Inc.

All rights reserved

Printed and bound in Italy

03 02 01 00   5 4 3 2 1

First Edition

PROJECT EDITING: Clare Jacobson

COPY EDITING: Andrew Rubenfeld

SERIES DESIGN: Sara E. Stemen

BOOK DESIGN: Mia Ihara

SPECIAL THANKS TO: Ann Alter, Amanda Atkins, Eugenia Bell, Nicola Bednarek, Jan Cigliano, Jane Garvie, Caroline Green, Beth Harrison, Leslie Ann Kent, Mark Lamster, Anne Nitschke, Lottchen Shivers, Jennifer Thompson, and Deb Wood of Princeton Architectural Press —Kevin C. Lippert, publisher

HALF–TITLE PAGE: *Temple crests of the Bank of New York Building (left) and the National City Company Building (center), and the tower of the Cities Service Building (right).* Museum of the City of New York

TITLE PAGE: *Constructing the concrete cofferdam walls for the Cities Service Building's foundation.* Collection of The New-York Historical Society

LIBRARY OF CONGRESS CATALOGING-IN-PUBLICATION DATA

Abramson, Daniel M. (Daniel Michael), 1963–

Skyscraper rivals : the AIG Building and the architecture of Wall Street / Daniel M. Abramson.

p.   cm.

Includes bibliographical references (p.   ) and index.

ISBN 1-56898-244-5 (alk. paper)

1. AIG Building (New York, N.Y.) 2. 40 Wall Street (New York, N.Y.) 3. One Wall Street (New York, N.Y. : 1931–) 4. 20 Exchange Place (New York, N.Y.) 5. Skyscrapers—New York (State)—New York. 6. Art deco (Architecture)—New York (State)—New York. 7. Wall Street (New York, N.Y.)—History—20th century. 8. New York (N.Y.)—Buildings, structures, etc. I. Title.

NA6233.N5 A363 2000

720'.483'09747109042—dc21   00-010034

IMAGE CREDITS

All photographs by Norman McGrath are © Norman McGrath, all rights reserved.

The Sanborn Map™ on page 9 has been reproduced with written permission from the Sanborn Library, LLC. All further reproductions are prohibited without prior written permission from the Sanborn Library, LLC.

The image on page 180 has been reproduced with written permission from Corbis Corporation. All further reproductions are prohibited without prior written permission from Corbis Corporation.

Reproductions from *Architecture and Building* and *Through the Ages* appear courtesy of Avery Architectural and Fine Arts Library, Columbia University in the City of New York.

All New-York Historical Society reproductions are © Collection of The New-York Historical Society.

New York Public Library reproductions from Photographic Views of New York City Collection, Milstein Division of U.S. History, Local History and Genealogy, The New York Public Library, Astor, Lenox and Tilden Foundations.

CONTENTS

TO MY PARENTS, GRANDPARENTS, AND BROTHER

KEVIN LIPPERT AT PRINCETON ARCHITECTURAL PRESS INVITED ME TO WRITE THIS book, for which I am most grateful. From start to finish the project was supported generously in resources and spirit by AIG. Tufts University provided a leave in fall 1999 to complete the writing. The Getty Research Institute funded a trip to Los Angeles that was facilitated by Beth Ann Guynn.

The research for this book benefited considerably from the assistance and expertise of John Lovett at the University of Oklahoma; Christine McKay at The Bank of New York; Jean Elliott and Shelley Diamond at Chase Manhattan; Annette Dennis at HLW International; Anne-Sophie Roure at Avery Library, Columbia University; Lisa Prats and Stephanie Oppenheimer at the Building Owners and Managers Association International; Suzanne F. W. Lemakis, Ellen Quinn, and Joan Silverman at Citibank; Eileen Kennedy Morales and Elizabeth Ellis at the Museum of the City of New York; Mary Daniels, Ann Whiteside, and Alix Reiskind at Loeb Library, Harvard University; Kenneth Cobb at the City of New York Municipal Archives; and Robert Cicciari at 20 Exchange Place. Meredith Arms Bzdak, Chris Cavalier, Jeffrey Leighton, Neil Levine, Robert Makla, and Paul Watson all helped as well, along with my spring 1999 seminar on skyscrapers at Tufts.

Carol Willis' contributions have been of vital importance, especially her detailed comments on a first draft of the manuscript. Norman McGrath's photographs bring the buildings to life in color. Clare Jacobson has been the most patient, flexible, and astute editor imaginable.

Julie Iovine and Kevin, Christopher, and Cooper Lippert made my trips to New York always a pleasure. My wife Penley Knipe sustains me everyday.

Marcus Samuel Abramson, my grandfather, spent his working life at 60 John Street. This book is dedicated to him and my family of New Yorkers: Marcus and Pnina Abramson, Albert and Annette Amitay, Lee and Frances Amitay Abramson, and Marc Abramson.

185:—DOWNTOWN SKYSCRAPERS, NEW YORK.

THE FINANCIAL CENTER OF THE WORLD.   44253

PREFACE

WALL STREET. THE SHORT NAME FOR NEW YORK'S FINANCIAL district and its economic activities is world famous, but the physical place is indistinct, even to many native New Yorkers. Its confusing colonial streets tend to curve like cow paths and have names (not sensible numbers) such as Pine, Cedar, and Maiden Lane. The Lower Manhattan skyline, likewise, is instantly recognizable, but, beyond a few key towers such as the Woolworth Building and World Trade Center, its skyscrapers are oddly anonymous. People everywhere know the Empire State and the Chrysler buildings, but the contemporary suite of Wall Street towers designed and constructed in the late 1920s and early thirties have remained obscure and unsung, until *Skyscraper Rivals*.

In the 1930s, the downtown skyline of stepped-back masses and slender spires established New York as *the* modern metropolis. Since the late nineteenth century, Lower Manhattan's skyscrapers offered the first glimpse of New York to millions of newcomers, but the harbor view in the thirties was different. Not just taller, the new towers were distinctive in shape, style, and scale. The striking period photographs and prints collected in this book illustrate the contrast of old and new. In previous decades, the downtown skyline was composed of boxy, elongated rectangles of various proportions, punctuated by a few ornate landmark towers. As late as 1925, the view of Lower Manhattan from the Brooklyn docks (*Fig. 1*) was still dominated by giants of the pre–World War I cycle of construction. They were (in ascending height), the Bankers Trust, Equitable, Singer, and Woolworth, respectively, the world's tallest banking structure, the largest office building, the tallest office building in 1908, and the reigning record holder in height.

By 1931, a similar East River view (*Fig. 2*) shows the city utterly transformed. Pyramids of various shapes and sizes, but with the same characteristic stepped form required by zoning, predominated. Soaring shafts of sixty or more stories clustered near Wall Street, dwarfing the Bankers Trust and making the once-commanding Singer and Woolworth buildings look like fancy toys. The simplified setback silhouettes cropped up all over the financial district, from the southern end of Broad Street near the tip of the island to the burgeoning insurance district around John Street to the north.

This formal transformation was all the more remarkable for its speed. The story of the four major towers of *Skyscraper Rivals* transpires in the years between 1928 and 1932. The boom cycle that began in the mid-1920s and flared out by 1932 added some thirty million square feet of office space to Lower Manhattan. Most of this space came on the market in 1930–31. Skylines grow in spurts because real-estate booms, like stock market highs, are part sound economics and part psychology. As a general rule, a skyline represents a three-dimensional graph of a boom in which the tallest buildings appear at the peak, when escalating land values, easily available financing, and a dose of competitiveness combine to drive up the number of tower floors.

Also astonishing is the extraordinary concentration of construction in the core of the financial district around the New York Stock Exchange and the major investment houses. Given its historically high land values and strong demand for prime office space, Wall Street was surprisingly slow to give way to skyscrapers. Perhaps the conservative and clubby world of bankers was the reason that the nineteenth-century buildings with their posh executive offices, but limited areas of work space, survived so long. When the change came, the older structures collapsed as if on a fault line. If one mapped all the sites under construction in 1928 to 1931, the area would cover about a quarter of the financial district. Think of it: during those four years, a major part of every block was, in succession, a hole in the ground, a staging area for materials deliveries by hundreds of trucks, a ruckus of riveters, a neck-craning spectacle of steel erection, then a shell alive with workers of the finishing trades. No wonder the vacancy rate downtown remained low through 1930; much of the district's office population was displaced during construction.

These new towers of the financial district were different in character from the Art Deco extravaganzas of midtown. For the most part, as Daniel Abramson carefully details, they were traditional in design and upscale in the use of materials, especially limestone on facades and rich marbles and metals in lobbies, as befitted the banking institutions and their associated professions. There were some flashes of glamour—for example, the red and gold mosaic reception room at One Wall Street—but otherwise the Art Deco styling, even in such glorious cases as the Cities Service/AIG Building at 70 Pine Street, was restrained by standards of midtown, where signature skyscrapers such as the Empire State, Chrysler, and RCA buildings monumentalized their modernity in two-story lobbies. The star-power towers and a chorus of Art Deco dolls such as the Chanin, Fred French, and Paramount buildings reflected midtown's more commercial character as a district that mixed business, shopping, and entertainment and that opened its storefronts to the street to seduce pedestrians. Downtown was a zone of work and an interior environment of privilege and status.

Skyscraper Rivals goes behind the scenes to try to understand this world. Abramson's text includes characters as colorful as the Cities Service Company president Henry L. Doherty or as faceless as the bank building committees who commissioned One Wall Street and City Bank Farmers Trust. His last chapter, "Skyscraper Lives," explores the interior, gendered world of the towers from the basement to the boardroom. The sumptuous banking halls, executive suites, and private luncheon clubs, so beautifully illustrated here in the companies' own commissioned photographs, were the male domain of the upscale tenants, mainly investment bankers, brokers, lawyers, and industrialists. The typical office was a hierarchic space that separated men and women as boss and secretary, or supervisor and typing pool. The building services were also segregated, with mail-room males and security guards and an unusual corps of female elevator operators at the Cities Service Building. The culture of business and the culture of buildings were consistent in the twenties and thirties.

The array of sources Abramson has mined for his collective portrait of the downtown towers shows how persistent digging can pay off. The resources are widely scattered. A trip to Oklahoma to the Cities Service Oil and Gas Corporation Collection yielded background information on the company's real-estate holdings, building directories, and some promotional literature. Albums on the City Bank Farmers Trust Building acquired from a dealer by The Getty Research Institute offered clues about that tower's development. Several corporate archives have preserved old company newsletters that announced building plans or memorandums that recorded dates or decisions about design. A few individual architectural studies, working drawings, or other documents dispersed in various New York museums and libraries helped to identify which member of a firm or which architect in a collaboration was responsible for the design. Skyscrapers were a popular subject in the contemporary press and among photographers and artists, and Abramson has used the texts and images of period observers to great effect.

At the same time, it is disheartening to realize how much material on these commercial buildings and others less spectacular has been lost. There are, for example, no surviving records for architectural firms as important to the development of the financial district as Clinton & Russell, whose partnership, established in 1894, was responsible for at least a dozen downtown high rises, including the Broad-Exchange Building at 25 Broad Street and the Hudson Terminals, which early in the century were two of the largest office buildings in the city and the world. As Abramson explains, the firm continued under the name Clinton & Russell after the death of the principals in 1910 and 1907 and was rechristened Clinton & Russell, Holton & George in 1926. As architects of the Cities Service Building the firm produced one of the most inspired Art Deco towers of the period and a building with numerous technological innovations, yet we cannot say with any certainty who in the office designed the tower or how the office functioned.

We also know little about the operations of architects such as Trowbridge & Livingston, the blue-chip firm that nearly cornered the market on commissions at the intersection of Wall, Broad, and Nassau streets—the Bankers Trust tower, the headquarters for J. P. Morgan, and the office annex of the New York Stock Exchange—or of the brothers Cross & Cross, architects of the tower for City Bank Farmers Trust, who practiced both design and real-estate development. There are few comprehensive collections of records of New York architectural practices in institutional collections. In cases where extensive office records of large firms do exist, such as for McKim, Mead & White or Cass Gilbert, academic attention has generally focused on the principals and on "who designed what" rather than on how a firm was organized to execute large commissions. In contrast, scholarship on Chicago architects—for example, the writings of Robert Bruegmann on Holabird and Roche and Sally Kitt Chappell on Graham, Anderson, Probst and White—has explored the nature of commercial practice. In New York, a city with far more skyscrapers, but far less public appreciation of its history, the drawings and records of major firms have not been preserved or interpreted with the same diligence.

Histories of major buildings can sometimes be pieced together from various sources, and the composite picture is instructive, for the assembled facts contradict oft-repeated stories that probably had their origin in the publicist's office. One of the most familiar tales is the race between the Chrysler Building and 40 Wall Street (or The Manhattan Company Building) to claim the title of world's tallest skyscraper. The drama has two aspects: one is the contest of height; the other is the rivalry between the architects William Van Alen and H. Craig Severance, who had once been partners. Many a television documentary has repeated the story of how each architect thought his tower might be tallest and so kept the final height secret for fear of being surpassed. In September 1929, when both buildings topped out their steel frames, the Chrysler Building staged a public relations coup: workers cranked up its 185-foot silver spike from inside the scalloped spire to establish the official height as 1046 feet, some 120 feet taller than the needle point of 40 Wall Street.

People love this anecdote, but the full story is more complicated, as Abramson's research suggests. Although Severance's name was the one most often associated with the design of 40 Wall Street, he was not the principal architect, but one of a team, each of whom represented the several investors' interests. Severance probably acted as the business manager of the project (the same role he played in his partnership with Van Alen), while the chief designer was likely Yasuo Matsui who, drawings record, developed the massing and the exterior treatment. Matsui maintained that there was no race and that the building's height related directly to economic calculations of cost and return. In fact, it is rarely the architect who decides how tall a skyscraper will be; that determination is made by owners in consultation with, especially, elevator consultants and rental agents.

While the notion of a deliberate race among the downtown towers is misleading, the idea of *competition* is essential for understanding any commercial architecture. Skyscrapers are business rivals, competitors for tenants, light and air, and prestige. Owners and architects like to distinguish their buildings from others, and height is one way to make a structure stand out. Great height has advertising value, because visibility and image-ability create a sort of skyline logo. Likewise, naming a tower for a large corporation, even if it is not the owner or major tenant, can lend cachet and help attract other upscale clients; this was the strategy at 40 Wall Street, where the building was promoted as The Manhattan Company Building by its speculative developers. The business of real estate—of erecting and owning buildings—is in large part the business of creating value. A good address, a prestigious name, an impressive lobby, or a distinctive crown is a device a developer can use to enhance a building's marketability.

Another supposed verity about skyscrapers, especially the tallest ones, is that they are driven up by ego. Abramson takes a clear-eyed view of the issue and has done his best to research the motives of the men who commissioned the Wall Street towers, but pronouncements of their reasons for building—especially self-promotional ones—are rare. If they intended to immortalize themselves in stone and steel, they fell far short, for until this book, they have remained virtually anonymous. The ambition most evident in their projects was one with which Wall Street remains very familiar: making money.

It is ironic, then, that the moguls, bankers, and investors who created the Wall Street skyscrapers played the real-estate market so badly, for their towers were all completed—indeed, some were begun—well after Black Tuesday in October 1929. The stock market crash did not dislodge the belief, fervently expressed by most of the leaders in the financial and building industries in 1930, that demand would rebound. The rising towers remained assertions of optimism; the costly colored marble lobbies and opulent executive offices and board rooms were installed without compromise. As Abramson shows, the original decisions to construct new buildings made in the heady days of the bull market seemed entirely rational. Still, one has to wonder how the men who undertook to erect such enormous containers of space could have ignored the scene before their eyes—that is, the nearly continuous construction site that was the financial district at the end of the twenties. How could they not have paused to consider who would fill all this new space or how the volume would affect their investments?

As the country slipped into the depths of the Great Depression, the vacancy rate downtown climbed toward twenty-five percent. The oversupply of office space would not be fully absorbed until after World War II, and, naturally, no new buildings were initiated until the twenties surplus (with its very competitive rents) was leased. The first postwar skyscraper erected in the financial district was One Chase Manhattan Plaza, completed in 1961.

While Lower Manhattan suffered the effects of overbuilding for nearly thirty years, commercial construction revived more quickly in midtown where, especially on Park Avenue near Grand Central Terminal, many major corporations established new headquarters. Some of these, such as the Lever House, the Seagram Building, and the Union Carbide Building, were striking statements of International Style modernism—prismatic towers rising from an open plaza. Their taut glass walls sealed in a new kind of office interior—an open plan, air-conditioned and brightly illuminated.

Downtown's identity remained frozen in stone. The black-and-white beauty of its masonry-clad towers was fixed in the photographs and prints of WPA artists of the thirties and *noire* films of the fifties, and etched in the memories of more than one generation as the iconic New York skyline. Larger—but lesser—towers of our present day, with their expanses of glass or prefab panels, have made many people nostalgic for the materials and the craftsmanship of the twenties. The sculpted limestone facade of One Wall Street, the tonal gradations of the bricks of the Cities Service tower, and the giant hooded figures atop the City Bank Farmers Trust silently assert affluence. The imposing banking halls and lavish lobbies, with their special artistic programs of murals or sculpture, celebrated democracy, industry, and abundance with absolute confidence. "Above the waters stands the magic mountain of steel and stone, shining and glorious, one of the crowns of human endeavor," effused the prominent architect and historian Fiske Kimball in his late-twenties text, *American Architecture*. Other critics, such as Lewis Mumford, held more skeptical views of the quintessential architecture of capitalism, but they, too, noted the symbolic power of the great stone pyramids.

For the first half of the twentieth century, the visual gravity of downtown's skyline and the center of gravity of New York's business community was Wall Street. But the centering forces began to weaken in the sixties. Downtown lost its dominance as the largest business district, slipping to third in the nation, after midtown Manhattan and Chicago, in the total volume of office space. A new shape and scale of construction overwhelmed the twenties towers. With the technology of fluorescent lights and cooled air, the floor plans of office buildings became solid rectangles without light courts. Reinforcing the aesthetics of the International Style, the 1961 zoning law replaced the setback form of base and slender spire with sheer-walled slabs, often surrounded by plazas. As working wharves receded into history, the biggest buildings rose at the edges of the island, along Water Street and on the west side. The twin towers of the World Trade Center, each 110 stories and nearly four million square feet of floor area, represented the extreme of this new scale, but through the boom of the late 1960s and early 1970s, most skyscrapers were exceptionally large, bulky boxes.

Bigger and better. An American maxim of the past century is a sentiment far less popular today, especially in New York City, where the politics of height generally oppose tall towers. Many of downtown's titans of the twenties and thirties have been overpowered or boxed in by blank giants. The romantic skyline of Lower Manhattan, dominated by the elegant, aspiring forms of the great Art Deco towers, survives only in a magnificent photographic record that is richly sampled in this book. Fortunately, the individual buildings survive in all their glory for us to visit and admire. What is astonishing is that such stars have for so long remained unknown, unstudied objects of reverie. With *Skyscraper Rivals*, at last they have a serious history.

Carol Willis
Founding Director, The Skyscraper Museum
New York City

Chapter One

INTRODUCTION

Financial district skyscrapers from the East River.

TOP: FIG. 1. *Lower Manhattan's prewar skyline seen from Brooklyn around 1925 with the Woolworth Building at the far right and in the middle the domed Singer Tower, the boxy Equitable Building, and the pyramid-capped Bankers Trust Building.* New York Public Library

BOTTOM: FIG. 2. *Lower Manhattan's 1931 skyline transformed by the central spires of the City Bank Farmers Trust Building, One Wall Street, 40 Wall Street, and the Cities Service (now AIG) Building, still under construction. 120 Wall Street dominates the waterfront, with 99 Wall Street to its left and One Cedar Street to its right.* Library of Congress

THE SKYSCRAPER EXPLOSION IN NEW YORK'S FINANCIAL DISTRICT OF THE late 1920s and early 1930s revolutionized the Lower Manhattan skyline. Instead of a broad plateau stretching from the Battery to City Hall, pierced by a few towers, there rose a great pyramid focused on Wall Street and surmounted by soaring new skyscrapers (*Figs. 1 and 2*). Celebrated in art and mass culture, the financial district skyline symbolized twentieth-century New York's congestion, dynamism, and modernity. Subsumed within the ensemble, however, were the new buildings' individual identities. Who owned and designed these Wall Street area skyscrapers, and why? How did the buildings accommodate their thousands of daily inhabitants within the life of the city?

FIG. 3. *The Cities Service Building (1930–32, Clinton & Russell, Holton & George) soars above South Street with 40 Wall Street in the background in this 1935 rendering by John Wenrich.* The Landmark Society of Western New York

This book began as a study of the Wall Street area's tallest skyscraper, the 66-story AIG Building (1930–32), first known as the Cities Service Building and Sixty Wall Tower, and now also as 70 Pine Street (*Fig. 3*). When completed, the 952-foot Cities Service Building was the world's third tallest skyscraper, after the Empire State and Chrysler buildings. Owned by a large utilities conglomerate, the brick-clad Cities Service Building was "considered off the beaten path," at the financial district's north-eastern corner.[1] Isolation enhanced the sculpted tower's prominence and helped its streamlined profile become a favorite subject of artists, including the photographer Arthur Fellig, known as Weegee, who thought it "the most beautiful building of all."[2] The building's architects, the firm of Clinton & Russell, Holton & George (with

FIG. 4. *Lower Manhattan c. 1950 seen from above the East River with the Cities Service Building, right of center, and, to its left, 40 Wall Street, the City Bank Farmers Trust Building, and One Wall Street.* Courtesy of AIG Archives Department

Thomas J. George as designer), embellished the Cities Service Building's lobby in an exuberant Art Deco style, and placed a jewel box of an observation gallery on the 66th floor. Inspired and directed by Cities Service founder Henry L. Doherty as well as company engineers, the skyscraper was filled with the latest technology, including hot-water heating and double-deck elevators, plus an in-house gymnasium and law library to attract tenants to the upper rental floors. Today, the Cities Service (now AIG) Building remains Lower Manhattan's third tallest spire (after the World Trade Center towers) and a classic example of twentieth-century skyscraper architecture.

Though rich in detail, an isolated narrative of the Cities Service Building's story misses the fullness of its situation within the financial district. A complete picture of its architectural typicality and uniqueness, its economic and social character, means studying the district in total. Hence this book draws a composite portrait of Wall Street's skyscraper development in the 1920s and 1930s, with a special emphasis on the Cities Service Building and its three main skyscraper rivals (*Fig. 4*).

FIG. 5. *40 Wall Street (1929–30, Severance and Matsui), home of The Manhattan Company, as seen from the west, and framed to the left by the pyramidal cap of the Bankers Trust Building and to the right by the Equitable Building's setbacks.* Library of Congress

After the Cities Service Building the financial district's next highest structure was the 927-foot 40 Wall Street (1929–30, also known as The Manhattan Company Building and now the Trump Building) (*Fig. 5*). Initiated as a speculative development by the banker George L. Ohrstrom and the builder William A. Starrett, 40 Wall Street became the home of The Manhattan Company when that banking corporation included its site with that of the new skyscraper. The lead architect H. Craig Severance and the probable designer Yasuo Matsui oversaw collaboratively the rapid construction of the brick-clad tower, capped by a pyramidal crest in a "modernized French Gothic" style, and with a Greek colonnade along its base.[3] Inside, The Manhattan Company's architect Morrell Smith, assisted by the firm of Walker & Gillette, designed a grand second-story bank hall and American colonial style executive offices. The 71-story building contained more total office space (845,000 square feet) than any other financial district building constructed between the wars, much of it rented to financial service firms.

FIG. 6. *The City Bank Farmers Trust Building (1930–31, Cross & Cross) facing west toward William Street with a chamfered corner to Beaver Street.* Getty Research Library, 940010

FIG. 7. *One Wall Street (1929–31, Voorhees, Gmelin & Walker), home of the Irving Trust Company, rising above Trinity Church and its graveyard.* Norman McGrath

Next in height the 760-foot City Bank Farmers Trust Building (1930–31, now 20 Exchange Place) made a distinctive impression at the financial district's southeast corner, its elegant chamfered shaft offset above the large trapezoidal base (*Fig. 6*). Designed by the commercial and country house architects Cross & Cross (with George Maguolo as chief designer), the 54-story City Bank Farmers Trust Building embodied the venerable institution's culture. Stone-clad in limestone to a greater height than any other building in the world, the "conservative modern" skyscraper featured emblematic art and a large wood-paneled senior officers' hall beneath the bank's eight floors of offices.[4]

The financial district's fourth highest tower, the 654-foot One Wall Street (1929–31) was built by the Irving Trust Company at the prestigious southeast corner of Broadway and Wall Street, a site chosen to draw maximum attention to the bank (*Fig. 7*). For similar reasons, the Irving Trust Company hired the artistically ambitious firm of Voorhees, Gmelin & Walker and, as a design consultant, Yale art school dean Everett V. Meeks. The 50-story skyscraper's fluted, rhythmic limestone wall hung like a textured curtain over the step-backed mass and tower. Inside One Wall Street the design team, including artist Hildreth Meiere, created a dazzling ground-floor reception room and a muraled tenants' lobby, plus a three-story-high penthouse lounge for bank officials.

Besides the four highest towers, a score of other major skyscrapers were erected in the 1920s and early 1930s in the financial district: an area defined by the real estate industry as roughly south of Maiden Lane between the Hudson and East rivers, with the John Street insurance district part of the area's northerly expansion (*Fig. 8*).[5] Large major office buildings by Ely Jacques Kahn, Shreve, Lamb & Harmon, and Clinton & Russell, Holton & George rose along John Street. Overlooking the Hudson River along West Street appeared skyscrapers by Starrett & Van Vleck and farther inland, on Greenwich and Rector streets, a 450-foot tower designed by Lafayette Goldstone. The district's prime north–south arteries of Broadway and Broad Street filled up with large corporate headquarters, including the Standard Oil and Cunard buildings along Broadway, and the Equitable Trust and Continental Bank buildings along Broad Street. Wall Street itself rose to new heights with a series of financial service headquarters by Trowbridge & Livingston, Benjamin W. Morris, and Delano & Aldrich, and, near the East River, a pair of austere blocks by Ely Jacques Kahn and Schwartz & Gross.

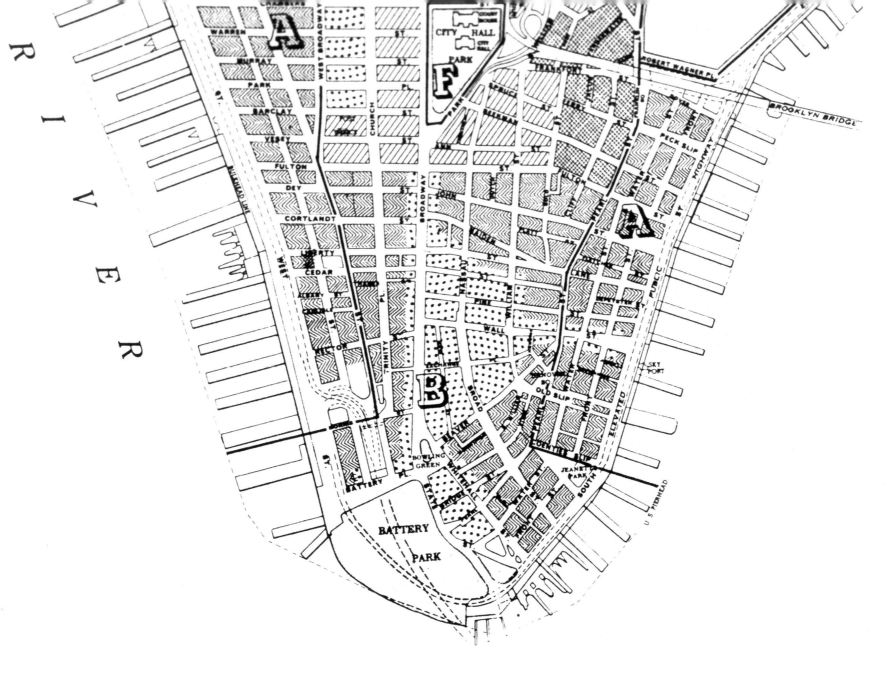

FIG. 8. *Map of Lower Manhattan c. 1955 showing the area dotted around Wall Street zoned for business use, surrounded by herringboned areas for unrestricted use.*

Copyright 2000 Sanborn Map Company

FIG. 9. *Wall Street looking west around 1850 to Trinity Church (1839–46, Richard Upjohn) with the flagged U.S. Custom House (later Sub-Treasury, 1834–42, Town & Davis) looking down Broad Street, and with various bank buildings in the foreground, including The Manhattan Company's at the right with Oceanus and his trident on the roof.*
Collection of The New-York Historical Society

WALL STREET'S ARCHITECTURE BEFORE 1920

Wall Street's skyscraper roots reach back deeply into the district's history. In the seventeenth-century, Dutch colonists laid out the district's uneven colonial street pattern, which helped produce the modern skyline character and distinctive massings. In the mid-nineteenth century, major monuments, built after a devastating 1835 fire, relate directly to the district's circa 1930 skyscrapers (*Fig. 9*). Richard Upjohn rebuilt Trinity Church (1839–46). Its Gothic verticality would echo across Broadway in One Wall Street's fluted walls. At the head of Broad Street, Town & Davis designed the Greek Revival United States Custom House (later Sub-Treasury, 1834–42, and now Federal Hall National Memorial). Its Doric colonnade influenced 40 Wall Street's nearby base. Isaiah Rogers designed at 55 Wall Street the great domed Merchants Exchange (1836–42, expanded 1901–7), which was connected by a rear bridge to the City Bank Farmers Trust Building.

Next, in the 1850s and 1860s, along Wall Street rose ornate five- to six-story brownstone palazzi for banks and insurance companies. In the 1870s and 1880s appeared the first nascent "sky-scrapers," a term introduced around 1883 to describe skeletal metal frame buildings of about a dozen stories that utilized modern elevators

FIG. 10. *60 Wall Street (1905, Clinton & Russell), where Henry L. Doherty established the Cities Service Company on the street front block's 14ᵗʰ floor, and later put his company sign over the Ionic entrance.* Western History Collections, University of Oklahoma Libraries

and accommodated a growing office worker population. The 1890s witnessed improvements to skyscraper structural and mechanical technologies, including pneumatic caisson foundations and central heating as well as new exterior articulations of buildings now topping twenty stories as a base, shaft, and attic, ornamented in light-toned, classical, textured surfaces of stone and terra cotta.

"Current American architecture is not a matter of art, but of business," wrote the critic Barr Ferree in 1893.[6] Skyscrapers in New York, Chicago, and other American cities were constructed primarily for profit, whether the owner was an investment syndicate or a corporation occupying several stories and renting out the rest. Architects, too, operated like businessmen, developing their own projects, and running offices along corporate lines with hierarchical divisions of labor. These turn-of-the-century professional trends would intensify in the production of Wall Street's later skyscrapers.

FIG. 11. *Wall Street looking west c. 1923 dominated by the pyramid-capped Bankers Trust Building (1909–12, Trowbridge & Livingston) and the foreground, colonnaded Merchants Exchange (1836–42, Isaiah Rogers; expanded 1907, McKim, Mead & White) with 60 Wall Street to the right.* Collection of The New-York Historical Society

In the 1900s Wall Street area skyscrapers grew in height and bulk, as developers assembled larger lots, and corporations and small businesses sought increased modern accommodations. At the intersection of Broad Street and Exchange Place, for example, the 20-story Broad-Exchange Building (1900–2; *Fig. 80*) encompassed some 340,000 square feet of rentable office space, making it the largest office building yet built.[7] The architects were Clinton & Russell, a firm founded in 1894 by the partnership of Charles W. Clinton with the younger William Hamilton Russell. One of the financial district's most prolific practices in the 1900s, Clinton & Russell also designed 60 Wall Street (1903–5), the first home of Henry L. Doherty and his Cities Service Company (*Fig. 10*). Long after Clinton and Russell died, the Cities Service Building (connected to 60 Wall Street by a 16th-floor bridge over Pine Street) would be the firm's swan song, produced under the guidance of partners Alfred J. S. Holton and Thomas J. George.

In the years around 1910 landmark towers with distinctive crests sprung up to satisfy corporate desire for publicity. The 612-foot Singer Tower (1906–8) by Ernest Flagg at 149 Broadway, with its domed mansard crest, rose higher than any other building in the world. The 539-foot Bankers Trust Building (1909–12) by Trowbridge & Livingston at Wall and Nassau streets terminated with a distinctive stepped-pyramid crest (*Fig. 11*). Topping all was the fantastic Gothic cap of Cass Gilbert's 792-foot Woolworth Building (1910–13) north of the financial district proper facing City Hall Park, and "a giant signboard" according to its owner.[8] Each of these major buildings would influence the design of later Wall Street area skyscrapers.

The turn-of-the-century building boom came to a resounding conclusion with a 1911 recession and the construction of the Equitable Life Assurance Building (1913–15) at 120 Broadway by the Chicago firm of Graham, Burnham & Company. This 38-story, 1.25 million square-foot behemoth completed the prewar skyline and seemed to embody the skyscraper's general ill effects on the city. Since the 1890s critics had assailed skyscrapers for blocking neighbors' light and views, congesting streets, offending aesthetic sensibilities, straining municipal services, devaluing adjacent properties, and endangering health by trapping noxious dust and vapors. Architects joined planners, engineers, public health experts, citizens, and businessmen in calling for restrictions on skyscraper building, leading to the 1916 passage of New York's landmark zoning law.

The new zoning code divided the city into use areas, with the financial district zoned to maintain the status quo of office business in the center and unrestricted commercial, mercantile, and light industrial activities along its edges (*Fig. 8*). To further protect property values and limit skyscraper bulk, the 1916 law also divided the city into height districts, with building massings determined by the width of adjacent streets. Again in accordance with the status quo, the financial district was allowed the maximum building sizes. The base of financial district skyscrapers could rise two and one-half times the width of adjacent streets. Above the base a skyscraper had to set back one foot for each vertical rise equal to its height district factor multiplied by two. Thus financial district buildings were step-backed one foot for every five-foot rise. On over a quarter of the lot area could be built a tower of unrestricted height. The 1916 zoning code created the characteristic pyramidal New York skyscraper formula: a full base, a set-back midsection, and a high tower.

The story of Wall Street's architecture up to 1916 has been ably told in Lois Severini's *The Architecture of Finance: Early Wall Street* (1983) and Sarah Bradford Landau and Carl W. Condit's authoritative *Rise of the New York Skyscraper, 1865–1913* (1996). The period from around 1920 through the early years of the Depression in New York City's architecture has been generally treated in Robert A. M. Stern and his colleagues' encyclopedic *New York 1930: Architecture and Urbanism Between the Two World Wars* (1987), which includes several sections on Wall Street area skyscrapers

FIG. 12. *The financial district skyline photographed in 1936 by Berenice Abbott from Pier 11 along the East River showing, left to right, the City Bank Farmers Trust Building, 63 Wall Street (1927, Delano & Aldrich), 40 Wall Street, 99 Wall Street (1930–31, Schwartz & Gross), the Cities Service Building, and 120 Wall Street (1930, Ely Jacques Kahn).* Museum of the City of New York

and their styles, particularly Art Deco (which Stern divides into "Modern Classicism" and "Modern Naturalism").[9] The present book, *Skyscraper Rivals*, also discusses the aesthetics of the Wall Street area skyscrapers, especially Art Deco masterpieces such as the Cities Service Building. But this book examines just as closely issues of planning, use, and technology as well as social, professional, urban, and financial matters. Highlighting economics and planning in skyscraper architecture has been the achievement of Carol Willis, culminating in her important book, *Form Follows Finance: Skyscrapers and Skylines in New York and Chicago* (1995). Willis' thesis is that "skyscrapers should best be understood both as the locus of business and as businesses themselves."[10] The present work follows Willis' premise and applies it in detail to the Wall Street area skyscrapers.

Skyscraper Rivals has been written for the reader interested in the financial district's skyscrapers, without requiring a specialist's knowledge. The sequence of chapters presents a general story about skyscraper architecture in the 1920s and 1930s, organized by theme and grounded in the particularities of the district's buildings. The first chapters are on the clients and architects, then skyscraper planning, construction, technology, interiors, and exteriors. The penultimate chapter examines skyscraper rituals, working lives, and the buildings' meanings within the New York metropolis and American culture. A postscript summarizes the story up to today. Overall, a picture takes shape of Wall Street area skyscraper architecture, many of whose points and conclusions apply equally to commercial office buildings and sky-scrapers in midtown Manhattan, Chicago, and other American cities. For specialists the book offers new primary material on all four major exemplars, plus extensive ref-erences to contemporary literature. From corporate and academic archive collections come publicity documents, construction drawings, photographs, and other valuable material which are detailed in the bibliography.

The building names used in this book follow original designations, since the book is about the skyscrapers when they were first built. The familiar marketing monikers are used for 40 Wall Street (rather than The Manhattan Company Building) and One Wall Street (rather than the Irving Trust Building). The current AIG Building is called the Cities Service Building, rather than Sixty Wall Tower, to avoid confusion with the present 60 Wall Street, and to emphasize the skyscraper's early and strong corporate identity.

The Cities Service Building and its contemporaries vied with each other for pres-tige, publicity, and tenants. Unique crests, fine materials, height, style, and beautiful lobbies distinguished one building from the other, bringing honor to owners and attracting tenants (*Fig. 12*). Skyscraper rivalries were a serious matter, with millions of invested dollars at stake in each project, as well as architects' and owners' reputa-tions. Still, there was a sense of commonality in the rivalry, a word whose Latin derivation, *rivalis*, means "one who uses a stream in common with another." All the architects believed in the skyscraper form's capacity for beauty, efficiency, and prof-itability. All the owners believed in Wall Street's primacy as a business district and in the virtues of capitalism. Out of these shared convictions, as well a sense of rivalry, came the efflorescence of the Wall Street area skyscrapers.

Chapter Two

THE CLIENTS

Proposed Cities Service skyscrapers at Battery Park.

FIG. 13. *The open-air stock exchange of the Curb Market on Broad Street c. 1914 before the exchange moved indoors and eventually to its own 1930 building on Trinity Place (now the American Stock Exchange).* Library of Congress

O N MAY 13, 1932, HENRY L. DOHERTY, FOUNDER AND PRESIDENT OF THE Cities Service Company, formally opened his corporation's new Pine Street skyscraper headquarters. Floodlights bathed the 66-story Cities Service Building's stainless steel mast 952 feet above the ground. Moonbeams powered Doherty's voice on radio nationwide. A year earlier the City Bank Farmers Trust Building and One Wall Street had been similarly inaugurated with visitors, telegrams, and flowers. In the spring of 1930 The Manhattan Company took occupancy of 40 Wall Street's lower floors.

Noticeably all these skyscrapers opened in the midst of a deepening recession. "As the stock averages have gone down, the average height of the buildings in the grand canyon of finance have gone up," wryly noted Charles Puckette in *The New York Times*.[1] In the same month that Doherty opened the Cities Service Building, tens of thousands of impoverished war veterans marched on Washington, D.C. On the surface of it, construction of the Wall Street area skyscrapers at the beginning of the Great Depression appears downright foolhardy. However, a look back to Wall Street in the 1920s illuminates the rationale for these skyscraper climaxes.

WALL STREET IN THE 1920s

On Wall Street, America's "Seven Fat Years of Prosperity" (1922–29) meant boom times and fundamental change. Evolved from its early days as a commercial port, Lower Manhattan in the 1920s superceded London as the center of world finance. Here

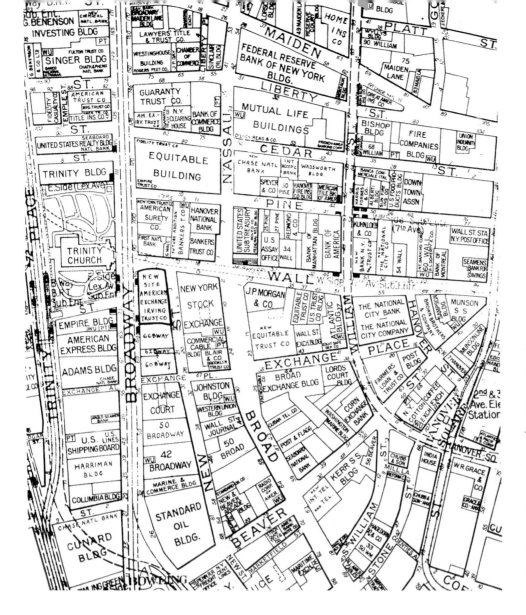

FIG. 14. *The financial district c. 1928 showing the site of the Irving Trust Company's One Wall Street at the intersection of Broadway and Wall Street, plus the various parcels of the future 40 Wall Street between the U.S. Assay Office and the Bank of Manhattan Building; the future City Bank Farmers Trust Building site in the trapezoidal block south of Exchange Place occupied by the Farmers Loan & Trust Company; and the future Cities Service Building site between Pine and Cedar streets in the open area east of the Downtown Association.* The Bank of New York Archives

traders dealt in commodities. Corporations and governments raised money. Investors speculated in securities (*Fig. 13*). Ten separate exchanges specialized in stocks, bonds, cotton, coffee, sugar, metal, rubber, and leather. In and around Wall Street big industrial corporations headquartered themselves close to their bankers. Hundreds of insurance companies, brokerage houses, law firms, and transport companies kept the financial machinery going. Meanwhile, stock ticker machines blossomed across the country and hard-selling brokers peddled Wall Street's latest offerings to prosperous middle-class Americans. Wall Street's banks, financing the booming stock market, merged to achieve economies of scale along with greater profits, market share, branch networks, and efficiency in serving corporate America. Consolidation was also the hallmark of the public utilities, railroad, telephone, and insurance industries. Massive holding companies headquartered around Wall Street, such as Standard Oil and the Cities Service conglomerate, aggressively marketed securities to finance their acquisition of subsidiaries.

Each day about half a million commuters streamed into Lower Manhattan, from executives and stock salesmen to cleaning women and file clerks. The financial district centered on Wall Street and the north–south thoroughfares of Broadway and Broad Street (*Fig. 14*). In this compact area businessmen clustered because of "the efficiency of proximity."[2] Even as the telephone enabled information to be transferred across continents and oceans, the "managerial function of coordination and control" stayed a matter of one-to-one relations. "The personal conference remains, after all, the method by which most of the important work is done," observed the Columbia University economist R. M. Haig in 1930.[3] "The financial district is in effect one big structure," Haig noted, linked together by interlocking webs of symbiotic interests.

In the late 1920s Wall Street had to grow vertically if it was to continue to be the nerve center of American and global business. Enlarged corporations needed space to amalgamate. Small firms needed space to expand. New firms needed to establish a foothold. And all needed to be close together to survive and prosper. Under these conditions a handful of corporations and developers pressed forward in the late 1920s with plans for the area's great skyscrapers.

CITIES SERVICE

The Cities Service Company was a classic creature of 1920s Wall Street. Its rise to prominence was based on financial cunning and public relations as much as on administrative and engineering expertise (*Fig. 15*). Organized to hold subsidiary companies' securities, Cities Service grew rapidly in the 1920s as national consumption of electricity, petroleum, and natural gas skyrocketed. The name captured the conglomerate's mission: to profit from utilities services for America's urban areas. Its formula for success was "acquire, rebuild, merge, refinance, infuse new life and new organization, and move on to the next field."[4] Starting in 1910 with a capital stock of $50 million, by 1930 Cities Service was worth $1.3 billion, making it one of the five largest electric and gas companies in the United States, and one of the nation's twenty largest nonbanking corporations. By 1932, when its skyscraper headquarters opened, Cities Service had half a million shareholders and 25,000 employees, and operated more than 200 subsidiaries in 33 states serving 3,000 towns and cities. It owned 6,000 oil wells, 1,300 miles of pipelines, 8 refineries, and 1,600 tank and gas stations from Texas to Massachusetts.

The Cities Service Company's "growing character" was epitomized by its "expanding circle" logo. The Greek delta's sides stood for industry, integrity, and imagination. Its circular ellipses represented engineering, finance, and sales.[5] Indeed, finance and sales were at the center of Cities Service's operations, as much as engineering, and made Cities Service more than a traditional utility company. In order to finance its acquisitions and capital investments, the Cities Service Company raised tens of millions of dollars from the general public by the sale of securities to tens of thousands of investors through a nationwide network of offices under the aegis of Henry L. Doherty & Company (the parent company of Cities Service).[6] Thanks to the Doherty Company's skilled stock salesmen, Cities Service securities were one of the most widely owned American stocks. One day alone in 1930, Cities Service stock represented seventy percent of the Curb Market's volume.

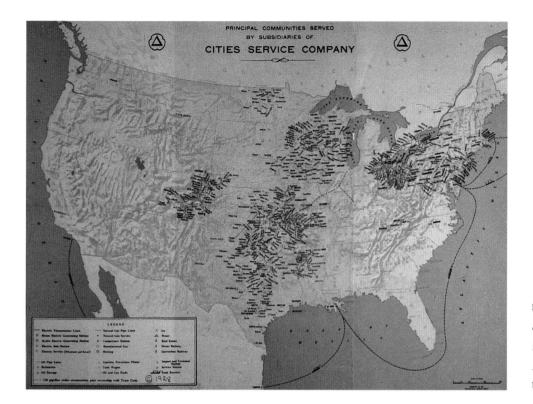

FIG. 15. *The billion-dollar Cities Service energy empire in 1928, at the time plans were first made in New York for the Cities Service Building.* Western History Collections, University of Oklahoma Libraries

The Cities Service Company relied on good public relations for its success with customers and stockholders, pioneering the use of mass media and advertising campaigns. It sponsored a Friday night Cities Service Hour on NBC radio, complete with a Cities Service march song. When it came time to build its new headquarters, the Cities Service Company had the experience to use the skyscraper for promotional purposes as well as considerable expertise in managing large office buildings.

The Cities Service Company's rapid 1920s expansion put pressure on its New York staff's space needs. To house its hundreds of Wall Street headquarters' workers, and also to rent out for profit and diversify its revenue flow, Cities Service became a holding company for real estate, too. Through subsidiary companies it controlled about four acres of land, mainly to the east and north of Battery Park, worth some $50 million, which made Cities Service one of the financial district's single largest landlords.[7]

As it grew the Cities Service Company developed a vivid corporate culture focused on teamwork and nourished by company beauty contests, sports teams, picnics, newsletters, celebrations of founder Henry L. Doherty's birthday, and a womens' club and a men's fraternity featuring secret handshakes, lapel pins, initiation ceremonies, and secret oaths. When the Cities Service Building was completed, corporate cohesiveness achieved architectural expression. Before the skyscraper's completion the company's culture and identity revolved most concretely around the figure and personality of its founder, Henry L. Doherty.

HENRY L. DOHERTY

Born in Columbus, Ohio, on May 15, 1870, the youngest son of an inventive waterworks superintendent, Henry Latham Doherty's life was a Horatio Alger tale (*Fig. 16*). Leaving school at age 12 to work for the local gas company, young Doherty taught himself engineering out of trade catalogs. By his mid-twenties Doherty was

LEFT: FIG. 16. *Henry L. Doherty, founder of the Cities Service Company, poses in his State Street penthouse apartment.* Western History Collections, University of Oklahoma Libraries

RIGHT: FIG. 17. *Doherty's electric bed on rails, equipped with its own telephone, on the open-air terrace of his State Street penthouse apartment.* World's Work

an accomplished engineer and an expert in public utility operations and reorganizations. At the age of 35, in 1905, Doherty set up in New York his own holding corporation, Henry L. Doherty & Company, in two 14th-floor rented rooms in 60 Wall Street, a 27-story building completed that same year by the leading commercial architecture firm of Clinton & Russell (*Fig. 10*). By all accounts Doherty possessed boundless energy for his job, traveling around the country in a personal Pullman railroad coach or self-contained "auto-trailer" complete with telephones and radios for keeping in touch with his corporate empire. "I get my fun out of work," Doherty told *Newsweek* in 1935, and he enjoyed repeating favorite aphorisms such as "Think straight and clear" and "Let nothing be impossible."[8] Doherty's personal fortune soared into the tens of millions of dollars, and though he was not as famous or rich as the Rockefellers and Mellons, the news of Doherty's death on December 26, 1939, made the front page of *The New York Times.*

Notwithstanding Doherty's success as an executive, financier, and salesman, his proudest achievements revolved around engineering. He always took the title of chief engineer in his businesses. After making his fortune Doherty applied for an official engineering license, declaring, "I would like to be known as a scientist and engineer."[9] Despite little formal education Doherty held some 150 patents on energy processes and apparatuses and authored several award-winning papers on oil conservation and production.

Doherty's fertile imagination expressed itself in household inventions as well. For much of the 1920s the workaholic millionaire resided in a penthouse apartment of one of his buildings, 24 State Street, overlooking the Battery close by his Wall Street office. Doherty's penthouse contained a gymnasium, squash court, physical and chemical laboratories, movable wicker furniture, and a suite of offices and conference rooms. Indulging his taste for gadgetry Doherty's bachelor aerie also featured various mechan-

FIG. 18. *The 66th-floor observation gallery of the Cities Service (now AIG) Building looking to the northeast; originally intended as the "watch tower" of a private penthouse apartment for Cities Service chairman Henry L. Doherty.* Norman McGrath

ical musical instruments, sixty-four telephone outlets, and a remarkable "automotive bed" equipped with telephone, electric fan, and heating pad connections, mounted on rails and capable of being self-propelled from Doherty's bedroom through remote-controlled swinging doors onto an adjacent open-air sun porch (*Fig. 17*).[10]

Doherty's penchant for technology influenced the character of the Cities Service Company's skyscraper headquarters. Company engineers helped design the building's innovative heating and ventilation systems. Doherty himself was widely credited with the initiative for the building's double-deck elevators and aluminum terrace railings. "Sixty Wall Tower is a tribute, of the noblest conception to the life, work and genius of Mr. Doherty, its builder," exclaimed publicist Edwin C. Hill in the promotional pamphlet, *Sixty Wall Tower*.[11] The Cities Service Building's glass observation gallery was meant to be part of a new penthouse apartment for Doherty (*Fig. 18*). Doherty never did reside atop the Cities Service Building, in part because he struggled for much of his later life with debilitating rheumatoid arthritis (thus explaining his penthouse's technological conveniences). From 1926 on he lived at the Kellogg Sanitarium in Battle Creek, Michigan, and in Florida before dying at the Temple University hospital in Philadelphia in 1939.

Although Doherty was never a long-term inhabitant of the Cities Service Building, he was the off-stage inspiration for its distinctive technological character. Doherty was president of the Pine Street Realty Company, Inc. (later Sixty Wall Tower, Inc.), established by the Cities Service Company in 1929, for tax and legal reasons, to build and manage the skyscraper. In this position Doherty transmitted his thoughts to the building's architects via August H. Fromm (Cities Service's experienced real estate manager), E. J. Smith (the skyscraper's eventual building manager), and W. Alton Jones (the Cities Service first vice president who would eventually rise to the head of the company).[12]

IRVING TRUST

Like the Cities Service Building, One Wall Street was built to accommodate recent corporate growth and enhance institutional identity. The Irving Trust Company

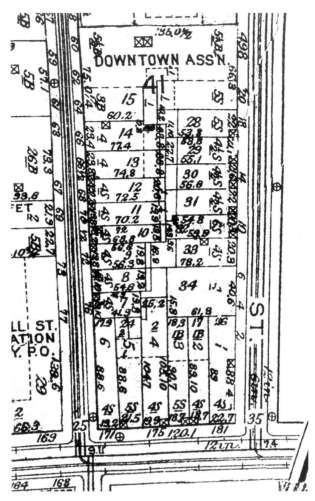

LEFT: FIG. 19. *Pine Street looking west in 1929 from beneath the Pearl Street elevated railroad just before the low buildings on the right were demolished for the Cities Service Building, including recalcitrant owner Nik Coutroulas' Lindy's Cafeteria in the background.* New York Public Library

RIGHT: FIG. 20. *Site of the Cities Service Building in 1921 showing some two dozen lots east of the Downtown Association totaling 30,875 square feet, which Cities Service purchased for $2 million in 1929–30.* Atlas of the Borough of Manhattan

was first established in 1851 and named after Washington Irving for instant credibility. In the 1910s and 1920s Irving Trust's growth typified the consolidation of the American banking industry. It merged with and acquired some half-dozen other New York banks, multiplied its resources six times over to $865 million, and established itself as a major banker to Wall Street's brokerage houses. However, its headquarters remained a half-mile north of the financial district in the lower floors of Cass Gilbert's opulent Woolworth Building (1910–13), which Irving Trust's head, Lewis E. Pierson, had been instrumental in financing for the discount store magnate F. W. Woolworth.

By the late 1920s Irving Trust's two-thousand-plus headquarters staff had outgrown its Woolworth Building accommodations. Deciding to relocate closer to its new stock market business, Irving Trust acquired in 1927–28 one of the most symbolically significant sites in the financial district—the southeast corner of Broadway and Wall Street—across from the Gothic tower of Richard Upjohn's 1846 Trinity Church, just around the corner from the New York Stock Exchange, and at the western head of Wall Street itself. Negotiations to purchase the site's four separate plots took place secretly with Irving Trust directors as frontmen. These were common tactics. If sellers knew the importance of their individual holdings to the real buyer's larger plans, then they would inflate their prices. For example, with the Cities Service Building, Pine Street cafeteria owner Nik Coutroulas held out for more money even as a dozen neighboring buildings were being demolished to make way for the new

skyscraper (*Figs. 19 and 20*).[13] In the case of One Wall Street, Irving Trust still paid somewhere in the range of $15 million for the site, making it possibly the most expensive piece of real estate in the world (versus the $2 million cost for the Cities Service Building's land on the financial district's periphery).

Irving Trust's desire "to produce a building which would be in harmony with the conceded dignity and importance of the site," as chairman Lewis E. Pierson explained at the 1930 cornerstone laying, led the bank to approach the skyscraper's design with unusual care (*Fig. 21*).[14] Irving Trust hired the artistically-minded New York architectural firm of Voorhees, Gmelin & Walker, and also Yale art school dean Everett V. Meeks as design consultant, and gave them plenty of time to develop the design, "a somewhat unusual experience in this day and age and particularly in high-speed New York," said architect Stephen Voorhees at the building's dedication ceremony.[15] "What the bank needs is a masterpiece, not rentable area," one of the bank directors told the architect Ralph Walker, perhaps having in mind the model of the bank's old Woolworth Building headquarters.[16] The desire to honor the site's prominence may also have reflected the personality of the executive "credited with a major responsibility" for One Wall Street's erection, Irving Trust president Harry Edwin Ward.[17] The Yale-educated Ward was a member of numerous colonial heritage associations, including the Society of Mayflower Descendants and the Sons of the Revolution. Ward's feeling for tradition may have influenced Irving Trust's sense of its historical site's dignity, just as Henry L. Doherty's engineering identity affected the Cities Service Building's technological character.

Of course the Irving Trust Company also saw economic advantage in erecting a well-planned landmark building to house its staff, draw bank customers, and attract tenants to the upper rental floors. To ensure functionality and attractiveness Irving Trust officials and consultants formed a broad array of committees to study One Wall Street's space layout, vault and built-in equipment, movable furniture, machines, communications, security, and staff utilities (*Fig. 22*). During the building stage additional committees oversaw architectural design, engineering, construction, renting, and eventual operation. Significantly, Irving Trust also designated an assistant vice president, Robert H. Elmendorf, to be its "consultant in publicity."[18] Elmendorf's department placed scores of articles and pictures in local publications, national newspapers, and trade journals—press releases often ran verbatim as articles in *The New York Times*—and staged elaborate cornerstone and opening ceremonies that presented One Wall Street's construction as an act of enlightened civic service. Elmendorf's greatest publicity coup involved having Irving Trust president Harry Ward send engraved letters in December 1929 to over five hundred of One Wall Street's neighbors apologizing for the loud riveting of the steel frame. "This never has been done," explained one of Elmendorf's assistants, "and there is opportunity not only to make a favorable impression for the Irving on the recipients

FIG. 21. *Lewis E. Pierson (above), chairman, and Harry E. Ward (below), president, of the Irving Trust Company. Pierson helped finance the Woolworth Building in the early 1910s. Ward oversaw the design and construction of One Wall Street in 1928–31.* The Bank of New York Archives

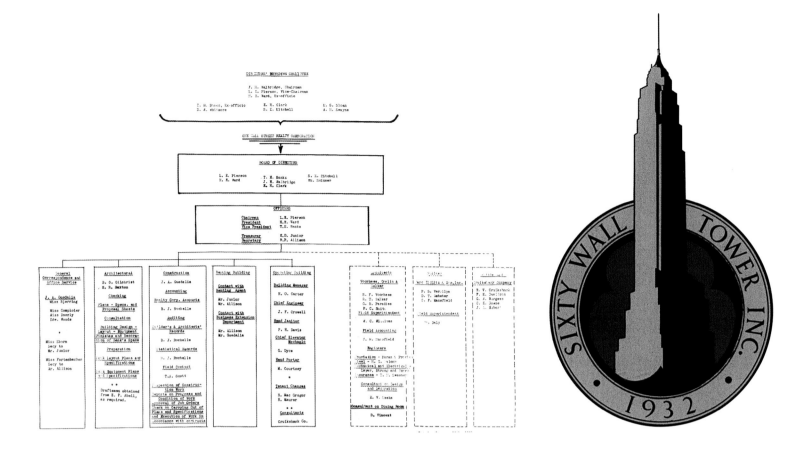

of the letter but to use the letter for incidental publicity purposes."[19] As planned, One Wall Street's neighbors responded with notes of surprised gratitude. The story of Irving Trust's consideration and politeness ran for days in the New York and national press.

Irving Trust's publicity campaign was unusual in its imagination and thoroughness but not unique. Skyscraper owners often issued press releases, staged ceremonies, and marked a skyscraper's opening with elegant illustrated publications, such as the Equitable Trust Company's *From Sheep Pasture to Skyscraper* (1926), the Cities Service Company's *Sixty Wall Tower* (1932), the City Bank Farmers Trust's *The Oldest Trust Company and Its Newest Home* (1931), and Starrett Brothers & Eken's *40 Wall Street: Designed for Working* (1930). These books supplemented the ubiquitous rental brochures that sales agents used to entice prospective tenants to the skyscraper offices with promises of convenient location, ample lighting, superior services, architectural features, flexible layouts, stable ownership, and a prestigious tenantry. The large color booklet *Sixty Wall Tower: The Aristocrat of Office Buildings* helped the Cities Service Building achieve a good 71% occupancy rate just a year after opening (*Fig. 23*).[20]

In the 1920s large staffs of "space salesmen" mounted aggressive campaigns to market skyscraper office space.[21] Marketing efforts included newspaper and direct mail advertising plus special planning services to suit tenants' needs. Often these techniques were aimed not at prospective tenants but at the specialist brokers that companies hired to locate the best and cheapest quarters. Skyscrapers that marketed heavily tended to adopt their prestigious addresses as names, which helped attract smaller tenants by allowing them to maintain separate identities from the owning corporation. Thus resulted the names 40 Wall Street, One Wall Street, and, for the Cities Service Building, Sixty Wall Tower, a moniker implying a prestigious Wall Street address that was justified by the 16th-floor bridge across Pine Street to 60 Wall Street.

The marketing and management of skyscrapers was becoming as commercialized and specialized as the skyscrapers' physical production. For example, the real estate management firm of Cruikshank & Company, with large offices on the 17th floor of One Wall Street, operated separate departments for renting, sales, leasing, appraisal, repair, and insurance.[22] To become a success a skyscraper needed a middleman's public relations and rental campaigns as much as an architect's good design.

CITY BANK FARMERS TRUST

Like the Irving Trust Company, City Bank Farmers Trust participated in the merger mania of the 1920s banking industry. Established in 1822 as the oldest American trust company, the Farmers Loan and Trust Company (as it was known from 1836 to 1929) specialized in investment and trust services for wealthy families and large corporations. Attempting in the 1920s to break into the middle-class market with minimum investment "uniform trusts" (the ancestor of the modern mutual fund), Farmers Loan and Trust, under the leadership of president James H. Perkins, found itself the object of a friendly takeover by the much larger National City Company. City Bank Farmers Trust became National City Company's trust subsidiary, still headed by Perkins (*Fig. 24*).

FIG. 24. *City Bank Farmers Trust president James H. Perkins presided over his company's skyscraper construction.* The Oldest Trust Company

Before the 1929 consolidation with National City, Farmers Loan and Trust had been planning to accommodate its growing business in a rebuilt headquarters on its 22 William Street site, just behind National City Bank's headquarters at 55 Wall Street. The merger with National City promised increased work for City Bank Farmers Trust, so the company's building plans grew upward to 54 stories (after an initial 75-story proposal), and also outward to encompass the whole of the trapezoidal block encompassed by William Street, Beaver Street, Hanover Street, and Exchange Place.

With no need to move or establish a prominent financial district identify, City Bank Farmers Trust proceeded with a less aesthetically ambitious design than Irving Trust. The personality of Harvard-educated Perkins was one of a "quiet, scholarly, [and] homespun...country banker."[23] This and Perkins' interests in woodcarving, carpentry, and oil painting perhaps influenced the City Bank Farmers Trust Building's "conservative modern" style and interior richness in stone and wood.[24] The skyscraper's restraint and solidity aptly expressed the trust company's fiduciary character.

The skyscrapers built by the Cities Service Company, Irving Trust Company, City Bank Farmers Trust Company, and other financial and industrial corporations accommodated growing businesses and symbolized corporate distinction.[25] They also represented gambles on the real estate market. Companies typically housed their own workers on a skyscraper's broad lower floors, while adding tower floors as rental

space to pay the building's cost and to produce future revenue. Building high was thus a matter of profit as much as prestige. Indeed, profit was the sole originating motive for the construction of the Cities Service Building's closest skyscraper rival, the 927-foot-high 40 Wall Street.

40 WALL STREET

The guiding hand behind the development of 40 Wall Street belonged to the young Michigan-born investment banker George Lewis Ohrstrom, who had downed the last German plane of World War I on Armistice Day morning before going on to found a multimillion dollar securities underwriting firm (*Fig. 25*).[26] Needing a partner to develop 40 Wall Street, Ohrstrom joined forces with the leading skyscraper builder William Aiken Starrett, another Midwesterner who had served in the war as a construction engineer (*Fig. 26*). Joining Ohrstrom and Starrett as the consortium's real estate broker was the Oxford-educated yachtsman Adrian Iselin II. Unlike the corporate owners of the Cities Service Building, One Wall Street, and the City Bank Farmers Trust Building, Ohrstrom, Starrett, and Iselin were professional real estate developers interested exclusively in making money from their skyscraper. Most of the Wall Street area's smaller 1920s and 1930s office buildings were in fact sponsored by developers. Elias Cohen built 99 Wall Street. The milliner-turned-developer Abe Adelson put up 29 Broadway. Hyman Schroeder headed the company that built 19 Rector Street.[27]

Ohrstrom and Starrett began 40 Wall Street with a smaller site in mind than was eventually developed, east of the government-owned Sub-Treasury Building (Town & Davis, 1834–42) and Assay Office (c. 1900). Ohrstrom assembled five plots on Wall and Pine streets in 1928 and then arranged to buy the Assay Office to prevent another tall building from blocking his project's western flank. Unexpectedly, in early 1929, The Manhattan Company banking group agreed to lease for $500,000 a year its abutting site just east of Ohrstrom's plot.

The Manhattan Company joined Ohrstrom's scheme for familiar corporate reasons. First established by Aaron Burr in 1799 as a water supply company (a business dropped in the mid-nineteenth century), by the 1920s The Manhattan Company was expanding its local, national, and international banking business. For The

Manhattan Company, joining Ohrstrom's scheme meant larger lavish quarters, yet still on the bank's original prestigious Wall Street site. However, unlike the Cities Service Company and Wall Street's other corporate builders, The Manhattan Company father–son executive team of Stephen Baker and J. Stewart Baker played no significant role in 40 Wall Street's construction and design.[28] The project remained Ohrstrom and Starrett's in conception and execution. As a developer's project 40 Wall Street was built relatively cheaply (with brick instead of stone facing, for example) and very quickly (in less than a year) to produce income as fast as possible for taxes and debts.

The Manhattan Company's passive contribution to 40 Wall Street consisted primarily of the enlarged lot size which allowed a building 71 stories high. The bank's long-term lease of the lower floors also allowed Ohrstrom to promote the skyscraper as "The Manhattan Company Building" once the financing was in place. The Manhattan Company would not let Ohrstrom trade on its good name for his initial money raising, specifically instructing the developer to this effect.[29] Ohrstrom would have to raise the funds on his own, relying on the mechanisms available to the 1920s real estate industry.

FINANCE AND THE REAL ESTATE MARKET

To finance the Cities Service Building, the Cities Service Company had employed the formidable stock-selling network of Henry L. Doherty & Company to market $15.7 million worth of shares to investors. Each local Doherty office was given a quota to meet by the end of October 1930, ranging from Spokane's $91,500 to New York's $3 million. This was the money used to build the Cities Service Building. Thus the Cities Service Company constructed its headquarters essentially debt-free, with "no mortgage whatsoever," and so could turn a modest profit even in the depths of the Depression.[30] Relying on more burdensome financing the developers of 40 Wall Street were not so fortunate.

Buying the land and building 40 Wall Street cost some $24 million, of which $19 million was raised through the sale of 6% mortgage bonds by Ohrstrom and Starrett's companies (for which the underwriters made tidy profits). Mortgage bonds, invented in the 1890s, allowed real estate developers to borrow money directly from the public instead of from banks, insurance companies, and trusts, which did not like risky loans on speculative skyscraper projects. At 40 Wall Street the economic difficulties of the 1930s kept occupancy rates below expectations and, much worse, drove down rental rates from an expected $8 per square foot to less than $3. From its opening in 1930, 40 Wall Street's income hardly covered its operating expenses— much less the mortgage bonds' $1 million annual interest payments—leading to a 1935 default and a sale offer of $1.2 million, "less than we paid for the 43 high speed elevators," lamented Ohrstrom.[31]

Opening seven months after the stock market's October 1929 crash, 40 Wall Street's financial wounds seem self-inflicted, the result of speculative developers "operating with a series of abstract physical and financial magnitudes, supported by a promise, a hope, a gambler's optimism, an opium-eater's dream," chided *The New Republic* in 1931.[32] Even later into the deepening recession One Wall Street, the City Bank Farmers Trust Building, and the Cities Service Building poured hundreds of thousands more rentable square feet into the financial district's office market. Excavation of the Cities Service Building's foundation did not even begin until summer 1930. In retrospect Wall Street's skyscraper owners and developers seem crazy to have gambled in such ominous times. Yet in the late 1920s, and even into the early 1930s, these skyscraper clients could reasonably expect their investments to pay off.

Lower Manhattan's financial district in the late 1920s and early 1930s possessed one of the tightest real estate markets in the whole country, with occupancy rates ranging from 96% to more than 99% between 1926 and early 1931.[33] Large corporations sought efficient modern buildings with updated infrastructures and wide open floor plans to accommodate their growing clerical staffs. Older and smaller buildings, sometimes constructed just a couple of decades earlier, became financially obsolete. These were sold in batches to developers who needed large lots for big buildings both to accommodate tenants and turn profits as land costs rose.[34]

The years 1929 and 1930 were the hottest for new developments.[35] Developers eyed whole blocks between Broad Street and Broadway and along Wall Street toward the East River as likely sites for skyscraper projects never completed. Louis Adler planned a $20 million, 105-story building at 80 Wall Street. A. M. Bing & Son and the General Realty and Utilities Corporation proposed a $50 million Battery Tower residential development along West Street and the Hudson River (six decades before Battery Park City arose on nearly the same site).[36] Perhaps the grandest real estate vision belonged to Henry L. Doherty. At the tip of Manhattan, around Battery Park, the Cities Service magnate had amassed by the mid-1920s some $3 million and four acres' worth of real estate.[37] With his holdings Doherty "contemplated spending as much as $100,000,000 developing an independent business centre for shipping and foreign interests."[38] A bird's-eye view of Doherty's scheme shows the edges of Battery Park dominated by two imagined pyramidal skyscrapers topped by the Cities Service logo (*Fig. 27*).[39] "We could have rented the new space by telephone at that time," Doherty later explained. "We were in the midst of a panic—a panic for fear of lack of space. Companies were looking everywhere for more room."[40]

In early 1929 several new Wall Street area office buildings opened 100% rented—when a 52% opening rate was considered average. In the summer of 1929 Manhattan real estate experts reported "little likelihood of overbuilding because of the steady demand for space" and "in the downtown field there seems to be no cause for uneasiness."[41] Even after the October 1929 stock market crash, developers remained opti-

mistic that lower labor and materials costs, along with capital fleeing stocks, would keep the building boom going. As late as October 1930 "realty brokers expressed the opinion that the high percentage of rentals which has been evident in the financial section during recent years will be maintained even with the additional space available."[42] Only in May 1931 did the financial district's overall occupancy rate dip below the normal industry standard of 90% (with the opening of the Empire State Building and other large midtown buildings), while the rest of the metropolitan and national markets had nose-dived to an 83% average. Wall Street's tight 1920s office market, corporate demand for accommodation, readily available financing, and the optimism persisting well after the 1929 stock market crash all help explain the mindset behind the construction of the Cities Service Building and its skyscraper rivals.

During the skyscraper building boom Wall Street area clients expected from architecture what clients and patrons had asked of architects for centuries: functional accommodation, good taste, and distinctive character. Owners and developers also expected their architecture to be a commodity: produced, bought, rented, and sold for money's sake. Around Wall Street, as in midtown Manhattan and business districts in cities like Chicago, architects since at least the 1880s had been made by their clients to approach design from a capitalist perspective, in which every cubic foot's value would be measured by its capacity for future returns. For centuries buildings had been constructed for economic gain, but not at this scale nor with the same intensive financing and market priorities. Little in an architect's schooling or professional training prepared him for this situation.

FIG. 27. *The Cities Service Company planned during the mid-1920s real estate boom to develop its Battery Park properties as a new skyscraper business center featuring imagined twin towers capped by pyramid crests bearing the Cities Service logo.* Courtesy of AIG Archives Department

Chapter Three

THE ARCHITECTS

A Building Planning Service committee of real estate experts meets with a skyscraper's owner, engineers, and architects.

V ISITING NEW YORK FOR THE FIRST TIME IN THE MID-1930S, THE
architect Le Corbusier remarked, "For the moment the skyscrapers
are greater than the architects."[1] Praising Manhattan's towers, the
famous modernist slighted their designers about whom he knew little or
nothing. Today, over sixty years later, the paradox remains. We admire
Manhattan's skyscrapers yet overlook their architects. Their names come at us shroud-
ed in anonymity in part because of the structure of commercial architectural practice.

Since the late nineteenth century American architects had produced skyscrapers in the context of large firms, with a firm's principal leading the project and
work divided among designers and assistants specializing in contracts, specifications,
engineering documents, interior design, statistics, building permits, and publicity.
"This is what is happening in our office today,—groups of men work on each problem," explained Ralph Walker, chief designer of One Wall Street, in 1930. "Mine
happens to be, for our office, the standard of taste. I am the analyst of beauty, so to
speak, but the final design is the work of many minds, each contributing something
to it."[2] At Cross & Cross an architect named George Maguolo received credit for the
design of the City Bank Farmers Trust Building, working in a drafting room of some
two dozen assistants and model makers.[3]

CLINTON & RUSSELL, HOLTON & GEORGE

The architects of the Cities Service Building, Clinton & Russell, Holton & George,
had been a leading skyscraper firm since the 1890s. In the 1900s, under the leadership of Charles Clinton and William Russell, the firm designed over half a dozen
office buildings in the financial district, more than any other practice, including 60
Wall Street (1905), Cities Service's first quarters (*Fig. 10*). After Clinton and Russell
died in 1910 and 1907, respectively, leadership transferred to the firm's junior associates. James Hollis Wells had been trained as a civil engineer and was New York
City's Inspector of Pavements before joining Clinton & Russell.[4] Alfred J. S.
Holton had been born and educated in Canada before being apprenticed-trained as
an architect.[5] Thomas J. George went straight from Cornell's architecture school to
Clinton & Russell where he was "in charge of almost all of the designs," according
to an official biography.[6]

The new principals kept the original partners' names for prestige and publicity
purposes and in 1926, after Wells' death, reconstituted the firm as Clinton & Russell,

FIG. 28. *60 John Street (1930–31) by Clinton & Russell, Holton & George features an Art Deco facade of tight-packed piers and a separate soaring tower.* Museum of the City of New York

Holton & George. The firm maintained a national practice designing office buildings in Houston, Toronto, Pittsburgh, Richmond, and Newark, plus internationally in San Juan and Cape Town. It also built hotels in New Bedford, Youngstown, and Atlantic City.[7] In Manhattan, Clinton & Russell, Holton & George designed interior corporate offices for Standard Oil of New Jersey (c. 1926), a large addition to the Herald Square Building (1930), the 73rd Street Level Club (1926) for Masons, and also finished H. P. Knowles' Arabian style 55th Street Masonic Mecca Temple (1925–27). Clinton & Russell, Holton & George continued its Lower Manhattan work with insurance district buildings at 85 John Street (National Board of Fire Underwriters Building, 1925–26) and 60 John Street (New Amsterdam Casualty Company Building, 1930–31) whose 31-story, Gothic finned tower was "the pride of New York's great insurance center" (*Fig. 28*).[8] Just north of Wall Street the firm designed One

FIG. 29. *Ralph Walker, the articulate designer of One Wall Street's rhythmic facade, whom Frank Lloyd Wright once called "the only other architect in America."* American Architect

Cedar Street (1929–30), a 24-story, set-back building whose balanced grid of piers and spandrels mirrored the base of the neighboring Cities Service Building (*Fig. 98*).

Clinton & Russell, Holton & George likely gained the Cities Service commission because of the client's long familiarity with the firm's work at 60 Wall Street and elsewhere in the financial district. Perhaps, too, company leader Henry L. Doherty felt a personal affinity with men from the provinces: Doherty from Ohio, Holton from Ontario, George from Rome, New York. Moreover, Clinton & Russell, Holton & George kept their offices in the financial district (at various locations on Nassau Street, John Street, and Maiden Lane) rather than moving to midtown where most architects had their practices. Like Doherty in his State Street penthouse, Clinton & Russell, Holton & George maintained a geographic allegiance to Lower Manhattan.[9] In any event, by the time Doherty commissioned the Cities Service Building the firm's best days were behind it. No more major projects came through the office after 1932. In 1936 Holton died. George retired at the beginning of World War II and upon his death in 1947 the firm dissolved itself. The Cities Service Building would be Clinton & Russell, Holton & George's last and greatest achievement.

VOORHEES, GMELIN & WALKER

Voorhees, Gmelin & Walker, the architects of One Wall Street, were another well-established commercial firm dating back to the late nineteenth century, established in 1885 by Cyrus L. W. Eidlitz. Stephen Voorhees, head partner in the 1920s and 1930s, energized the firm's design by hiring MIT-educated Ralph Walker (*Fig. 29*)—whom Frank Lloyd Wright once called "the only other architect in America"[10]—plus Columbia graduate Perry Coke Smith as Walker's assistant. Walker gained renown for the firm with the Barclay-Vesey Building (1923–26) and Western Union Building (1928–29) in Lower Manhattan, which featured faceted facades, twisting towers, and an absence of historical ornament.

Voorhees, Gmelin & Walker offered clients commercial expertise combined with aesthetic sophistication, both sought by the Irving Trust Company for its landmark skyscraper at the intersection of Broadway and Wall Street. In its interview with Irving Trust's executives, the firm "outlined a strategy for the design," recalled Ralph Walker, "that captivated his prospective employers and ultimately won the competition for his office."[11] Part of the strategy included collaborating with Yale art school dean Everett V. Meeks as "Consultant on Design and Decoration," plus a cross-country research trip of bank executives and architects to study skyscrapers from Boston to Chicago. Personally, Yale-educated Irving Trust president Harry E. Ward, who was involved in colonial American history organizations, may also have felt a connection with the Princeton-educated Voorhees, whose Dutch ancestors dated back to seventeenth-century New Amsterdam. After One Wall Street, Voorhees, Gmelin & Walker continued its successful practice. Today the firm is known as HLW International (previously Haines, Lundberg & Waehler).

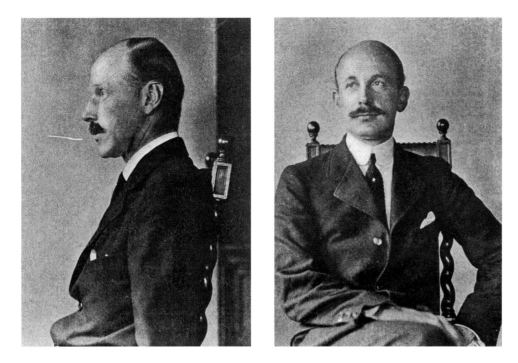

CROSS & CROSS

Founded by brothers John and Eliot in 1907 (*Figs. 30 and 31*), Cross & Cross, architects of the City Bank Farmers Trust Building, also produced in the 1920s sumptuous country residences as well as Manhattan apartments, social clubs, luxury retail stores, and branch banks, plus in the financial district, the Doric-columned Lee, Higginson & Company Bank Building (37 Broad Street, 1929; *Fig. 80*), the 38-story Harriman (later Fred French) Building (39 Broadway, 1928), and the grid-fronted Stone & Webster Building (90 Broad Street, 1931).

Cross & Cross generally favored historical associations. The firm's midtown masterpiece, the 40-story RCA Victor Building (later General Electric Building, 1930–31) rose on Lexington Avenue behind St. Bartholomew's Church. The skyscraper's Gothicized crest and chamfered tower echoed its ecclesiastical neighbor and served as the model for the downtown City Bank Farmers Trust Building's own spire. Professionally, Cross & Cross ran an exemplary office whose rationalized practices were detailed in a 1930 *Architectural Forum* profile. The lead designer for the City Bank Farmers Trust Building was the St. Louisian George Maguolo, who had studied at the Ecole des Beaux-Arts in Paris in 1921–23.[12]

Cross & Cross's taste and efficiency doubtlessly appealed to its conservative trust company client. The well-bred Cross brothers had between them attended Groton, Harvard, Yale, Columbia, and the Ecole des Beaux-Arts and were active Manhattan clubmen. These additional social factors perhaps favored the firm with the gentlemanly, Harvard-educated bank president James Perkins.[13]

SEVERANCE, MATSUI, SMITH, AND WALKER & GILLETTE

The clients of 40 Wall Street rather than hiring a single firm instead assembled a team of architects each representing a different investor's interests. The credited lead architect for 40 Wall Street was H. Craig Severance, a real estate investor and commercial architect whose work included 50 Broadway (1926–27), the Central

Mercantile Trust Company Building (c. 1928) at Fifth Avenue and 44th Street, and the Court-Montague Building in Brooklyn. Between about 1914 and 1924 Severance had been the business partner of designer William Van Alen, later of Chrysler Building fame. At 40 Wall Street, Severance likely coordinated the other architects' work. He represented the interests of lead developer George L. Ohrstrom whose golden boy image as a war hero and Greenwich, Connecticut, gentry mirrored Severance's own high-living exploits as a yachtsman and public persona, known for a drunk driving fracas with a New Jersey police officer. "My husband had been drinking a lot of highballs and that is what caused the trouble," explained Mrs. Louise Severance to the judge in August 1931.[14]

Investor and builder William Starrett's interests at 40 Wall Street were represented by Japanese-born and MIT-educated Yasuo Matsui, who had served stints as a draftsman in the offices of George B. Post, Ernest Flagg, Warren & Wetmore, and the Starrett Brothers organization. Matsui was a valued associate architect working elsewhere in the financial district on the planning of Delano & Aldrich's 63 Wall Street (another Starrett project) as well as early massing schemes for the City Bank Farmers Trust Building. On his own, Matsui designed the Japanese Pavilion at the 1939 World's Fair, the innovative swept-curve glass corners of the Starrett-Lehigh Building (1931), and an unbuilt 1928–29 project for the so-called Houston Tower on Madison Avenue. This last building's striped shaft and pyramidal cap with dormers and finial so closely presaged 40 Wall Street's shape and crowning feature that it strongly suggests that Matsui, and not Severance, designed the Wall Street skyscraper's exterior.[15]

For 40 Wall Street's interior bank quarters The Manhattan Company employed the architect Morrell Smith, who had built several of its branch banks, and paired Smith with the larger firm of Walker & Gillette, whose greater experience included work for the International Acceptance Bank, recently merged with The Manhattan Company. The divided design work for 40 Wall Street reflected the skyscraper's complex financial structure.

OTHER FINANCIAL DISTRICT ARCHITECTS

Besides the architects who worked on the Wall Street area's four major towers, other firms worked actively in the district while building elsewhere, too. Dominating the prime intersection of Broad and Wall streets was Trowbridge & Livingston, designers of the northwest corner's 41-story, pyramid-capped Bankers Trust Building (1909–12, *Fig. 11*); the southwest corner's 26-story, elegant marble-clad addition (1922) to the New York Stock Exchange; the southeast corner's pretentiously low J. P. Morgan Bank Building (1915); and, wrapping this last structure, the hulking 43-story Equitable Trust Company Building (1925–28; *Fig. 82*). Besides these four landmarks Trowbridge & Livingston also designed the 29-story Bank of America

Building at 44 Wall Street (1926) as well as other Manhattan banks, stores, residences, the American Museum of Natural History and Hayden Planetarium, and, the firm's swan song, the Oregon State Capitol in Salem. Columbia-educated Goodhue Livingston, the firm's surviving principal after 1925, hailed from an old New York family and resided in Southampton, Long Island, social factors doubtlessly related to his firm's success from the 1890s through 1930s.

After Trowbridge & Livingston the other dominant architect in the financial district's heart was Benjamin Wistar Morris, whose Wall Street area career commenced on lower Broadway in 1919–21 with the monumental 25 story Cunard Building (*Fig. 79*). On Wall Street itself Morris designed the American colonial style 32-story Bank of New York and Trust Building at 48 Wall Street (1927–29) and the polychromatic Seamen's Bank for Savings Building (1926) at 74 Wall Street (*Fig. 81*). Morris moderated his historicizing tendencies when he and his new partner and son-in-law, Robert O'Connor, erected the plain 48-story Continental Bank Building (1929–32) at 30 Broad Street (*Fig. 105*). Outside the financial district Morris built in 1912 the Architects Building at 101 Park Avenue (abode to numerous midtown firms including his own) and Hartford's Wadsworth Atheneum, two Princeton University dormitories, several luxurious New York country estates, and Manhattan's elite Brearley School. The cultured son of an Episcopal bishop, educated at St. Paul's, Trinity College, Columbia, and the Ecole des Beaux-Arts, Morris achieved success through his talents, background, and close connections to the Morgan banking family for whom he worked in Hartford, Princeton, and New York.[16]

Assisting Morris with the Cunard Building was the firm with which he once trained, Carrère & Hastings, designers of the New York Public Library (1897–1911) and, downtown in the financial district, the massive curving bulk of the 31-story, ziggurat-capped Standard Oil Building (1922–26) across Broadway from the Cunard Building (*Fig. 61*). This renowned firm's surviving design partner in the 1920s, Columbia-educated Thomas Hastings, came from an old New York family and personified the traditional artist-architect. "An eager, concentrated figure in a shiny working jacket, hair in disarray, hands smudged, bending over a drafting table," wrote a contemporary about Hastings. "He believed that no matter how great the demands on an architect's time might become he should always draw and design every day and most of the day."[17]

Although the Standard Oil Building was Carrère & Hastings' only financial district building (in the 1920s the firm produced mostly midtown retail shops), the firm's influence was felt as the training ground for other area architects, including Morris, Severance, Chester Aldrich, William Delano, and Richmond Shreve and William Frederick Lamb, whose firm of Shreve & Lamb (and later Harmon) consulted on the Standard Oil Building (and 40 Wall Street) and took over Carrère & Hastings' practice.

Like Carrère & Hastings, the firm of Shreve, Lamb & Harmon found fame and fortune outside the financial district with the Empire State Building (1931) and other skyscrapers in midtown Manhattan as well as numerous northeast educational buildings. In Lower Manhattan, Shreve, Lamb & Harmon designed the 26-story Bankers Trust addition (1931–32) on Wall and Nassau streets, featuring a magnificent Art Deco banking hall, as well as the 25-story, striking metallic Insurance Company of North America Building (1933) at 99 John Street (*Fig. 106*).

Besides these architects, other architectural firms operating in the financial district's core included Delano & Aldrich, builders of plutocratic country homes and the 37-story Gothic-crested Brown Brothers and Harriman Building at 63 Wall Street (1927). McKim, Mead & White designed the 35-story, temple-topped National City Company Building at 52 Wall Street (1928). Under the designing hand of T. Markoe Robertson, the firm of Sloan & Robertson put up for the developer Abe Adelson, a 30-story modernistic black-and-white banded slab at 29 Broadway (1930–31; *Fig. 94*) as well as the massive 38-story Maritime Exchange Building at 80 Broad Street (1931), whose vertical stripping, central light court, and flanking setbacks resembled the same firm's midtown Art Deco masterpiece, the Graybar Building (1925–27).

Working mainly on the financial district's margins, no firm built more area buildings in the 1920s and 1930s than Starrett & Van Vleck. After Goldwyn Starrett of the famous building family died in 1918, the surviving Nebraska-born design partner Ernest Van Vleck, educated at Cornell, led the design of five skyscrapers along the financial district's edges: the classically-styled Westinghouse Building (150 Broadway, 1924) and Royal Insurance Company Building (150 William Street, 1927); then the Art Deco New York Curb (now American) Stock Exchange Building (86 Trinity Place, 1930) and Downtown Athletic Club Building (19 West Street, 1929–30); and, finally, the modernistic glass-cornered 21 West Street (1930–31)— "probably the first commercial building in America to be so designed"[18]—whose ground-floor brick arcade, overlooking the Hudson River, evoked recent northern European expressionist architecture (*Fig. 95*). Outside Lower Manhattan, Starrett & Van Vleck specialized in department stores for Abercrombie & Fitch, Abraham & Straus, Lord & Taylor, Saks, Lerner's, and Bloomingdales.

After Starrett & Van Vleck, Ely Jacques Kahn was the second most prolific architect working along the financial district's periphery. Trained as an architect and painter at Columbia and the Ecole des Beaux-Arts, Kahn produced some of the Wall Street area's most aesthetically ambitious works, beginning with the small Lefcourt Exchange Building at 60 Broad Street (1926–28), then effervescing with the insurance district buildings at 80 and 111 John Street (1926–27 and 1928–29; *Figs. 92 and 93*), whose jazzy Art Deco textures closely resembled Kahn's midtown skyscrapers, especially 2 Park Avenue (1924–27) and the Bricken Textile Building (1928–30). Then Kahn's design turned plain and modernistic with the 36-story, stepped-back gray box of 120 Wall Street (1929–31; *Fig. 107*). Kahn also may have had a hand in the design of the 38-story International Telephone & Telegraph Building (1930) at 67 Broad Street, which is generally credited to Louis S. Weeks.[19] Kahn ran a highly successful business—he presided over the corporation that built 111 John Street—and he was named by Allene Talmey in *The New Yorker* as one of "three little men," with Ralph Walker and Raymond Hood, "who build tall buildings, and who probably rake into their offices more business than any other architects in the city."[20] The firm Buchman & Kahn continued as Kahn & Jacobs until 1966 when it merged with the St. Louis-based firm now known as HOK (previously Hellmuth, Obata & Kassabaum).

On the financial district's western edge Lafayette A. Goldstone produced the dynamic Art Deco set-back tower of the 38-story 19 Rector Street building (1929–30), with Robert D. Kohn as architectural consultant (*Fig. 62*). Elsewhere in Manhattan, Goldstone built scores of tenements and luxury apartment buildings (including one on the Park Avenue site of Ludwig Mies van der Rohe's 1954–59 Seagram Building).[21]

On the financial district's eastern perimeter, at 99 Wall Street (1930–31), appeared a stark box produced by the firm of Schwartz & Gross, both of whose partners, Simon I. Schwartz and Arthur Gross had trained at the city's Hebrew Technical Institute (*Fig. 108*). This was the only financial district building by "one of the leading architectural firms in the city," which elsewhere in Manhattan produced numerous office buildings, luxury apartment buildings, and residential hotels.[22]

EDUCATION

The architects who led the firms designing the Wall Street area skyscrapers of the late 1920s and early 1930s were born mainly in the late 1870s and early 1880s, thus producing their major buildings while in their forties and fifties. These men were among the earliest generation of American architects to receive graduate-level educations at American schools of architecture. Prior to the late nineteenth century, apprenticeship had been the dominant route of entry into the profession, taken for example by A. J. S. Holton, who trained with Clinton & Russell, and by Lafayette A. Goldstone, who trained with Cleverdon & Putzel. These, however, were exceptional cases. By the early twentieth century, university education had become the prerequisite for leading a successful practice.

Among Wall Street area architects roughly half had attended Columbia University, housed at Fourth Avenue and 50th Street until 1897, and thereafter at its new Morningside Heights campus.[23] Columbia, along with Harvard and Yale, provided not only a first-rate education but also important social cachet for aspiring architects from elite families. MIT and Cornell tended to attract bright middle-class students, often on scholarship, like Thomas J. George (Cornell), Ernest Van Vleck (Cornell), Ralph Walker (MIT), and Yasuo Matsui (MIT). A few Wall Street area architects

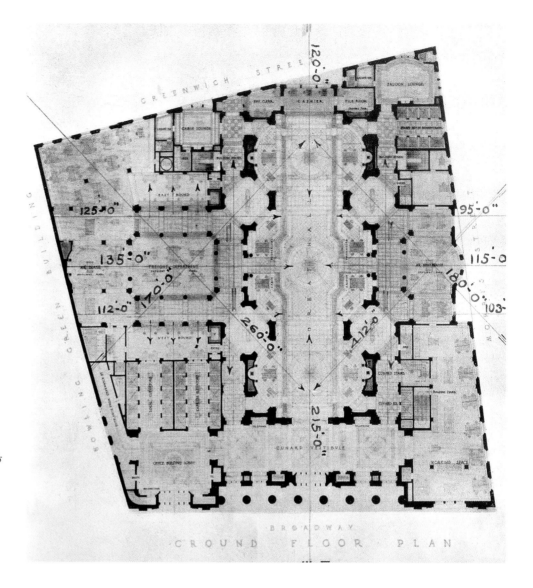

FIG. 32. *The ground plan of the Cunard Building (1917–21) by Benjamin Wistar Morris exemplifies the Beaux-Arts classical planning principles taught in American architecture schools: symmetry, cross-axes, a variety of walled spaces, and a central focus, here on an octagonal dome.* Architectural Forum

attended the University of Pennsylvania and New York University. Two Jewish architects later in partnership, Simon I. Schwartz and Arthur Gross, attended New York's Hebrew Technical Institute in the early 1890s (whose 1915 building at Stuyvesant and Ninth streets was designed by Lafayette Goldstone).

In the late 1890s and early 1900s, when most of the architects who would lead the production of Wall Street's skyscrapers were in school, a four-year architectural curriculum, like that at Columbia, provided students with a design-based rather than pragmatic education. Students practiced drawing skills and studied the classical principles of historic buildings. Following these examples students learned to lay out buildings horizontally along major and minor symmetrical axes with clear circulation patterns and a hierarchical build-up of spaces into a bodily whole, often focused on a domed center. Application of these principles appears vividly in Benjamin Wistar Morris' Cunard Building great hall and ground floor plan (1921) (*Fig. 32*), and also in Cities Service Building designer Thomas J. George's youthful 1904 proposal for a municipal center on Blackwell's Island in the East River (*Fig. 33*). Submitted to the New York City Planning Commission, George's scheme featured an array of domed and colonnaded buildings laid out axially in ample fields of space and linked to the rest of the metropolis by broad avenues and bridges.

The design approach taught in turn-of-the-century American schools of architecture derived from the curriculum of Paris' famous Ecole des Beaux-Arts, which had been attracting since the 1840s Americans such as Richard Morris Hunt, H. H. Richardson, and Charles McKim. Following in the footsteps of these leading practitioners, roughly half of the architects who would work around Wall Street polished their educations at the Ecole in the late 1890s and 1900s, including John Walter Cross, Everett V. Meeks, Benjamin Wistar Morris, Ely Jacques Kahn, and several others. Attending the Ecole or traveling in Europe on fellowship (as H. Craig Severance did) not only completed a young man's education but also provided social finishing and a rich store of memories to share in the future. "After a day of grueling work at the *atelier*, it was customary to drop in at the *Café Deux Magots* to discuss with friends the problems of art and architecture over an urbane liqueur," remembered Meeks.[24]

The New York architects who attended the Ecole des Beaux-Arts received the most advanced education available and represented the New York profession's social elite, institutionalized in 1894 with the founding of the Society of Beaux-Arts Architects, open only to Paris-schooled architects. But the opinion generally held by the 1920s was that Ecole-style training inadequately prepared students for the realities of American professional practice. "The great difficulty is that it has tried to make draftsmen and not broadly educated men," complained Walker. "The average student gains at college the impression that architectural design consists in making pretty pictures of buildings."[25] "I had the usual college training in New York and spent over five happy years at the Ecole des Beaux-Arts in Paris," recalled Ely Jacques Kahn. "When I returned home, I little suspected that I would be plunged into an activity far removed from what I had dreamed might be my career."[26]

FIG. 33. *Thomas J. George, later designer of the Cities Service Building, imagined in 1904 a new civic center for New York City on Blackwell Island in the East River, featuring classical colonnades, arches, and bridges focused on a municipal building domed like St. Peter's in Rome.* House & Garden

SKYSCRAPER CHALLENGES

The design of office skyscrapers was based on the hard fact, not taught in school, that in commercial work "the production of income (or its equivalent) is the primary purpose of building," declared Richmond Shreve.[27] "The design of the high office building is unfortunately only in a very limited sense a purely aesthetic consideration," explained Kahn.[28] Before ever placing drawing pencil to paper, architects might help clients determine a building's economic feasibility with tables, charts, and diagrams analyzing land and building costs, variable lot and floor areas, zoning envelopes, rentable volumes, and potential expenses and income.[29] "In commercial work [the architect] is called in more and more to help determine the financial return of the contemplated project," explained Ralph Walker.[30] "In the presentation of preliminary information to the bankers it is essential that the facts be reduced to an outline that can be immediately translated, through cubic contents, net and gross floor areas, to the simple statement of cost and return," wrote Kahn.[31] Even for corporations seeking architectural prestige—like Irving Trust, City Bank Farmers Trust, and Cities Service—preliminary calculations ensured profitability and helped rationalize in economic terms otherwise subjective desires for greater height and beauty.

Once under construction a skyscraper's physical size and complexity demanded from its architects considerable managerial and administrative skill, again subjects not taught at school. Hundreds of drawings, specifications, subcontracts, and material orders had to be produced with great accuracy and speed to meet tight construction schedules so that a skyscraper produced income as soon as possible to pay off its debt and taxes. "Time has become more and more an element of building cost," reported Yasuo Matsui.[32]

In further contrast to school exercises that assumed the individual architect's mastery over the design process, the production of skyscrapers since the late nineteenth century had necessitated collaboration with an array of contractors and tradesmen, structural and mechanical engineers, and scores of suppliers. In the 1920s there also arose a cohort of new interests to challenge the individual architect's prerogatives. At a project's earliest stages institutional investors, such as banks and mortgage companies, often used their own experts to challenge and revise architects' and clients' financial projections and building plans. Later, insurers might demand that their own experts review a skyscraper's fire and building code compliance, moving stairs and fire walls.

In the mid-1920s there arose the figure of the "office layout specialist" whose field of expertise combined "certain functions of efficiency engineers and architects," asserted office layout man Warren D. Bruner, and represented "a new field for the application of specialized knowledge."[33] At One Wall Street, for example, it was not Voorhees, Gmelin & Walker who arranged tenants' partitions, furnishings, and equipment, but rather individually hired specialists like Gibbs &

Ernest ("Equipment Architects"), John Barnaby, Inc. ("Modern Office and Building Planning"), and the Seitz & Sanborn Company ("Office Planning and Equipment"), as well as architecture firms like Cross & Cross for a 31st-floor office, and Delano & Aldrich which arranged the Fiduciary Trust Company's 30th-floor premises.[34]

Challenges to architects' control came also from the Chicago-based National Association of Building Owners and Managers (NABOM), which in 1924 initiated a Building Planning Service to help prospective skyscraper owners "develop space of the greatest possible rentability" (*Fig. 34*).[35] Among the Building Planning Service's dozens of consultations each year, in January 1929 a group assembled for two days in Chicago to analyze plans for the City Bank Farmers Trust project. This group consisted of half a dozen experienced building managers from Chicago, Pittsburgh, Detroit, Buffalo, and New York as well as representatives from the bank, the architectural firm, the engineering firm, the construction company, and the rental agent.[36] This committee's exact contributions to the eventual design of the skyscraper remain unknown, but typically the Building Planning Service produced reports up to five hundred pages long analyzing factors such as building investment charge per square foot of rentable area, and advising owners about their proposed building's siting, rental strategy, floor layout, mechanical equipment, elevator distribution, and eventual operation.

The Building Planning Service's purpose was in part "to give building managers professional standing" in the skyscraper production process.[37] Architects responded defensively, recognizing the challenge to their authority and autonomy. "The reaction of architects to the Building Planning Service was at first one of amazement that uninitiated building managers should presume to offer suggestions to them," recalled NABOM executive Earle Shultz, "and some apprehension, perhaps, that the association was trying to undermine or belittle them."[38]

FIG. 34. *In January 1929 the City Bank Farmers Trust Building's plans were reviewed by an outside committee of building managers, rental agents, and publicists, plus the skyscraper's architects, engineers, and owners; a group similar in composition to this pictured 1928 committee, led in both cases by building manager association executive Earle Shultz, seated at far left.* Courtesy of BOMA

PROFESSIONAL PRACTICE

The rigorous demands of skyscraper building elicited responses from architects at several levels. Some architects such as Kahn, Goldstone, and Schwartz embraced the business environment and sometimes presided over their projects' ownership corporations.[39] Following in the footsteps of late nineteenth-century businessmen-architects, such as the Chicagoan Daniel Burnham, other Wall Street area skyscraper architects operated as professional real estate investors, such as Severance, John Sloan, and Eliot Cross who in 1922 founded the prominent real estate investment firm of Webb & Knapp. Many of Wall Street's 1920s architects had also learned about large-scale building administration through military and government service during World War I.

In previous wars architects had served in combat, such as the Philadelphian Frank Furness, a Civil War cavalry hero, and Clinton & Russell associate Colonel James Hollis Wells, who participated in Theodore Roosevelt's 1898 charge up San Juan Hill. By contrast, World War I's unprecedented logistics sent architects to postings more appropriate to their professional training. Stephen Voorhees served as an engineering major in the Sanitary Corps; A. Stewart Walker in the Overseas Transport service; Arthur Loomis Harmon, John Sloan, and William F. Lamb as builders for the Army. The Housing Division's architects included Alfred J. S. Holton (of Clinton & Russell) as well as John Walter Cross and Lafayette Goldstone. In military service these architects honed management skills relevant to skyscraper construction. As the builder-developer William Starrett, himself a reserve colonel, declared in 1928, "Building skyscrapers is the nearest peace-time equivalent of war."[40]

Tempered by their wartime duty, Wall Street's architects in the 1920s hummed a mantra of economy, functionality, and collaboration to attract clients and acclimate themselves to commercial circumstances. Explaining his firm's business mentality, Arthur Loomis Harmon wrote, "Conscience, self respect and self preservation demand that we meet the useful, economic and structural requirements. Unless these are met squarely, aesthetic values may be false."[41] Skyscraper architects abandoned the ideal of the autonomous architect-artist with his "heavy black pencil, long hair and temperamental disposition," in Richmond Shreve's derisive characterization (thinking perhaps of Frank Lloyd Wright).[42] Instead of lone genius, Ely Jacques Kahn "very quickly learned the importance of team play, the amount of permissible freedom and the rigid limitations as well."[43] "The architect has his role, but as part of an organization,—not as a despot," explained Shreve, laying out an ideal skyscraper planning and design board of owner, bankers, real estate agents, architect, engineers, builder, subcontractors, and suppliers.[44] While accepting a cooperative process, skyscraper architects still insisted on their leading role. "Coordination is properly the architect's work, and his relationship to the several specialists should be that of leader," explained Walker. "The architect because of his humanistic training, is the best fitted for that task."[45]

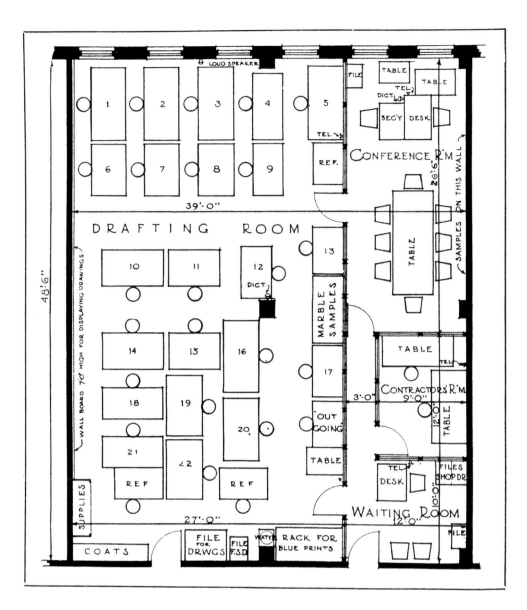

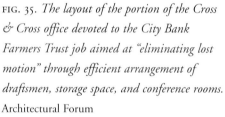

FIG. 35. *The layout of the portion of the Cross & Cross office devoted to the City Bank Farmers Trust job aimed at "eliminating lost motion" through efficient arrangement of draftsmen, storage space, and conference rooms.* Architectural Forum

One way architects maintained leadership of the skyscraper production process was through mimicking their business clients' rationalized office practices. Adapting scientific management principles of efficiency, specialization, hierarchy, and segregation, skyscraper architecture firms confronted "the problem of the drafting room [which] is to reduce the number of drawings and also the time spent on each drawing to a minimum."[46] Just as factories and corporate offices worked to rationalize their production processes, so large skyscraper firms like Cross & Cross rationalized the manufacture of their chief product—architectural information in the form of drawings, specifications, and subcontracts.

In 1932 *Architectural Forum* published a description and plan of the portion of Cross & Cross's large office at 385 Madison Avenue used for the City Bank Farmers Trust Building job (*Fig. 35*). In the middle of the main workroom stood the isolated desk of the chief draftsman (with adjacent dictaphone) under whose watchful eye twenty or so draftsmen worked on plan, design, and shop drawings. Storage cabinets and enclosed conference, contractors, model, sample, and waiting rooms were segregated along the workroom's periphery, along with desks for the supervising executive architects. This office organization aimed to eliminate "lost motion," to provide "close and easy supervision of the job," and to save "time in the distribution of authentic information."[47] Only large well-managed architectural firms could hope to secure skyscraper commissions and see them through efficiently, successfully, and profitably.

TRADITION, MODERNITY, AND TEXTURE

The architects who produced Wall Street's skyscrapers readily articulated their practical solutions and businesslike attitudes toward the challenges of modern skyscraper building. Less volubly did they publicize their aesthetic ideas. Theorizing ran against their identity as working pragmatists. "Let us understand each other," Arthur Loomis Harmon declared, "Mr. Harmon is writing this article in Mr. Lamb's absence from his office. He is out in the drafting room, designing office buildings."[48] Among the architects who designed Wall Street's skyscrapers only Ralph Walker and Ely Jacques Kahn articulated their aesthetic principles in writing during the late 1920s and early 1930s. Without letting these two speak too much for their contemporaries, their words help explain the aesthetic ideas behind the design of Wall Street's skyscrapers.

After World War I had unsettled complacent attitudes toward the past and emboldened avant-garde experimentation, many architects in the 1920s felt caught between the divergent poles of tradition and modernity. While some staked out hard-line claims (Gothicists like Ralph Adams Cram versus modernists like Frank Lloyd Wright), most were left in the middle seeking some form of compromise. The architects of Wall Street's skyscrapers mainly occupied this middle ground. On the one hand the deep appeal of the familiar was acknowledged. "Our people will always want a tie with the past," believed the Cross brothers of the City Bank Farmers Trust Building; "they will not feel at home in a house which does not acknowledge precedent." On the other hand the past's particular forms seemed ossified and irrelevant. "Mr. Cross says there has been too much archaeology and not enough architecture."[49]

This ambivalence about tradition echoed in similarly conflicted attitudes toward modernity. On the one hand Kahn voiced the period's general desire for contemporaneity. "Nothing is modern other than that it represents its own time," he wrote; "the demand is for a rational interpretation of our own problems controlled by what good taste we possess."[50] Machine technology would produce "greater accuracy, finer precision, a delicacy, refinement and subtlety," Walker argued, leading to a "more universal" architectural culture.[51] On the other hand there was resistance to the severe functionalism of European "extremist" architects such as Walter Gropius, Le Corbusier, and Ludwig Mies van der Rohe who, wrote Kahn, "demand purity in mass as well as detail." "The difficulty of the purist is that a certain hardness and cold quality is likely to develop because of this conscious restraint."[52] Americans were not yet ready for the stark articulation of the skyscraper's steel-frame structure, believed Arthur Loomis Harmon: "it would not now, at least, please the eye nor satisfy the mind; later perhaps it will."[53] From a political point of view, Hildreth Meiere, muralist for One Wall Street, attacked "Left Wing Modernists" on the grounds that "human nature demands interest and relief from barrenness by some sort of enrichment."[54] Everett Meeks, One Wall Street's design consultant, considered 1920s European functionalism to be the particular result of that continent's postwar privation: "elementary functionalism governed by rigid economy."[55] By the reasoning then of Wall Street's skyscraper designers, modernist European functionalism was alien to American aesthetic, economic, psychological, and political conditions.

The architects who designed Wall Street's skyscrapers negatively rejected the extremes of traditionalism and modernism. Positively, they promoted the expression of the skyscraper's "vertical urge," as Walker put it. They also accepted the New York City zoning code's "setback régime," in Kahn's words, which mandated low bulky bases surmounted by stepped-back floors and then, if desired by the client, soaring towers. [56] "Gradually something evolved that was modern architecture," wrote Kahn.

New York's skyscraper architects also developed a theory of the skyscraper wall as textured fabric. As early as 1922 the critic John Taylor Boyd, Jr. noted that in Starrett & Van Vleck's midtown office buildings "wall surfaces and windows tend to merge in a broad pattern of tiny tones...commingled as in a tapestry," creating a "unity and consistency of design."[57] Using similar terms Kahn said he "was thinking of the texture of fabric" when he designed his skyscrapers' facades.[58] Likewise, Walker declared, "the ornament of the skyscraper...should be first thought of as textured relief."[59]

Texture and color, Kahn argued, were economical from the point of view of the "enterprising city developer" and allowed the "artist" great freedom of design.[60] Drawing his own inspiration from exotic pattern sources as varied as Han Chinese buildings, Maori canoes, Moroccan courtyards, Persian pottery, Benin sculpture, Mayan temples, and Wright's architecture, Kahn's textured aesthetic envisioned New York as a modern imperial skyscraper metropolis drawing unto itself the world's cultural as well as economic threads.

Ralph Walker's textured aesthetic pursued psychological rather than global ends. Walker valued texture's modernity—"who has seen the end of the textures of the machine craft or those made possible by chemistry"—as well as its natural "ever-changing light and pattern," and its unclassical "unity not easily comprehended...pattern that is not easily read at a glance."[61] Intricate textures, Walker believed, provided "mental escape" from modern work pressures and "recreation for the mind" among increasingly leisured people.[62] Out of Walker's belief in individual happiness as architecture's metaphysical aim, the architect conceived a counteraes-

FIG. 36. *A study of One Wall Street's base illustrates the fluted curtain wall's textured surface, which designer Ralph Walker believed could psychologically ameliorate the tensions of modern life through beholders' visual engagement with the facade's complex rhythm.* © HLW International LLP

thetic to tectonic functionalism. "The vital part of architecture is not structure but shelter," Walker argued; "It is a place in which to be physically comfortable and mentally happy."[63] Walker's notion of the sheltering rather than structurally articulate wall generated the treatment of One Wall Street's surfaces (*Fig. 36*). "The quality of the walls developed from a then current thought that the exterior of a building was in the nature of a curtain wall covering the structure of the building," Walker explained.[64] As Walker records, the notion of the curtain wall draped over a skyscraper's framed structure permeated late 1920s architectural design. Many Wall Street area skyscrapers from this period, including the Cities Service Building and the City Bank Farmers Trust Building, present flowing unified surfaces more or less visually independent from the underlying structure—in contrast to earlier stacked classical compositions (for example, the Cunard Building; *Fig. 79*) and later more tectonic expressions (for example, 99 Wall Street and 120 Wall Street; *Figs. 107 and 108*).

In effect, New York architects enveloped skyscrapers in textured walls to help mediate ambivalent feelings toward tradition and modernity. On the one hand the textured wall abjured historical plagiarism in favor of integrally expressed modern materials. On the other hand the textured wall maintained the traditional architectural idea of an applied, unified facade whose beauty masks and gives meaning to underlying structure. Thus the practice of the textured wall allowed New York architects to tread an aesthetically progressive middle path between the extremes of reactionary traditionalism and radical modernity.

A composite portrait now comes into focus of the men who led the firms that designed the Wall Street area skyscrapers. In their fifties, they had been educated at elite eastern architecture schools, and perhaps also at the Ecole des Beaux-Arts in Paris, before gaining practical professional training in the offices of leading New York commercial firms where they learned the business of skyscraper building. Rising to partnerships, or setting up their own firms, they delegated authority and rationalized their large office practices with draftsmen numbering in the dozens, so as to best serve the interests of business clients. Learning the lessons of wartime construction management, New York's skyscraper architects adapted themselves to the rigors of skyscraper building, including its financial and functional imperatives and collaborative design procedures. At the same time they held fast to the architect's traditional leading role and the importance of meaningful representational design. The motif of the textured curtain wall, cloaking New York's set-back vertical masses in the late 1920s, satisfied contradictory desires for modernity and tradition.

Le Corbusier had characterized New York's skyscrapers as being "greater than the architects" because he could not empathize with their architects' professional situation. Loyal to the ideal of the individual architect-artist-genius, Le Corbusier was blind to the fact that to meet the rigorous demands of modern capitalism and building production—to get these skyscrapers actually built—architects had to give up romantic control and artistic identity. In effect, Le Corbusier, the great modern stylist, failed to recognize the equally fundamental modernity of the architectural system that produced the Cities Service Building and its skyscraper rivals.

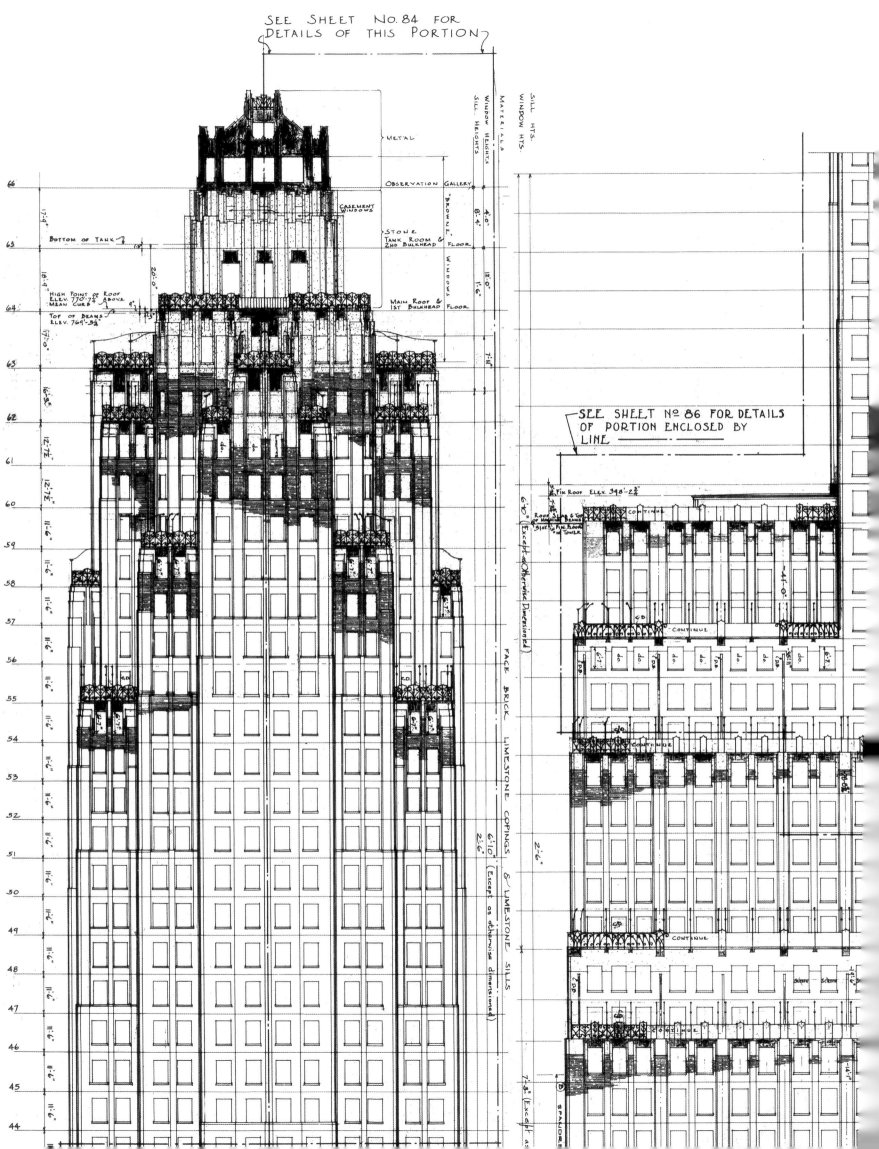

SEE SHEET NO. 84 FOR
DETAILS OF THIS PORTION

METAL

OBSERVATION GALLERY

CASEMENT
WINDOWS

Bottom of Tank

STONE
TANK ROOM &
2ND BULKHEAD FLOOR

High Point of Roof
ELEV. 770-7½ ABOVE
MEAN CURB

Top of Beams
ELEV. 769-3½

MAIN ROOF &
1ST BULKHEAD FLOOR

SEE SHEET NO. 86 FOR DETAILS
OF PORTION ENCLOSED BY
LINE ——————

FACE BRICK, LIMESTONE, COPINGS, & LIMESTONE, SILLS

MATERIALS

WINDOW HEIGHTS
SILL HEIGHTS

"BRONZE"

WINDOWS

SILL HTS.
WINDOW HTS.

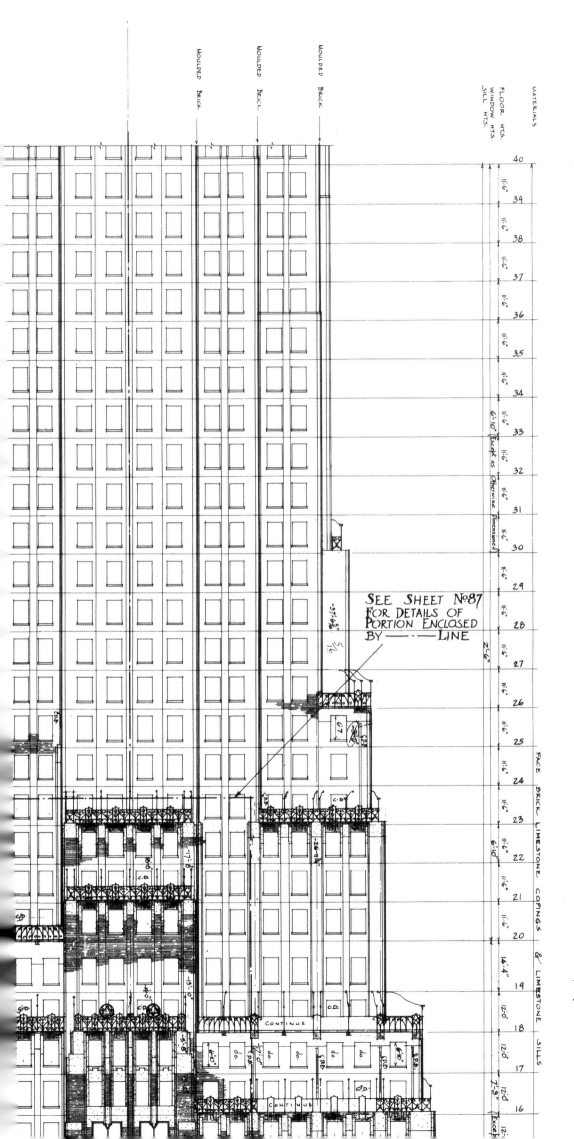

Chapter Four

PLANNING

SEE SHEET Nº87
FOR DETAILS OF
PORTION ENCLOSED
BY ———·—— LINE

*Detail of construction drawing for the Cities
Service Building's Pine Street facade.*

I N SEPTEMBER 1924 AND AGAIN IN JUNE 1930 *ARCHITECTURAL FORUM* PUBLISHED special numbers on office building architecture with articles by Ely Jacques Kahn, William F. Lamb, Richmond Shreve, and others discussing skyscraper design, management, construction, financing, mechanics, and layout.[1] American architects needed up-to-date guidance on these matters because the traditional design procedures they had learned in school were unsuited to the challenges of skyscraper planning.

Classical Beaux-Arts education taught the architect to arrange various sized and shaped rooms and buildings along horizontal axes, in ample fields of space, and with dramatic pedestrian circulation routes leading to the most important, usually centrally placed element. The goal was to create an aesthetic unity of well-proportioned parts, ornamented by classical decoration and composed in terms of symmetry, hierarchy, and concatenation.

In contrast, skyscraper designing was vertical, cellular, and economically motivated. The skyscraper architect's first design steps involved economic calculations and height massing studies, not the laying out of a unifying floor plan. Zoning restrictions and profitability operated more intensely than ever before and in vertical dimensions alien to classical theory. Skyscraper architects stacked identical open floors to be partitioned by each tenant. Inside, people moved by elevator and down short corridors rather than along processional axes. Ultimately, the skyscraper designer's goal was not to create a beautiful building but rather "a machine that makes the land pay," in Woolworth Building architect Cass Gilbert's famous phrase.[2]

MASSING

Laws and economics determined the Wall Street area skyscraper's massing. New York's 1916 zoning regulations established a basic three-part composition: 1) a massive lower base that in the financial district could rise to a height two and one half times the adjacent street width, usually about fifteen stories; 2) a middle set-back zone in which buildings in the financial district had to recede one foot for every five-foot vertical rise, usually up to about the 30th floor; and 3) a tower that could rise unlimitedly over an area equal to a quarter of the underlying lot. Out of these parameters flowed basic economic and design principles.

In the late 1920s boom years, when millions of dollars poured into office building construction, analysts attempted to make a science of skyscraper planning. In 1930, for example, the economist W. C. Clark and the architect J. L. Kingston (of the firm of Sloan & Robertson) published *The Skyscraper: A Study in the Economic Height of Modern Office Buildings*. Clark and Kingston determined that for a typical midtown Manhattan site the maximum annual profit of 10.25% would be returned by a 63-story, 1.6-million-square-foot skyscraper shaped as a high central tower with flanking set-backs and recessed light courts.[3] But as 40 Wall Street's architect Yasuo Matsui understood, "There can be no standardized plans . . . height and bulk may be arranged to produce effective and efficient designs which will differ from each other in many ways."[4] The variety of different solutions can be seen in the massing of the Wall Street area's four major towers, each derived from particular histories and circumstances.

CITIES SERVICE BUILDING

The genesis of the Cities Service Building lay in the company's desire to consolidate its workforce, spread in offices across the financial district, within an enlarged 60 Wall Street. This 15-story block, surmounted by a rear 27-story tower, had been the Doherty empire's headquarters since the building's completion and the conglomerate's founding in 1905 (*Fig. 10*). In March 1927 the architect Thomas J. George presented a study for a new modernistic finned slab tower soaring perpendicularly above the retained and westward extended lower Wall Street block (*Fig. 37*). In October 1927 George enlarged the scheme with a high turreted tower rising some 60 stories up through the perpendicular skyscraper slab, now set above a rebuilt lower base (*Fig. 38*). City planning authorities, however, denied permission to George and Cities Service's scheme, presumably because it was too large a skyscraper for the site. Instead, Cities Service constructed its skyscraper headquarters just to the north at 70 Pine Street.

Early height, massing, and financial analyses for the Pine Street Cities Service Building suggested that 48 stories would be the "maximum economical height for a building on this plot," recounted Cities Service's real estate executive August Fromm.[5] But further research indicated that if double-deck elevators could be used to supplement single elevators, then the tower could go up another dozen stories without sacrificing rentable floor area. Within these parameters and those of the lot and the zoning code, the architects worked to fit the maximum amount of space within a unified soaring shaft (*Fig. 39*).

The Cities Service Building rose from a site between Pine and Cedar streets that slopes downward to the narrower eastern end along Pearl Street. The irregular plot created a slightly trapezoidal base plan, while the change in elevation produced a midsection that begins its set-backs first at its lower eastern end, then its higher western portions (*Fig. 40*). To fill the midsection with the maximum rentable space, the set-backs recede at as near a diagonal line as possible. In plan (*Figs. 41–43*) the set-back zone, from the 11th to 31st floors, carves back the trapezoidal base into an angled fish-like outline with its head pointed toward Pearl Street and a flared tail bringing up the

LEFT: FIG. 37. *Thomas J. George's March 1927 scheme for an enlarged 60 Wall Street, to house the Cities Service Company's growing workforce, preceded plans for the company's eventual Pine Street skyscraper.* Courtesy of AIG Archives Department

CENTER: FIG. 38. *An October 1927 scheme by Thomas J. George for a rebuilt 60 Wall Street features vertical fins similar to the same firm's later 60 John Street, plus a spired crest resembling the Cities Service Building's eventual crown.* Courtesy of AIG Archives Department

RIGHT: FIG. 39. *The Cities Service (now AIG) Building as built (1930–32, Clinton & Russell, Holton & George), seen in a perspective view that emphasizes the tower's sculpted verticality and also shows the 16th-floor bridge over Pine Street to the back of 60 Wall Street.* Museum of the City of New York

western rear. The slab tower then rises from the 32nd to 54th floors where the corners cut back to produce the tapered crest that culminates in the 66th-floor observation gallery (*Fig. 44*). The overall effect of the Cities Service Building's shape is of a continuously upthrusting, narrowing pinnacle echoing the set-back zone's syncopated rhythm and diagonal massing (*Fig. 45*). From its narrow sides the Cities Service Building reads as a nearly continuous spire. The tower's slightly swelling sides convey an impression of a sculpted, almost breathing bodily mass (*Figs. 46 and 47*). The other Wall Street area skyscraper whose massing comes closest to the Cities Service Building's integrated verticality is One Wall Street, home of the Irving Trust Company.

ONE WALL STREET

In May 1928 Irving Trust announced plans for a new 46-story headquarters building on the compact site at the southeast corner of Wall Street and Broadway (*Fig. 48*). Two months later the architects Voorhees, Gmelin & Walker produced a new proposal, called "Scheme B-1," for a 52-story building with staggered set-backs and a broad, stepped-pyramid cap vaguely reminiscent of Mesoamerican temple forms (*Fig. 49*). This scheme was modified in a detailed August 1928 question-and-answer

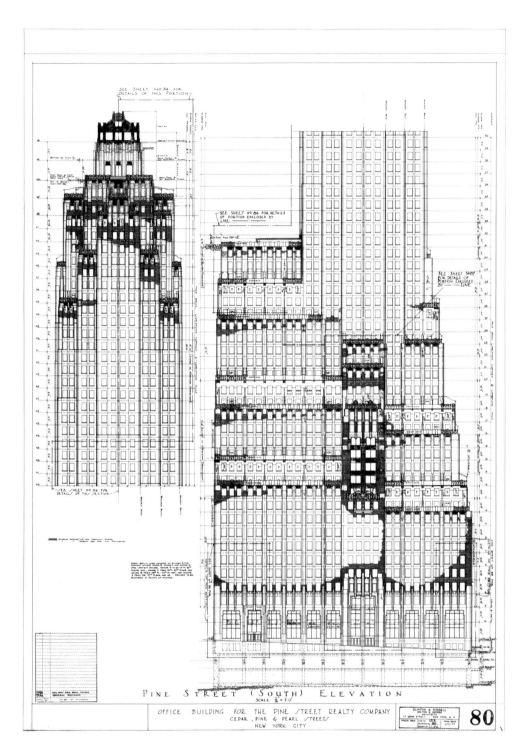

PINE STREET (SOUTH) ELEVATION

OFFICE BUILDING FOR THE PINE STREET REALTY COMPANY
CEDAR, PINE & PEARL STREETS
NEW YORK CITY

80

FIG. 40. *A construction drawing of the Cities Service Building's southern Pine Street elevation that illustrates the slope of the site and the complex rhythm of set-backs at the midsection and crest.* American International Realty Corporation

memorandum between architect and client, which determined that bank employees' elevator use should be segregated from that of the buildings' tenants; that the inclusion of luncheon clubs, public restaurants, and retail stores would "detract from the prestige of the bank"; and that Scheme B-1's initial pair of ground-floor banking rooms should be omitted in favor of a simple "reception lobby."[6] Needing more rentable floor space than regulations allowed to cover the site's high land costs, Irving Trust in early 1929 received a zoning variance for higher base street walls, shallower set-backs, and a tower occupying more than twenty-five percent of the lot.[7]

As built One Wall Street's set-backs began at the 21st floor, with the 60-by-80-foot tower running from the 37th to the 48th floors, with two more high floors for

TOP: FIG. 41. *Plan of the Cities Service Building's compact tower floors from the 44th to 54th stories, which were favored by tenants for their superior light, air, views, and sense of exclusivity. The staggered outline helps create the tower's external streamlined sculptural appearance.* American International Realty Corporation

CENTER: FIG. 42. *Plan of the 29th story of the Cities Service Building shows a typical set-back midsection floor retracted back from the trapezoidal base with a staggered exterior outline to maximize window area.* American International Realty Corporation

BOTTOM: FIG. 43. *The third-floor plan of the Cities Service Building reflects the site's trapezoidal shape and shows the open office area for Cities Service clerical departments encircling the service core that includes a fire stair to Cedar Street.* American International Realty Corporation

OPPOSITE, LEFT: FIG. 44. *The Cities Service Building crest's alternating sequence of set-backs and terraces, commencing at the corner and then switching side-to-side, creates a rhythmic tapering form that culminates at the 66th-floor observation gallery, here still under construction.* Collection of The New-York Historical Society

OPPOSITE, TOP RIGHT: FIG. 45. *The Cities Service Building from the southeast showing its faceted sculptural form juxtaposed to a later flat modernist glass curtain-wall facade.* Norman McGrath

OPPOSITE, BOTTOM RIGHT: FIG. 46. *The Cities Service Building's faceted southern face dilates in the bright sunlight beneath a mast still under construction.* Collection of The New-York Historical Society

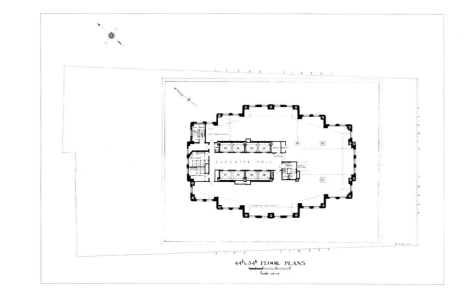

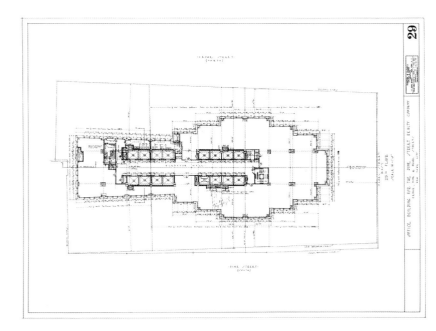

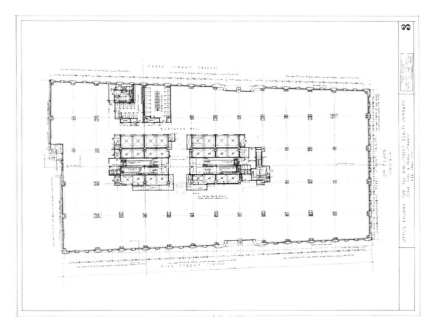

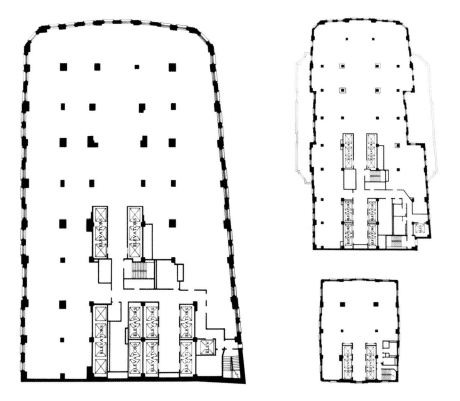

ABOVE: FIG. 49. *A preliminary 1928 study of One Wall Street's massing by Voorhees, Gmelin & Walker shows early ideas for the facade's vertical fluting and base articulation.* History of the Skyscraper

RIGHT: FIG. 50. *Plans of One Wall Street's typical base, set-back, and tower floors show office areas awaiting subdivision and wrapping in a J-shape service core that abuts the compact site's south end.* The Bank of New York Archives

the penthouse (*Fig. 50*). As at the Cities Service Building, One Wall Street's designer, Ralph Walker, alternated set-backs from one side to another—first Broadway, then Wall Street, then again Broadway, Wall Street, and so on—creating the impression of a unified rising mass. Still, in comparison with the Cities Service Building, Walker's corner and tower treatments appear blocky and conventional. For Walker it would be the subtly angled articulation of the 654-foot building's wall surface, not the overall massing, which would be the building's aesthetic hallmark.

40 WALL STREET

Of all Wall Street's skyscrapers 40 Wall Street most closely approximates the shape of Clark and Kingston's ideal economical skyscraper, reflecting in part the building's speculative character. In February 1929 the development consortium led by George Ohrstrom announced initial plans for $3.3 million, 47-story skyscraper for the 34–38 Wall Street site. Two months later, with the addition of The Manhattan Company's property, new plans envisioned a $20 million, 64-story tower. As late as November 1929, with construction underway, the associate architect Yasuo Matsui drew up extensive but unrealized plans for an additional 50-story tower on the adjacent Assay Office site at 30 Wall Street.[8] In the end the consortium and its architects decided that a 71-story, $22.5 million building with a 150-foot frontage on Wall Street and 209 feet on Pine Street for a rear wing represented the most lucrative building arrangement (*Figs. 51–53*).

40 Wall Street's massing consists essentially of a high, square central tower bolstered to the north and south by a set-back and projecting wings. The building's pyramidal cap—a traditional skyscraper device seen, for example, nearby in the Banker's Trust Building (1909–12)—has the visual effect of pulling upwards the otherwise bottom-heavy massing, endowing 40 Wall Street with an overall verticality which the buttressed composition otherwise lacks.

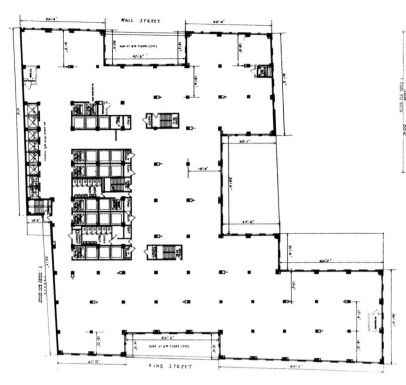

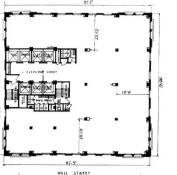

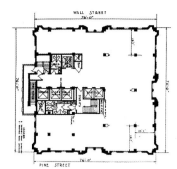

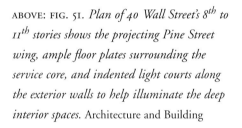

ABOVE: FIG. 51. *Plan of 40 Wall Street's 8th to 11th stories shows the projecting Pine Street wing, ample floor plates surrounding the service core, and indented light courts along the exterior walls to help illuminate the deep interior spaces.* Architecture and Building

ABOVE RIGHT: FIG. 52. *Plans of 40 Wall Street's 51st to 55th and 60th stories, showing the tower retracting back into a perfect square and the service core's evolving arrangement.* Architecture and Building

RIGHT: FIG. 53. *The buttressed tower of 40 Wall Street (1929–30) by Severance and Matsui looms over the Sub-Treasury's Doric temple front in Hugh Ferriss' rendering, a variation of which appeared in Ferriss'* The Metropolis of Tomorrow *(1929).* Avery Library

CITY BANK FARMERS TRUST BUILDING

The major Wall Street area skyscraper with the most unusual massing is the City Bank Farmers Trust Building at 22 William Street, two blocks south of the Cities Service Building, which features a chamfered square tower offset above an irregular trapezoidal base (*Fig. 54*). Business growth in the 1920s first led the Farmers Loan and Trust Company and its architect Cross & Cross to file plans in February 1929 for a modest 25-story base and set-back building (without tower) on the William Street site occupied by the bank since 1852 (*Figs. 55 and 56*). This scheme featured chamfered corners to mediate the acute angles with Exchange Place and Beaver Street. In April 1929 the Farmers Loan and Trust Company merged with its larger corporate neighbor across Exchange Place, the National City Bank, leading to new skyscraper plans, first for a 40-story building to fill the whole block (including the eastern portion occupied by the Canadian Bank of Commerce), then for a 52-story tower whose feasibility was studied by Yasuo Matsui (who proposed an exterior remarkably close to that of 40 Wall Street, complete with colonnaded base and dormered pyramidal cap).[9] In October 1929, with National City anticipating a merger with the Corn Exchange Bank to create the world's largest financial institution, new plans announced on the front page of *The New York Times* called for a 75-story skyscraper (incorrectly reported as 71 stories), which would resemble the Woolworth Building's Gothicized verticality and feature at its peak "a specially illuminated bronze sphere fifteen feet in diameter supported by four colossal bronze eagles" (*Fig. 57*).[10] This was the moment, too, when Wall Street's real estate market was red hot: "As the economic factors became more and more important the shape and size of the building changed accordingly," explained Cross & Cross.[11] But when the planned National City–Corn Exchange merger fell through, and the stock market crash dampened real estate expectations, plans for the City Bank Farmers Trust Building were scaled back to a 65-story then 54-story skyscraper. As the building's shape changed the architects worked to elaborate the design of the skyscraper's crown, set-backs, corners, and overall surface treatment. At one point lead designer George Maguolo used plasticine models to study the skyscraper's relationship to its neighboring buildings.[12]

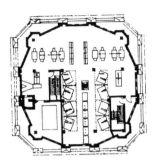

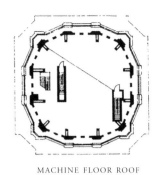

MACHINE FLOOR NO. 2

MACHINE FLOOR ROOF

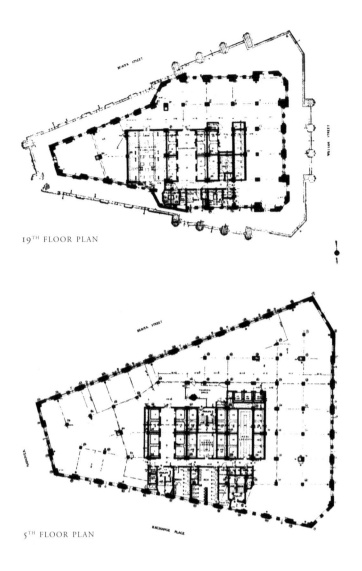

19ᵀᴴ FLOOR PLAN

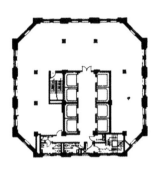

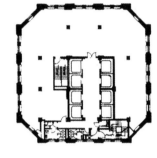

30ᵀᴴ FLOOR PLAN

31ˢᵀ FLOOR PLAN

5ᵀᴴ FLOOR PLAN

ABOVE LEFT: FIG. 58. *Plans of the City Bank Farmers Trust Building's 5ᵗʰ and 19ᵗʰ floors with the service core and its elevators abutting the northern Exchange Place entrance so as to maximize the south-facing office space overlooking New York harbor.* Architectural Forum

ABOVE RIGHT: FIG. 59. *Tower floor plans of the City Bank Farmers Trust Building show compact squares chamfered at the corners to create octagonal massings with the uppermost penthouse floors filled with elevator and other machinery.* Architectural Forum

RIGHT: FIG. 60. *From its corners the City Bank Farmers Trust Building's high square tower rises offset and seemingly twisting above the irregularly shaped base and set-back midsection.* Norman McGrath

As built the 54-story City Bank Farmers Trust Building rests on a 15-story stone-clad base, chamfered at its western William Street corners and narrowing dramatically at its eastern Hanover Street edge. Three set-back stages follow the base's trapezoidal plan to the 28th floor, where a square tower rises as an independent mass up the building's remaining 30 stories (*Figs. 58 and 59*). Except along William Street, the tower's planes diverge from those of the base and set-back zones, creating a dynamic interplay between the skyscraper's upper and lower elements (*Fig. 60*).

The City Bank Farmers Trust tower's twisting effect appears elsewhere in the financial district, notably at the Standard Oil Building on Broadway (Carrère & Hastings, 1922–26) (*Fig. 61*) and most dramatically at Lafayette Goldstone's 19 Rector Street (1929–30), where the view upwards from the corner of Rector and Greenwich streets reveals a cubist sequence of staggered set-back floors and rising tower mass (*Fig. 62*). Unlike midtown Manhattan's rationally planned nineteenth-century grid, the Wall Street area's irregular colonial street pattern derived from the shape of Lower Manhattan's tapering shoreline, converging at the Battery and creating irregular skyscraper plots (*Fig. 8*). Above these the dynamism of the skyscraper massings results from the juxtaposition of right-angled towers and irregular bases. In effect it is the natural topography, mediated through the colonial street pattern, which generated the financial district's dynamically twisting skyscraper towers.

LEFT: FIG. 61. *At the Standard Oil Building (1922–26, Carrère & Hastings), the bend of Broadway generates the curved palazzo base's shape, while the offset square tower rises into a stepped-pyramidal crest reminiscent of the ancient Mausoleum of Halicarnassus.* Museum of the City of New York

RIGHT: FIG. 62. *The dynamic set-back midsection of Lafayette Goldstone's 19 Rector Street (1929–30) mediates the difference between the irregular base and regular rectilinear tower. The polychromatic terra cotta Art Deco parapet decoration accentuates the cubist composition.* Norman McGrath

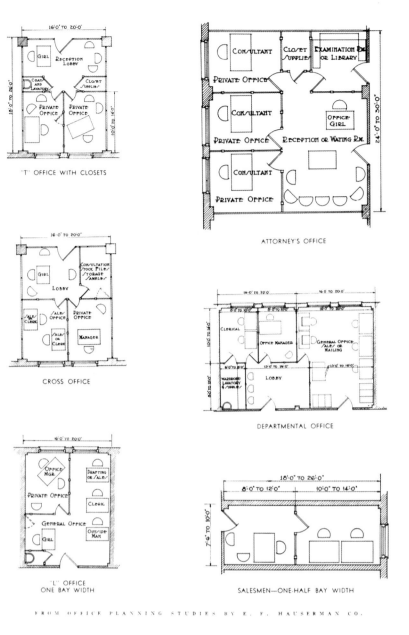

FIG. 63. *Basic two-bay office units, on the left, could be partitioned to tenants needs, or combined for larger attorney's or departmental offices, or divided in half for a small salesmen's office.* Architectural Record

FROM OFFICE PLANNING STUDIES BY E. F. HAUSERMAN CO.

INTERIOR PLANNING

Running up the heart of each skyscraper was its service core consisting of elevators, stairs, bathrooms, corridors, mail chutes, machine closets, and risers for water, heat, electrical, and telephone utilities. These service spines were a skyscraper's nervous and circulation systems combined. Architects designed service cores to be as compact as possible on each floor, to maximize usable or rentable office area. They ideally placed the service core in the building's center to avoid wasting valuable window area. Safety codes, however, required fire stairs along exterior walls for ventilation and quick ground-floor egress. In practice then service cores abutted one edge of the plan (usually toward an inferior view or an adjoining building) with open office areas wrapping the core in either a "U" shape (as in the Cities Service Building; *Fig. 41*) or an "L" shape (as in One Wall Street; *Fig. 50*).

The ultimate goal of skyscraper planning was to attract and please tenants. Considerable study went into determining tenants' desires. The results of a 1933 survey by the Institute of Research in Land Economics showed that many top tenant wishes were extraneous to a building's form (for example, location, proximity to clients and prestigious neighbors, cleanliness, and efficient service). Other tenant desires were unmistakably architectural: flexible floor plans, efficient circulation (including wide corridors and quick elevator service), well-appointed public spaces, signature features such as floodlighting or a distinctive skyline profile, and, most important, good ventilation and lighting.[13] In the days before fluorescent illumination, tenants paid twice as much for a 15-foot deep office than for a 50-foot deep space. As building management expert Earle Shultz pointed out, "An efficient floor plan is not the plan that gives the largest amount of space on the lot, but one that produces the largest amount of light space that will command the highest rate per square foot."[14]

THE OFFICE UNIT

The commercial skyscraper's identity as a spatial commodity meant that its planning began with its most basic sellable element: the single office unit. As the architect Richmond Shreve explained, "The important element in economic design is the establishment of the basic office unit, the cell whose multiplication around the central group of building utilities may be said to make up the typical floor plan and so to produce the total structure."[15] In the late 1920s market expectations for a first-class office unit meant a room depth of between 23 and 28 feet (deeper was considered loft space); a pair of windows each 4 1/2 feet to 5 1/2 feet wide and 5 to 8 feet high; ceilings 10 to 12 feet high; and a bay width between exterior wall columns of 15 to 22 feet, which could then be subdivided into individually fenestrated sub-bays.[16] Experts also recommended that exterior wall and window surfaces be roughly equal in proportion. "Many windows of average size are preferable to a few large openings," advised architect and writer Harvey Wiley Corbett; "too much glass surface causes economic waste and physical discomfort."[17]

Basic office units could be subdivided by partitions or agglomerated into open areas to suit tenants' needs (*Fig. 63*). Individual businessmen or firms with just a handful of employees could rent a single office unit and subdivide it with small exterior private offices partitioned off from an interior reception lobby or clerical workroom. Larger concerns, such as brokerage houses, might rent out the better part of a skyscraper floor, as Bear Stearns & Company did on One Wall Street's tenth floor, having their layout specialist (F. J. Horvath & Company; W. A. Zwicke, designer) combine and subdivide a series of units into private and general clerical offices, partners, conference, and trading rooms, reception spaces, runners' lobbies, order, file, wire, store, and machine rooms, customer lounges, and mail, statistical, supply, and margin departments. Law firms might take all or part of a skyscraper floor, lining the window walls with conference rooms and different-sized partner, associate, and

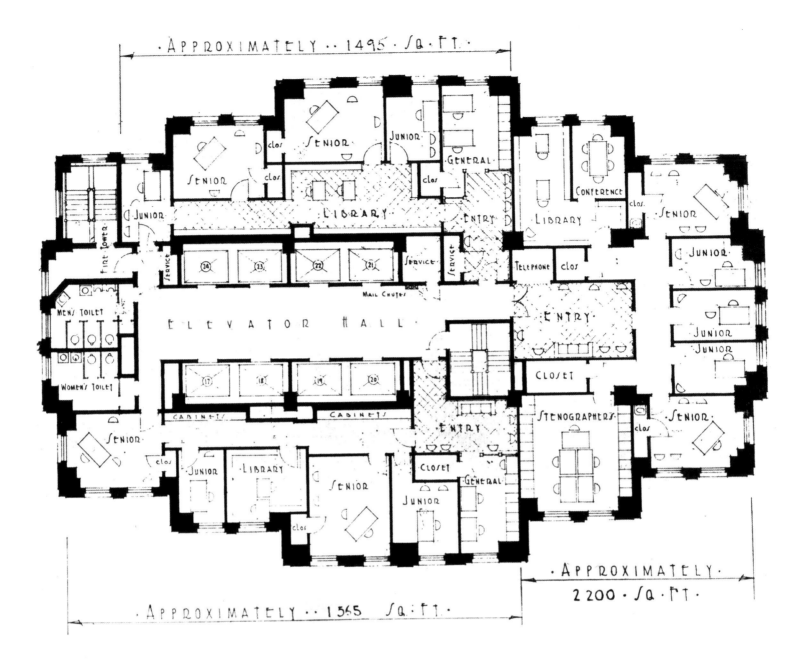

FIG. 64. *A tower floor of the Cities Service Building is partitioned into law firm suites of various sizes in this demonstration layout, with windows for nearly all rooms and senior partners allotted the largest corner offices.* Western History Collections, University of Oklahoma Libraries

investigator offices; grouping stenographers together in big, deep spaces; and placing libraries and reception spaces on the interior (*Fig. 64*). Rental experts noted that law firms liked to rent out whole tower floors, "for clients receive an impression of dignity and privacy in these comparatively small areas where limited traffic is encountered."[18] Tower floors rented at higher rates because of better views, light, air, elegant marble or terrazzo elevator halls, and lower populations (in the dozens rather than the hundreds) compared to broader lower floors closer to the street.

Businesses with large numbers of clerical employees—such as insurance companies, banks, and corporations—often filled up skyscrapers' broad base stories with open general offices for low-level clerks and machine operators. Here the basic office units were agglomerated into large loftlike areas. For example, on One Wall Street's second floor the Irving Trust Company located its bookkeeping department and personal trust and investment service department.

Above all flexibility in accommodating the whole range of tenant types and needs represented "the keynote of the success of the building," declared Yasuo Matsui about 40 Wall Street.[19] While big companies on their own might rent whole floors, building owners generally preferred smaller tenants because they paid more per square foot, put less pressure on the elevator service, and represented less of a loss if they moved out. Standardized office units allowed skyscraper layouts to accommodate a varied tenantry and their changing needs. As Matsui put it, "The subdividing of rentable area tests the magic of the plan."[20]

Chapter Five

CONSTRUCTION

*The steel frame of the Cities Service Building
in January 1931.* Western History Collections,
University of Oklahoma Libraries

FIG. 65. *To make way for the Cities Service Building, workers in July 1930 demolish low brick buildings on the north side of Pine Street, as seen from beneath the Third Avenue El tracks along Pearl Street.* New York Public Library

SKYSCRAPER CONSTRUCTION REPRESENTED ONE OF THE MARVELS OF modern urban life. *Fortune* magazine described 40 Wall Street's building site in the summer of 1929: "In August the steel was well up in the air, the masonry was only a few floors below it, and the terra cotta workers and carpenters and ornamental iron people were all over the lower floors. There were about 2,000 workmen in the building. . . . Hoists were vanishing up dusty chutes. Donkey engines clattered. There was no order or sense to anything."[1]

Speed was of the essence in skyscraper construction to begin recouping expenses as soon as possible. In a year, by May 1930, the 71-story 40 Wall Street was finished, its steel frame rising four floors a week. The 54-story City Bank Farmers Trust Building ascended just as quickly, from February 1930 to February 1931. Slightly slower, the 50-story skyscraper at One Wall Street took from May 1929 to March 1931 to build. The area's tallest tower, the 952-foot Cities Service Building, with the most advanced technological systems, remained under construction for two whole years, from May 1930 to May 1932.

During this process the architects' role diminished. Having completed the design, firms during construction mechanically churned out hundreds of drawings of details, floor plans, and elevations, and coordinated the engineers' separate production of drawings for the steelwork, fixtures, wiring, risers, and plumbing. Representatives from the architect's office kept an eye on construction to make sure plans were followed, but the complex work of building fell to others.

DEMOLITION, EXCAVATION, FOUNDATION

Around Wall Street construction always began with demolition—no Manhattan skyscraper rose on an empty, economically untested site. Sometimes the demolition

FIG. 66. *Bystanders in November 1930 look down into the waterproof concrete foundation floor, elevator pits, and cofferdam walls of the Cities Service Building, with mast-and-boom derricks ranged down the center of the site.* Western History Collections, University of Oklahoma Libraries

process could be tricky. At One Wall Street razing old ten-foot-thick masonry walls required advice from Columbia University engineering professors. At the Cities Service Building site, cafeteria owner Nik Coutroulas refused to vacate his Pine Street eatery, even "as the house wreckers were demolishing buildings all about his place" (*Fig. 65*).[2] Demolition for 40 Wall Street took place simultaneously with new foundation laying, to quicken the skyscraper's completion.[3]

Digging for foundations in Lower Manhattan could be complicated. Workers used steam, gasoline, and compressed air shovels, plus electric tunnel muckers and old-fashioned manual labor to excavate thousands of cubic feet of earth, rock, and silt. Existing subway tunnels had to be avoided, as at the Cunard Building and the City Bank Farmers Trust Building. Neighboring streets, buildings, and foundations had to be braced, shored up, and underpinned.

Next, the sinking of foundation piers presented its own set of problems. In Lower Manhattan solid bedrock lay as deep as 183 feet beneath strata of sand, clay, gravel, rock, quicksand, and water, not to mention ancient streams, shorelines, and old building foundations. At the Cities Service Building, 49 foundations piers, sunk 24 feet in four parallel rows, supported the skyscraper's steel frame with the center piers thickened to bear the heavy tower. At 40 Wall Street foundation workers jacked down 60 feet to solid bedrock and set dozens of foot-wide hollow steel caisson cylinders plus hundreds of steel piles clustered into piers. These pilings were filled with concrete then capped with steel billets to bear column loads up to 950 tons.

After the foundation the excavation received concrete flooring and cofferdam walls to keep out the earth and water (*Fig. 66*). A coating or two of impermeable cement made it watertight. A skyscraper's foundation, often so complicated to construct, became invisible, hidden forever. Rising next, the skyscraper's steel frame was both more predictable to build and more impressive to see.

LEFT: FIG. 67. *The structural steel frame of the City Bank Farmers Trust Building rises in mid-1930. Knee and corner diagonal bracing stiffens the slender tower against lateral wind forces.* Getty Research Library, 940010

RIGHT: FIG. 68. *"Gun-Man" George Smith and a "Bucker-Up" named Bowers from South Carolina were members of one of the riveting gangs employed at 40 Wall Street, here seen at work on another Manhattan skyscraper.* Fortune

STEEL FRAME

Architects and consulting engineers designed a skyscraper's structural steel frame as a "web system of rigidity," in 40 Wall Street designer Yasuo Matsui's words.[4] The frame bore the skyscraper's gravity load and supported the building's mechanical operations, exterior walls, and interior partitions. Diagonal and knee bracing stiffened the frame against lateral wind forces (*Fig. 67*).

Ideally, from an engineering standpoint, framing plans spaced steel columns apart at equal distances for uniform loading. But architectural conditions always altered the regular grid, for example, with closer column spacing around elevators to suit shaft arrangements and support heavy machinery, or with wider spacing to accommodate large ground floor public halls. As the architect Walter Kilham, Jr., explained, "the frame of a building should not be designed from the point of view of the most practical engineering, but from the standpoint of what the space it encloses is to be used for."[5]

A 1920s skyscraper's steel frame was composed of horizontal girders, beams, and trusses, plus two-story-high column units with horizontal connectors and vertical splices. All components had to be transported from the manufacturer to the building site. 40 Wall Street's steel parts traveled in eight hundred railcars from a Bethlehem, Pennsylvania, fabrication shop to Jersey City, then across the Hudson River in lighters to the East River's Old Slip, and finally by truck to Wall Street. Hoists and mast-and-boom derricks raised the steel up the building, and also lifted themselves upwards two stories at a time with the ascending frame. At the skyscraper's peak one derrick remained to elevate the last steel parts into place.

Assembling the steel frame was the most highly skilled skyscraper job and the most spectacular. The huge horizontal and vertical parts were swung and bolted temporarily into place. Then four-man riveting gangs permanently secured the steel. The work was dangerous and loud, requiring experience and coordination. First the riveting gang's "heater" fired inch-long rivets in a coke furnace and with his tongs tossed the red-hot pieces of steel dozens of feet upwards or downwards into the "catcher's" waiting metal bucket. Then the "catcher" placed the glowing rivet into the column and beam's lined-up holes. The gang's "bucker-up" braced himself against the rivet's capped end. Then the "gun-man" drove the still-hot chunk of steel into permanent position with a 35-pound air-compressor driven, steel-tube pneumatic hammer, firing in 60-second bursts a thousand rapid-fire blows per minute (*Fig. 68*). The process was repeated hundreds of times a day as the structural steel frame rose piece-by-piece. When riveting was replaced eventually by electric arc welding, skyscraper construction lost its characteristic spectacle of slung glowing steel and the machine-gun clatter of pounded rivets and pneumatic hammers.

FACADE AND FINISH

While the riveting gangs completed the skyscraper's steel frame, the lower floors assumed their finished form. On the exterior the enclosing curtain wall was hung floor-by-floor from steel shelf angles or outriggers attached to beam edges.[6] Whereas traditional masonry structures rose from the ground up, the steel-frame skyscraper's walls defied gravity (*Fig. 69*). Each floor's wall hung independent of the walls above and below. Upper floors filled in above empty bottom bays. Front facades took form while sides remained naked.

Typically, skyscraper curtain walls consisted of two layers. A backing layer of common brick provided fireproofing and took the interior finish. Then the outward facing exterior cladding was applied. This veneer could be brick (as at the Cities Service Building and 40 Wall Street) or terra cotta in various shades, colors, and shapes (as in many skyscrapers before 1914). Fancier masonry facing, such as limestone, represented "the accepted badge of dignified gentility," in the builder William Starrett's estimation. Marble was "more of an aristocrat than limestone."[7] Granite

FIG. 69. *Skeletal steel construction allows 40 Wall Street's brick enclosing walls seemingly to float above the open lower floors along Wall Street, unclad for the moment to avoid damaging the facade's future stone work.*
Avery Library

made good facing for a skyscraper's base, as at the Cities Service Building, being hard, dense, and durable. At the skyscraper's tip the roof was typically covered with tile or, in the case of 40 Wall Street's pyramidal peak, lead-coated copper.

Meanwhile on the inside dozens of other trades set to work. Incombustible terra cotta tiles or concrete wrapped and fireproofed the steel columns and beams. Over wooden forms workers laid hollow tiles or poured a concrete mixture over wire mesh to make fireproof flooring. Electricians ran wires and raceways. Plumbers ran pipes. Plasterers lathed walls. Other workers installed elevators, laid tiles, set windows, erected steel and wood partitions, and installed plumbing, electrical, ventilation, heating, and security systems. Floors were covered with linoleum or cork, and in public spaces with terrazzo and marble. Walls and columns were painted, paneled in wood, or veneered in fine stone, according to tenants' needs. Murals were painted on bank hall walls. Mosaics were laid into floors and ceilings. Metal grilles, banisters, and frames were installed. "The air was filled with the descending dust of a dozen trades sifting down through the hatches and shafts."[8]

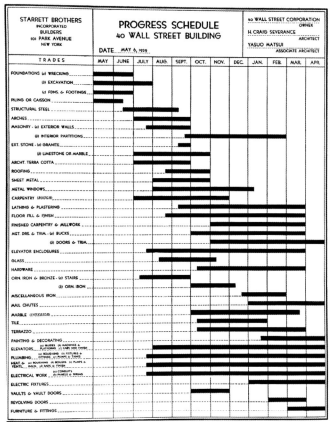

FIG. 70. *40 Wall Street's progress schedule charted the sequence of overlapping work completed in a record one year, so that investors could begin earning income on the heavily mortgaged project.* Fortune

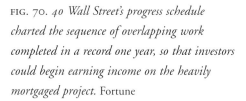

MANAGEMENT AND LABOR

The trick to constructing a skyscraper was to get all the work going in sequence, with all the materials delivered to the right spot at the right time. Each skyscraper's construction was mapped out by its "progress schedule," showing the overlapping commencement and conclusion of every major job (*Fig. 70*). 40 Wall Street's progress schedule began in May 1929 with the foundations, then forecast in June the commencement of the structural steel and almost at the same time the erection of the exterior walls and the laying of floor arches.[9] With the steel still going up and the walls being enclosed, work began later in summer on the windows, floor fills and finish, elevator enclosures, plumbing, heating, ventilation, electrical system, lathing, plastering, and roofing. With the building enclosed for winter, in came the trades responsible for partitions, carpentry, doors and trimwork, hardware, interior finishes, painting, electrical fixtures, and furniture. According to the progress schedule 40 Wall Street would be finished and ready to receive tenants on May 1, 1930, the traditional date for annual leases to start.

Implementing the progress schedule was the skyscraper builder's responsibility. The major New York building organizations included James Stewart & Company (builder of the Cities Service Building), Marc Eidlitz & Son (One Wall Street), Starrett Brothers & Eken (40 Wall Street), and the George A. Fuller Company (City Bank Farmers Trust Building).[10] The builder managed the site work and synchronized each project's hundreds of separate contracts and subcontracts, which provided everything from structural steel and mail chutes to bank vaults and building progress photographs, as well as the usual fittings, fixtures, insulation, iron work, masonry, bricklaying, and engineering services.[11] The builder also made sure the site

FIG. 71. *City Bank Farmers Trust workers pose with framed craftsmanship certificates awarded by the New York Building Congress at a January 15, 1931, ceremony, in an unfinished lower floor of the skyscraper.* Citibank

and structure were code compliant when city inspectors came to check the iron and steel, plumbing, drainage, electrical work, and elevators.

The builder's organization managed construction out of temporary wooden "shanties" or "bungalows" on skyscraper building sites. Beneath a superintendent worked auditors and timekeepers (twenty-four of them at 40 Wall Street) who checked attendance at the beginning, middle, and end of the day.[12] Job runners (seven at 40 Wall Street) coordinated materials deliveries and the distribution of drawings between the architect and subcontractors. The chief labor foreman managed the movement of men and materials on elevators, hoists, buckets, platforms, and sometimes small-gauge rails across unfinished concrete floors. The chief labor foreman also oversaw the work of the thirty or so trades active on the site. These included asbestos workers and bricklayers, derrickmen and gas-fitters, masons and roofers, riveters and steam-fitters, apprentices and water boys. At the City Bank Farmers Trust Building an estimated five thousand workers in total labored on the skyscraper, with an average daily number of two thousand, and a single-day high of about three thousand.[13]

The thousands of men who built Manhattan's skyscrapers with their hands, tools, and machines remain mostly anonymous. Often the only time a worker would be acknowledged individually was when he lost his life. Four died constructing 40 Wall Street and this was considered an average number for a building of that size.[14] Different ethnic groups gravitated toward particular trades, according to skyscraper architect Alfred Bossom. "The Germans and Italians go largely into the plastering trades. Scotsmen almost monopolize the stone work. The French are particularly to the fore in decorative painting. Brick work is largely in the hands of the English."[15] The riveting gangs and steelworkers, aristocrats of the site, were more of a nomadic brotherhood, moving from project to project and often state to state. One of the riveting gangs at 40 Wall Street, "Eagle's Gang," was led by E. Eagle of Baltimore working with a pair of brothers named Bowers from South Carolina and a New Yorker named George Smith (*Fig. 68*).[16] *Fortune* magazine profiled another 40 Wall Street steelworker, a skilled rivet-gunman and connector from Providence, Rhode Island, named Ed Radigan.[17] A seaman in his youth and a World War I veteran, Radigan had learned his trade on tanks and boilers across America before working on skyscrapers. A four-story fall once broke his arm and leg, but Radigan showed little desire to settle at home with his wife. "He has a Rickenbacker car, no children, and a two-family house in Providence. When he can't work steel, he'll live in the other half. Maybe." Radigan's possessions suggest that a decent living could be made working skyscraper construction. In terms of pay in New York City in 1933, the highest compensated trades—steelworkers, hoisting engineers, stone masons, and bricklayers—earned on average $13.20 a day. The poorest paid unskilled laborers took home about half that.[18]

The occasion in New York City where labor's achievement received formal recognition was a skyscraper's Building Congress awards ceremony, held if an owner was interested in honoring its workers toward the end of construction. On a cold January day in 1931 thirty-two City Bank Farmers Trust building workers received gold buttons and ornate certificates honoring their craftsmanship (*Fig. 71*).[19] A photo taken in one of the skyscraper's unfinished floors shows seventeen proud, necktied workers holding their framed certificates, flanked by their fellow workers, and posing in front of the suited bosses.

MAGNITUDE

The complexity and scale of skyscraper construction defied easy comprehension. Other than the evidence of the skyscraper itself, often the only other means of representing the architecture's magnitude was in material statistics. Builders and owners had these numbers easily on hand as part of their recordkeeping. Skyscraper publicity often focused on such tallies. For the Cities Service Building: 106,000 tons of excavated dirt; 24,000 tons of steel; 23.5 million pounds of cement; 10 million bricks; 3 million man hours of work; 9 miles of window caulking; 236 miles of wiring; 3000 windows; 100,000 square feet of glass; 25,000 light outlets; and so on.[20]

In an age of records the skyscraper's stupendous construction quantities appeared virtuous in and of themselves. On the day in July 1929, for example, that 40 Wall Street's first rivet was driven, an aviator broke a record for continuous flight, circling an airfield in Culver City, California, for over 200 straight hours.[21] In this era skyscraper construction quantities represented yet more evidence of the progress of human achievement.

Chapter Six

TECHNOLOGY

*Raceways for electrical wiring and telephone
lines being laid in the concrete flooring of the
City Bank Farmers Trust Building.*

THE VITAL PART OF ARCHITECTURE IS NOT STRUCTURE BUT SHELTER," asserted One Wall Street architect Ralph Walker; "it is a place in which to be physically comfortable and mentally happy."[1] Walker favored environmental over tectonic thinking in architecture. Similarly, in skyscraper engineering the most important advancements in the 1920s involved the systems that made skyscrapers good shelter: transportation, heating, ventilation, and communications technology. By the 1920s structural techniques for frames and foundations were well established. Comfort and convenience, architects and building owners understood, attracted tenants and made skyscrapers successful economically. One of the Chrysler Building's engineers summed matters up: "The building is no better than its mechanical equipment."[2]

VERTICAL TRANSPORTATION

Elevators are a skyscraper's most indispensable technology and riding them perhaps the quintessential skyscraper experience. Without elevators tall buildings would not exist. As long as people had to walk up stairs, six floors represented the upper limit of commercial office building. The first passenger office building elevator was introduced at 120 Broadway in 1871. Over the following decades engineers electrified elevators, grouped them in banks with express service to upper floors, and learned to control the cab's movement with variable-voltage and microleveling systems. By 1932 an estimated 18,000 passenger elevators in New York City transported 12.2 million riders daily.[3]

In skyscraper planning elevator service represented the key factor in calculating height and volume. The profit to be gained by adding extra tower stories and tenants had to be balanced against the need then produced for more elevators, whose shafts decreased each floor's rentable area. With tenants in first-class buildings expecting to wait in the lobby no more than about twenty seconds for an elevator, a Wall Street area skyscraper's elevator service needed to transport about twelve percent of the building's population within a five-minute period during the peak morning commute.[4] As a rule of thumb there had to be one elevator for every 25,000 square feet of rentable area in a building.[5] By this measure Wall Street's four major towers possessed superior service. 40 Wall Street (43 elevators) possessed one elevator per 19,600 square feet of rentable space. The City Bank Farmers Trust Building (27 elevators) had one elevator per 18,500 square feet. The Cities Service Building's system (25 elevators, including 8 double-deck) averaged one elevator car (counting

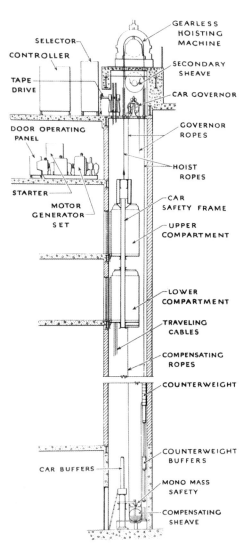

ABOVE: FIG. 72. *The Cities Service Building's innovative double-deck elevators saved space, time, and money by serving passengers on two floors at a time.* Western History Collections, University of Oklahoma Libraries

LEFT: FIG. 73. *Cities Service Building elevator attendants pose surrealistically in the twin cabs of the double-deck elevator system.* Western History Collections, University of Oklahoma Libraries

FIG. 74. *Escalators running from the Cities Service Building's lobby through the six lower floors accommodated rush hour, lunchtime, and interoffice traffic and introduced a sophisticated mode of vertical transport into the world of office work.* Museum of the City of New York

the 8 double-decks as two cars) for every 20,000 square feet of rentable space, and so could convey an estimated 10,000 people per hour.

The Cities Service Building's novel double-deck elevators allowed twelve more floors to be added to the skyscraper's tower without losing valuable rental space for additional shafts (*Figs. 72 and 73*). The Otis-manufactured double-deck cars ran as a high-rise express service from the building's two lobby levels up to the 29th through 60th floors. Besides carrying twice a single car's passenger load, the system decreased overall trip times. With each car one cab would stop at even floors and the other cab at odd floors, with the banks arranged so that from any floor visitors could choose either odd or even destinations. During off-peak hours the cars could be run as single cabs with the top compartment stopping at all floors. The Cities Service Building's double-deck elevators were widely publicized, attracting tenants and public interest to the skyscraper.[6] It was the first time double-deck elevators running in a single shaft had been used in an office building (the type had been invented for mine transport and used at the Eiffel Tower since 1889). The Cities Service Building's double-deck elevators continued to operate until 1972 when they were replaced by modern single cab elevators.

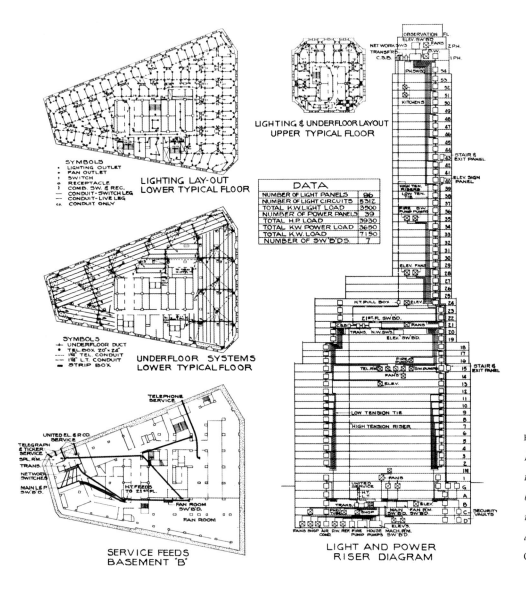

FIG. 75. *The City Bank Farmers Trust Building's electrical system powered the rest of the skyscraper's technology and ran from the basement via vertical risers and horizontal underfloor systems to a multitude of outlets and switches in individual offices.*
Getty Research Library, 940010

The Cities Service Building's innovative transportation technology also included escalators serving the skyscraper's first six stories, which housed the large clerical departments of the Cities Service Company (*Fig. 74*). Cheaper and more efficient to operate than elevators, the five pairs of escalators could convey six thousand people per hour, handling the floors' heavy commuting and interstory traffic. This was the first time escalators had been used extensively in an office building, introducing into office life a technology previously associated with department stores and exhibitions.[7]

ENVIRONMENTAL SYSTEMS

After elevators, environmental systems represented the skyscraper's most essential technology. Without water, heat, and electricity skyscrapers would hardly be habitable, much less functional as office buildings. A skyscraper's electrical system powered the rest of its machinery, including elevators, telephones, pumps, fans, office machinery, fire alarms, and, in the case of banks, vault protection systems (*Fig. 75*). Municipal utility companies typically supplied Wall Street's skyscrapers with high-voltage power running through steel-armored cables into basement transformer vaults, up conduits to brick-lined transformer rooms, then along

FIG. 76. *This view of the City Bank Farmers Trust Building's underfloor electrical wire raceway system also shows the skyscraper's steel columns before and after encasement in fireproof tiles, the raw ceiling surfaces, and the poured concrete flooring in the background.* Architectural Forum

underfloor raceways to individual electrical outlets on floors, columns, and ceilings, which provided tenants with the flexibility to arrange furniture and office machinery as needed (*Fig. 76*). Altogether a large skyscraper might possess upwards of one thousand miles of wiring.[8]

Of all a building's environmental technologies artificial illumination was probably the most important to tenants. Windows simply did not provide enough light for close clerical work, especially on broad lower stories where the majority of the floor area could be over twenty feet away from the nearest window. Overhead general illumination, rather than individual desk lamps, served the general population of office workers. Incandescent mazda lamps, introduced in 1926, proved particularly popular for their "soft rays."[9]

Just as extensive and necessary as the electrical system, a skyscraper's plumbing system supplied hot and cold running water, ozonated drinking water, and water for the building's fire protection system. Brass hot water pipes and steel cold water pipes fed hundreds of separate fixtures. The potentially bursting pressure was obviated by dividing the building vertically into separate zones with independent house tanks and pressure reducing valves. Integrated into the plumbing, a skyscraper's fire fighting system featured reserve water tanks on several floors, corridor hose racks, and separate telephone systems for firefighter use. To prevent fires to begin with, New York City skyscrapers had to be built with externally ventilated fire stairs and fireproof window frames and interior floor, wall, and partition finishes.

Intimately related to its plumbing, a skyscraper's heating technology usually employed vacuum steam heating systems. Outside utilities, such as the New York Steam Company, supplied steam via basement machine rooms and upper floor pressure-reducing valves in separate zones to hundreds of under-window copper radiators (3200 in 40 Wall Street). Larger unit heaters typically warmed skyscrapers' broad lower floors. The heating engineers at the Cities Service Building, Tenney & Ohmes, inspired and assisted by Henry L. Doherty and Cities Service engineers, installed an experimental system that substituted hot water for conventional steam heating (a method invented around 1831 and previously employed for smaller offices and homes). At the Cities Service Building, high-velocity pumps forced hot water through small pipes into copper "fin and tube" radiators placed beneath the skyscraper's windows in steel enclosures designed to blend into the office's decorative features. The hot water was heated up to a maximum of 210 degrees (120 degrees on mild days) with a watch engineer in the basement maintaining temperature control by balancing the system's water flow. Cities Service Building tenants could control the heat by opening or closing air louvers on the radiators; they had no access to valves as in conventional steam heating systems. In contrast with conventional steam heating, the hot water system was more precise and economical, avoided corroded pipes and burnt radiator dust particles, and accommodated late-working tenants by taking longer to cool down. Engineers also anticipated circulating chilled water or brine through the system in summer to cool down the building's lower six floors.[10] Like the double-deck elevators, the Cities Service Building's dual hot water heating and chilled water cooling system was a distinctive technological attraction for the skyscraper and "an experiment that will be watched with interest by architects and builders all over the country," commented G. W. Gray in the magazine *World's Work.*[11]

Connected to the Cities Service Building's experimental hot water heating system was the building's equally innovative unit ventilation system. Compartment space between window sills was provided for fan units to draw fresh air through aluminum sills, filter the air with cotton fiberpacks, warm it using the adjacent hot water radiators, and then blow the air up into ceiling ducts where it could be ventilated down into the center of the room. Adjustable baffles allowed air to be drawn from either inside or outside. In summer the air could be cooled by the brine-chilled radiators. Compared to conventional forced central ventilation, the Cities Service

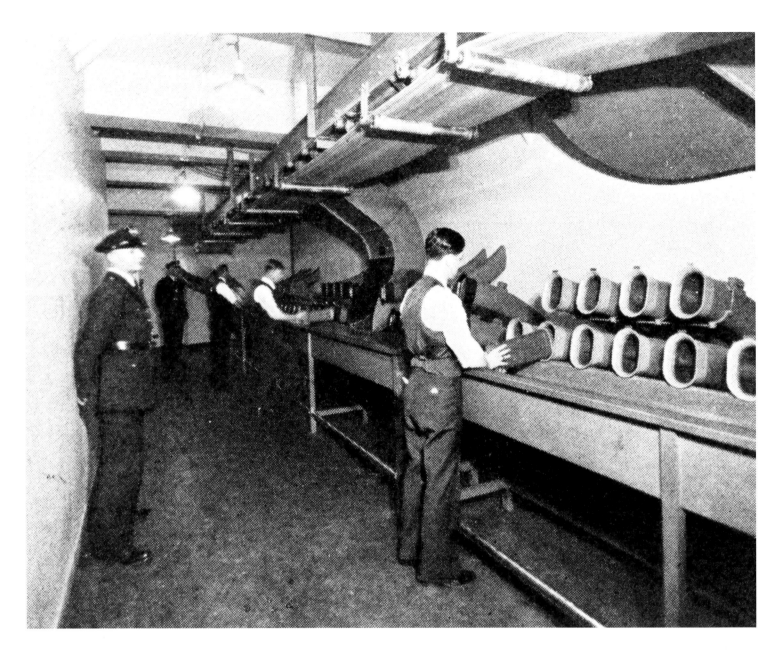

FIG. 77. *Pneumatic tube systems kept vital streams of information flowing smoothly from office to office. In the City Bank Farmers Trust Building's transfer station, workers direct leather oval carriers to their destinations according to coded numbers and tabs.*
Architectural Forum

Building's unit ventilating system replaced centralized and space-consuming fan rooms and ducts with small, economical, flexibly installed units. These were first provided in the Cities Service Building's lower stories above the fifth floor; tenants above could install the fan units in the built-in compartments as needed. Again, technology was put at the service of increased flexibility, comfort, and profit.

COMMUNICATIONS

On Wall Street information is the ultimate commodity, its circulation in person, on paper, by phone, wire, mail, ticker-tape, and messenger the area's life-blood. Since the turn of the century, telephones had supplemented the hand messenger system that circulated letters, contracts, securities, buy and sell orders, and the like. Telephones also connected far-flung national and global commercial networks. In February 1931 City Bank Farmers Trust president James Perkins officially opened the "largest private telephone exchange in the world" on the 15th floor of his bank's new skyscraper.[12] Staffed by some forty operators, City Bank Farmers Trust's No. 702-A

Dial PBX (private branch exchange) system was capable of handling more than a hundred thousand calls per day, carried over ten thousand individual extensions. All this was linked together via riser shafts in the skyscraper's service core, control closets on each floor, and miles of wires in underfloor conduits, baseboard raceways, and behind corridor and office picture moldings.

Besides telephones many Wall Street area skyscrapers, including all four major towers, also possessed extensive pneumatic tube systems (*Fig. 77*). Invented in the nineteenth century, these systems used air compression to transport through brass tubes at twenty m.p.h. mail, telegrams, securities, and interoffice communications. These were packed in leather carriers marked with coded address numbers, colors, and dials which guided them on their journey from terminal to terminal via central transfer stations where the pouches were sorted according to their destinations.[13] Such technology proved especially valuable in skyscrapers with busy "private banking and brokerage houses whose functions require rapid transfer of stocks and papers," explained the architect Yasuo Matsui. He helped design 40 Wall Street's pneumatic tube system which featured mezzanine-level terminals to keep messengers from clogging the building's lobbies and elevators during the trading day.[14] Because superior, reliable communications meant time and money for tenants, this type of technology was perhaps the most important in any skyscraper's infrastructure, from a purely business point of view.

ENCLOSURE AND CONCEALMENT

The overall aim of skyscraper technology was to engineer integrated, flexible, and efficient systems in the name of a more perfect interior environment. In line with this goal, building hygiene ranked as one of tenants' top priorities. "Next to the lighting and ventilation of his office, the tenant is probably more concerned with the matter of cleanliness than anything else," reported B. H. Belknap in 1924.[15] New technologies satisfied these desires. All four major financial district towers incorporated modern centralized vacuum cleaning systems, snaking their way behind the scene via basement machinery and separators, rooftop exhaust tanks, turbo blowers, and hoses on every floor that stretched dozens of feet down halls and into offices. The City Bank Farmers Trust Building also featured a building-wide liquid soap system for its bathrooms, with basement soap-making and storage facilities and intermediate auxiliary tanks feeding every bathroom's individual dispensers.

The desire to engineer cleanliness was a reaction in part to the surrounding city's dirt, noise, and disorder. One of the Cities Service Building ventilating system's advantages was that "with it in operation, the window can, of course be kept closed," wrote C. H. Fister for *Building Investment* in 1932.[16] Closed windows and conditioned air meant less street noise and dust, producing more efficient workers. "Health engineers assert that twenty-five percent better work can be done in offices so heated and

FIG. 78. *The Cities Service Building's set-back terraces featured open aluminum railings, suggested by company president Henry L. Doherty, which enabled winds to clean the terrace floor and let tenants enjoy fresh air and sweeping metropolitan views.* Western History Collections, University of Oklahoma Libraries

ventilated," claimed Edwin Hill about the Cities Service Building's systems.[17] Wall Street area skyscrapers' environmental technology aimed to insulate the buildings from the financial district's increasing pollution and congestion, a situation that, ironically, the skyscrapers had helped produce in the first place and continued to aggravate.

At the same time that skyscraper engineers and architects strove to separate inside from outside, a strong desire remained to connect with nature, achievable through technology and architecture. Skyscraper analysts W. C. Clark and J. L. Kingston looked forward in 1930 to the advent of all-glass skyscraper walls, "or even of glass through which the ultra-violet radiations of the sun may pass, thus permitting sunlight to exercise its full therapeutic and aesthetic effects."[18] From the Cities Service Building's rooftop observation gallery visitors could enjoy fresh air and bright sunlight. Along the same building's set-backs, open aluminum railings, rather than the usual parapets, were installed at Henry L. Doherty's suggestion to create "usable promenades" so that tenants could "stroll out on the terraces" and "enjoy the exhilaration" of harbor breezes and metropolitan vistas (*Fig. 78*).[19] The experience from the Cities Service Building's terraces encapsulates what architect and theorist Rem Koolhaas has called the skyscraper's "metropolitan paradox: the greater the distance from the earth, the closer the communication with what remains of nature (i.e., light and air)."[20]

A similar paradox existed between the celebration of skyscraper technology and its invisibility in the building itself. In the 1920s and early 1930s infrastructure machinery represented the skyscraper's most modern aspect. Advanced technology could endow a skyscraper, such as the Cities Service Building, with a distinctive image as much as could a signature skyline profile. From the architect's point of view, however, technology needed only discreet accommodation. The architect's job was to house not honor technology.

In skyscraper design architects aimed to concentrate and conceal skyscraper technology. In part the reasoning was financial. Compact vertical service cores, packed with risers and utilities closets, freed up maximum amounts of valuable rentable office area. Practically, basements and penthouses were the best for machine, motor generator, and fan rooms, storage space, water tanks, and elevator equipment. Spaced throughout the skyscraper, intermediate soundproofed machine floors, "upstairs cellars" one writer called them, like the City Bank Farmers Trust Building's 15th floor, accommodated telephone switchboards, water tanks, and electrical vaults housed together to minimize disruption to rentable floors and building tenants.[21] Everywhere infrastructure remained out of sight. Ducts, pipes, raceways, conduits, and shafts were all furred into walls and columns and buried beneath floors. At the Cities Service Building, "completely concealed" risers were "a very desirable feature" and specially designed steel radiator enclosures were embedded into the floor to avoid "unsightly gaps at the base."[22]

Although dependent upon and proud of technology's services, architects, owners, and tenants remained embarrassed by technology's visual and physical presence. As with the human body's own earthy parts, a skyscraper's structural and technological necessities seemed best hidden behind adorned walls, floors, and ceilings. In part this may have been because architects had no hand in engineering the skyscraper's infrastructure. Separate firms of consulting engineers, specializing in steel, electrical and plumbing systems, elevators, and vault systems, did all that work, laying out plans, organizing drawings, producing specifications, ordering materials, and overseeing construction. The architects of Wall Street's skyscrapers had no direct stake in the buildings' technologies and so neither celebrated nor represented them. When it came to decorating Wall Street area skyscrapers, architects had other ideas to express, about society, beauty, and history.

Chapter Seven

EXTERIOR
EXPRESSION

Wall Street's skyscrapers, 1930.

ITHIN LITTLE MORE THAN A DECADE, FROM THE LATE 1910S TO early 1930s, Wall Street area skyscrapers developed stylistically from an assured use of tradition to an Art Deco experimental period and then to a nearly complete disavowal of exterior decoration. In this evolution the financial district's architecture reflected generally the dynamic in western architectural culture of the 1920s between adherence to familiarity and authority, on one hand, and a desire for more modern expression, on the other. In between the extremes of these two poles the architects working around Wall Street sought a progressive middle ground between tradition and revolution.

LITERAL TRADITION

Before World War I architects ornamented Wall Street area skyscrapers with a profusion of classical and Gothic ornament. Immediately after the war the same tendencies prevailed, though more sober in tone and monumental in scale, as seen in the Cunard Building (1919–21) by Benjamin Wistar Morris (*Fig. 79*), and its pendant across Broadway, the Standard Oil Building (1922–26), by Carrère & Hastings with Shreve, Lamb, & Blake (*Fig. 61*).

In these buildings traditional ornament continued to be applied literally. Massive columns and pilasters paraded across street fronts and skyline pavilions. Full-bodied cornices, quoins, and balustrades defined facade edges and subdivisions. Sculptural pediments, shields, capitals, obelisks, urns, friezes, and door frames enlivened key passages. In the literal tradition, too, architects reproduced whole large-scale motifs from the past. Both the Cunard and Standard Oil buildings feature rusticated and arcaded bases in the manner of sixteenth-century Italian town palaces. Atop the Standard Oil Building's offset tower the architects raised a stepped-pyramid surmounted by a gigantic urn, recalling the ancient Mausoleum of

Halicarnassus and the similar prewar pyramidal caps of the Woolworth Building (1910–13) and the nearby Bankers Trust Building (1909–12). The pyramidal crown accentuated the skyscraper's verticality and like all distinctive pinnacles differentiated the building from its skyline competitors.

The literal application of traditional motifs helped unify skyscraper elevations into cohesive compositions of built-up horizontal masses laterally contained. The style, assurance, and solidity of the Cunard Building's facade seemed nearly "Medicean" to the critic Royal Cortissoz in 1921: "You have a sense of business raised to a higher power, taking luxury in its stride."[1]

The literal tradition's validity lasted around Wall Street through the late 1920s. The Lee, Higginson & Company Building (1929) at 37 Broad Street, by Cross & Cross, effectively employs a Doric entrance frame and upper Ionic colonnade to convey the bank's dignity and prestige (*Fig. 80*). At this late date, however, the rest of the elevation has simplified into ashlar planes rather than rusticated textures. Eventually the literal tradition became exhausted and even ridiculous. A dainty pair of literal Greek temples perch incongruously next to each other atop the Bank of New York Building at 48 Wall Street (1927–29, B. W. Morris) and the neighboring National City Company Building at 52 Wall Street (1928, McKim, Mead & White), utterly without relation to the massive buildings below.

TRADITION ABRIDGED

As the 1920s advanced architectural taste curtailed traditional ornamentation. Architects, increasingly aware of European modernism, desired to loosen the past's grip and express in simpler terms the character of contemporary times. Clients, for their part, strove for expression of rational efficiency. Restraint in decoration connoted modernity and economy.

Traditional motifs persisted but now diminished in mass, legibility, quantity, and coherence. Classical motifs flattened into smooth ashlar, grooved pilasters, low-relief panels, stripped entablatures, and stylized keystones and volutes. Windows lost frames. Spandrels became abstract patterns. In quantity, too, ornament abated. Sometimes only the barest moldings and projections remained to define a facade's abbreviated sense of proportion and historical association. Classical detailing as well as Gothic corbels, balconies, turrets, and crenellation hung isolated on bare brick surfaces.

Facades ornamented in this abridged fashion lost the force of specific historical associations. At the Seamen's Savings Bank Building at 74 Wall Street (1926, B. W. Morris) the facade's venerability, symbolizing the bank's security, derives not from the vaguely northern Italian historical motifs but from the polychromatic quarry-faced Plymouth granite blocks whose "split surfaces have been exposed for ages to the weather," noted a publicity pamphlet (*Fig. 81*).[2]

At the intersection of Wall and Broad streets, in the financial district's heart, Trowbridge & Livingston specialized in monuments of abridged tradition. At the

FIG. 80. *The Lee, Higginson & Company Building (1929, Cross & Cross) on Broad Street features a Greek Doric portico and upper Ionic colonnade applied to a plain ashlar facade that exemplifies the simplification of wall surfaces in the late 1920s. To the left is the Broad-Exchange Building (1900–02, Clinton & Russell).* Norman McGrath

LEFT: FIG. 81. *The granite facing of the Seamen's Bank for Savings Building (1926–27, B. W. Morris) on Wall Street conveys an air of weathered venerability that complements the northern Italian styling of the portal, balconies, and rooftop arcade.* Norman McGrath

RIGHT: FIG. 82. *The hulking Equitable Trust Building (1925–28) wraps the low-lying Morgan Bank Building (1915), both by Trowbridge & Livingston, at the corner of Wall and Broad streets.* Architectural Record

OPPOSITE: FIG. 83. *40 Wall Street (1929–30, H. C. Severance and Y. Matsui) towers above the neighboring temple crests of the National City Company (1928, McKim, Mead & White), in the near foreground, and Bank of New York (1927–29, B. W. Morris) buildings, and, in the background, the pyramidal cap of the Bankers Trust Building and the unglazed penthouse of One Wall Street.* Museum of the City of New York

southeast corner the firm's Morgan Bank Building (1915) featured ashlar walls, frameless windows, and simplified entablatures (*Fig. 82*). In 1922, across Broad Street, the firm erected in similar plain beautiful granite finish a 26-story addition to the New York Stock Exchange. Then, between 1925 and 1928, Trowbridge & Livingston built the massive 43-story Equitable Trust Company Building—more capacious in floor area (750,000 square feet) than every other area skyscraper built between the wars except 40 Wall Street. Wrapping the ostentatiously small Morgan Bank Building, the Equitable Trust's limestone-clad facades extended the earlier building's march of frameless windows and reduced entablature and cornice lines. The peak's pyramidal set-backs were articulated with only the slightest horizontal cornices, "splendidly handled, with great simplicity," approved the modernist critic Lewis Mumford, "being unadorned by useless architectural detail."[3]

At its best the tendency to abridge tradition could produce skyscrapers of powerful abstract effect, yet still retaining the solidity of classical masonry massing. Other examples in the financial district include the Federal Reserve Bank Building (1921–24, York & Sawyer), the Westinghouse Building at 150 Broadway (1924, Starrett & Van Vleck), the Bank of America Building at 44 Wall Street (1926, Trowbridge & Livingston), 50 Broadway (1926–27, H. C. Severance), the Fred F. French (Harriman) Building at 39 Broadway (1928, Cross & Cross), and the International Telephone & Telegraph Building at 67 Broad Street (1930, Louis Weeks). Traditional ornament could, however, be abridged to such a degree as to erode a skyscraper facade's overall coherence and consistency, dissolving the links between individual parts, as in the case of 40 Wall Street.

FIG. 84. *40 Wall Street's parade of stylized classical piers and windowed frieze along the skyscraper's rear Pine Street elevation represents a modern reinterpretation of the neighboring Sub-Treasury Building's Greek Revival Doric facade from the 1840s.* Courtesy Chase Manhattan Archives

40 WALL STREET: HYBRID HEIGHTS

The symmetrical tapered mass of 40 Wall Street (1929–30) is divided vertically into the three disconnected parts of its base, shaft, and crest (*Fig. 83*). The four-story-high limestone-clad frontages at the base along Wall and Pine streets feature solid vertical fluted piers and geometric caps framing recessed windows and terra cotta spandrels, with windows punched through at the entablature frieze level in place of traditional classical metopes (*Figs. 84 and 85*). The rear, 10-bay Pine Street base rests directly on a low stylobate; the lower Wall Street level required a high ground floor podium. Both fronts' rhythm of strong vertical solids and dark recessed voids resemble stylized Greek temple colonnades. In fact the associate architect Yasuo Matsui carefully studied 40 Wall Street's podium height and entablature level in relation to the nearby Wall Street Doric colonnade of the Sub-Treasury Building (1834–42, Town & Davis), the financial district's great Greek Revival temple at the head of Broad Street.[4] 40 Wall Street's stylized Greek base thus gives visual support to the skyscraper above and blends the building into a prestigious streetscape.

To mark the skyscraper's main Wall Street entrance Walker & Gillette, one of The Manhattan Company's architects, commissioned for $7000 the well-known sculptor Elie Nadelman to cast a reclining, 10-foot-long bronze of Oceanus, the Greek Titan (1929–30, present location unknown) (*Fig. 85*).[5] Nadelman modeled his *Oceanus* from a nineteenth-century Manhattan Company stock certificate, the figure having been featured on the corporation's official seal from its early days as a water utility company. *Oceanus* advertised the building's corporate identity and claimed validity for the continued use of traditional allegorical sculpture on modern skyscrapers. The stylized Italian baroque languor of the figure also underscored the skyscraper base's classical mien.

At the skyscraper's crest the architects pursued a different historicist strategy, topping the soaring brick shaft with a pyramidal cap in a "modernized French Gothic" style (*Fig. 86*).[6] Closely resembling Matsui's unbuilt 1928–29 Madison Avenue Houston Tower, 40 Wall Street's copper-clad crown features buttressed terraces, diaper-work patterning, tiny dormer windows, and a glass lantern surmounted by a thin

FIG. 85. *40 Wall Street's main entrance was crowned by a reclining bronze* Oceanus *(1931), designed by the sculptor Elie Nadelman. Oceanus was the emblem of The Manhattan Company banking group from its early days as a water supply company.* Courtesy Chase Manhattan Archives; photographer, Edward Ozern

FIG. 86. *40 Wall Street's lead- and copper-clad pyramidal cap, complete with crystal ball finial, brought the 71-story skyscraper to a "modernized French Gothic" climax. The tapering penthouse floors accommodated machinery, observation rooms, and a small 66ᵗʰ-floor residential apartment.*

Norman McGrath

mast and crystal ball finial. The crest's pyramidal shape stretches the square tower upwards, accentuating the building's verticality visually and by association with Gothic cathedrals and town hall spires.

40 Wall Street's classicized base and Gothicized crest digress in style, pursuing their own independent effects and meanings. The classicized base emphasizes context and support. The Gothicized crest underscores the building's verticality. The stylistic disparity between the two is smoothed out by the abridgement of motifs, and by the base and crest's disconnection on either end of the high brick shaft. The same hybrid of classical and Gothic traditions had appeared earlier at the 37-story Brown Brothers and Harriman Building (1927) at 63 Wall Street, another Starrett Brothers development (with Matsui assisting Delano & Aldrich).

CITY BANK FARMERS TRUST: "CONSERVATIVE MODERN"

While 40 Wall Street was being completed, the architect brothers John and Eliot Cross, and their designer George Maguolo, had well in hand the construction of the City Bank Farmers Trust Building. Finished in 1931 a block south of Wall Street, the City Bank Farmers Trust Building soared 54 stories into the air, its tall square tower offset above the irregular trapezoidal base.

As cladding the architects employed primarily Alabama Rockwood limestone with New York Mohegan granite along the basement and Exchange Place portal. This expensive and elegant veneer announced the City Bank Farmers Trust Building's allegiance to tradition, as opposed to brick utilitarianism. Classical repose and harmony were given by the heavy base and in the tower by intermittent horizontal bands and the chamfered angles (*Fig. 87*), which provided a measured containment resembling the Beaux-Arts styling of the landmark Singer Tower by Ernest Flagg two decades earlier. The City Bank Farmers Trust Building's stacked classical articulation was integrated vertically by projecting piers running up the building's height, culminating in a simple three-stage octagonal cap (*Fig. 88*). This terminus resembled the Gothicized crest atop Cross & Cross's 50-story RCA Victor Building, here abstractly classicized with round arches. Along with the nearly octagonal tower, the crest helped compose the entire skyscraper into a single soaring "graceful whole," as Cross & Cross intended.[7]

Other factors contributed to the City Bank Farmers Trust Building's traditionalist appearance, including the liberal application of sculpted ornament along the base, including spandrel rosettes, acanthus grillwork, Greek profile medallions, and hypertrophied triglyphs in the fenestrated frieze. All along the base an array of motifs emblematized the bank's character, from a pictographic combination of eagle ("national"), sheaf ("farmer"), and lock and key ("security"), to more general allegorical images of scales ("honesty"), hourglasses ("interest"), cornucopias ("prosperity"), caducei ("finance"), ships ("navigation"), and a compass with a model of the skyscraper ("architecture") (*Fig. 89*).[8] Humorously, a conventional classical bucranium

ABOVE LEFT: FIG. 87. *Along William Street the City Bank Farmers Trust Building's base and tower rise in parallel planes (1930–31, Cross & Cross). The skyscraper's overall verticality is harmoniously balanced by light horizontal banding in the tower shaft.* Norman McGrath

ABOVE RIGHT: FIG. 88. *At its crest the City Bank Farmers Trust Building's tower changes from a chamfered square to a pair of stacked polygonal penthouse floors.* Norman McGrath

LEFT: FIG. 89. *At the corner of William Street and Exchange Place, stylized Greek and Art Deco ornament frames emblems of commerce, plenty, and security at the bronze doorway into the City Bank Farmers Trust Company's original ground-floor headquarters.* Norman McGrath

LEFT: FIG. 90. *The arched Exchange Place entrance portal into the elevator and tenants' lobby of the City Bank Farmers Trust Building is framed by sculpted foreign coins representing the overseas offices of the parent National City Bank.* Norman McGrath

RIGHT: FIG. 91. *Four of the fourteen "giants of finance" heads designed by British sculptor David Evans at the 19th floor of the City Bank Farmers Trust Building, alternately smiling and frowning to symbolize economic cycles of plenty and scarcity.* Norman McGrath

(an ox-skull with garland) was denoted by the architects "In Memory of the Bull Market Catastrophe of '29."[9] Framing the round-arched Exchange Place portal eleven carved national coins represented the global branches of National City Bank (Farmers Trust's parent) (*Fig. 90*). Much of this ornamentation was the work of the British sculptor and Cranbrook Academy professor David Evans, who also designed the fourteen giant stone heads at the skyscraper's set-back 19th floor (*Fig. 91*). Seven of these helmeted, vaguely Greek and Assyrian "giants of finance" bear scowling visages, while the alternate seven smile benignly. This symbolized Wall Street finance's mercurial cycles of bust and boom and referred perhaps to Joseph's biblical prophesy to pharaoh of "seven years of plenty" followed by "seven years of famine" (unintentionally apt commentary on the verge of the Great Depression).

Alongside its traditional sense of harmony, elegance, and decor, Cross & Cross strove also to give a modern character to the City Bank Farmers Trust Building and insisted that function guided their design. "The architects hold no brief for any particular architectural style" averred a large July 1931 feature story in *Architectural Forum*, "and have been at some pains to clothe structure in material and form to serve as frank expression of the mechanical and economic forces

involved.... The buttresses of the 15th floor will serve as an illustration of this point. They were designed to give a visual support to the tower above and to serve as a concealment for the exhaust vents which are conducted through their backs to invisible louvered outlets."[10] Notwithstanding the traditional concealments of Cross & Cross's functionalism, the City Bank Farmer Trust Building's smooth stone facade was unmistakably modern in its top-to-bottom, light toned veneer quality, especially at the chamfered corners which were the visual opposites of traditional heavy corner quoining.

The City Bank Farmers Trust Building represented the financial district's finest example of abridged tradition. Cross & Cross blended discrete traditional details and an overall sense of harmonious unity with more modern tendencies toward flatness, abstraction, and lightness. The *Real Estate Record and Guide* called the City Bank Farmers Trust Building "conservative modern in style and of classic proportions."[11]

ART DECO
Simultaneous with the abridged traditionalism of 40 Wall Street and the City Bank Farmers Trust Building, other Wall Street area skyscrapers foreswore historicist associations altogether in favor of direct expression of material, structure, and verticality. Sometimes called "moderne" at the time, and now generally denominated Art Deco, these skyscrapers' style was suffused with a sense of energy and optimism.

LEFT: FIG. 92. *The jazzy textures of Ely Jacques Kahn's 80 John Street facade (1926–27), especially at the mezzanine level, inaugurated a period of Art Deco experimentation in the financial district's architecture.* Norman McGrath

RIGHT: FIG. 93. *The overall texturing of 111 John Street (1928–29) continued Kahn's experimentation with abstract ornamentation that could knit together massive skyscraper elevations using a distinctly modern decorative idiom.* American Commercial Buildings of Today

FIG. 94. *The banded brick facade of 29 Broadway (1930–31, Sloan & Robertson) contrasts with its traditional neighbors and echoes the horizontal stripped windows of contemporary European International Style modernism, though here the windows are not actually continuous.* Norman McGrath

The Art Deco tendency around Wall Street began with Ely Jacques Kahn's 27-story Insurance Center Building at 80 John Street (1926–27) where a richly textured mezzanine frieze features pillowed string courses and blocks, surmounted by a rhythmic run of zigzag ornament in front of whirling circular shields (*Fig. 92*). Echoing this dynamic abstract pattern the spandrels above were subtly studded with brick droplets and the set-back corners vibrate with tight-packed vertical ribs. Soon after, Kahn designed the much larger Indemnity Building at 111 John Street (1928–29) with a more evenly textured surface, featuring broad belts of striated brick wrapping the corners, woven into the patterned spandrels and simpler mezzanine (*Fig. 93*).

Kahn's all-over patterning and integral surface treatment, in these buildings and his similar midtown Two Park Avenue Building (1926) and Bricken Building (1928–30), reunified the skyscraper's exterior after 40 Wall Street's and other abridged elevations' loss of coherence. Some of Kahn's contemporaries thought they recognized archaic Mesoamerican echoes in his patterning, such as the Chilean architect Francisco Mujica who remarked on Two Park Avenue's "surprising likeness with the decorations and polychromes of the primitive monuments of America."[12] Kahn himself wrote, "The texture of its surface, the rhythms of the elements that break that surface either into planes or distinct areas of contrasting interest, becomes ornament."[13]

Kahn's John Street skyscrapers were the most high-spirited examples of financial district Art Deco. Other examples made the area around Wall Street fertile ground for experiments in the style. At 19 Rector Street (1929–30) architect Lafayette A. Goldstone designed a 38-story, brick-clad skyscraper with starburst railings and low-relief polychrome terra cotta chevron paneling (*Fig. 62*). Spectacularly, the set-back midsection rotates between the base and tower (to accommodate the irregular lot), casting into gigantic three-dimensional form the dynamic cubism of its Art Deco ornament. Nearby at 29 Broadway (1930–31) Sloan & Robertson produced a 31-story slab of alternating horizontal white and black enameled brick bands, resembling modernistic strip windows, to go with the Art Deco portal's high banded pylons with abstract scrolled tops and aluminum grill (*Fig. 94*).

Other fine Art Deco exteriors were produced in the western section of the financial district by Starrett & Van Vleck, led by surviving partner Ernest Van Vleck, including the 15-story New York Curb Exchange (1930, now the American Stock Exchange Building) at 86 Trinity Place, whose gray monotone facade featured stylized flat arches and keystones, broad fluted piers and plain mullions. With similar restraint Starrett & Van Vleck sheathed the Downtown Athletic Club (1930–31) at 19 West Street in a warm brick facing, which concealed the club's array of facilities including an indoor golf course (*Fig. 95*).

The trend toward plainer skyscraper exteriors continued through the early 1930s. 7 Hanover Street (1931, Chester B. Storm), 90 John Street (1931), and 116 John Street (1931, Louis Abramson) all featured ashlar bases, simple brick shafts with projecting

piers and mullions, recessed spandrels, and bare set-backs. Having moved well away from both literal and abridged tradition, Wall Street's Art Deco skyscrapers, with their overall surface patterning and expression of material and verticality, embodied qualities of coherence, sobriety, economy, and efficiency. These were especially appropriate in the early years of economic recession and imminent depression.

ONE WALL STREET: RHYTHM AND REMEDY

One Wall Street (1929–31) was the financial district's most self-consciously ambitious work of art, built by the Irving Trust Company for its new headquarters at the prominent intersection of Broadway and Wall Street (*Fig. 96*). Art Deco in many respects, One Wall Street reflected architect Ralph Walker's articulate vision of modern design.

FIG. 96. *The overall verticality of One Wall Street's facade (1929–31), designed by Ralph Walker, is varied by the subtle lateral rhythm of its fluting, synchronized with the staggered heights of its Broadway ground floor openings.* Museum of the City of New York

Walker made the most of the height of the shortest of the financial district's four major towers, accenting what he called architecture's "vertical urge."[14] Directly up out of the sidewalk sprung incised Art Deco stalks carved into the limestone walls (*Fig. 36*). No horizontal breaks whatsoever interrupt the elevation's verticality. Chamfered corners meld the Indiana limestone facades into a single whole. "A man on the street looking up," Walker explained, "should feel the power of that vertical lift upwards throughout the entire wall height."[15] (*Fig. 156*)

Verticality, however, was not Walker's primary aim. "We had started with a concept of a building with curtain walls which would have the appearance of surface movement," he noted.[16] Independent of the underlying frame structure, this "allows the wall to be treated at will," observed John Shapley about One Wall Street's design

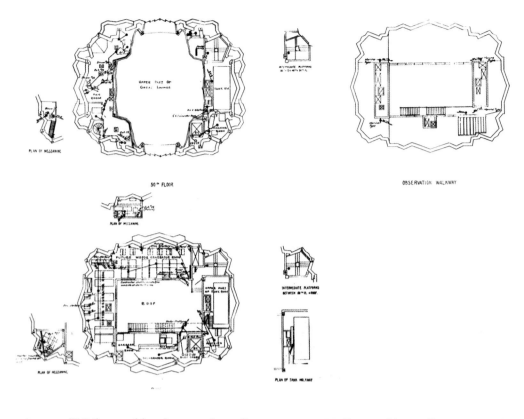

in 1929.[17] Liberated by the curtain wall conception, Walker and his colleagues "tried to do something different."

> We have tried to superimpose one rhythm upon a basic rhythm. We have one rhythm which goes around the entire building. These rhythmic motifs are not the same size. Although we endeavored to break them up, still they didn't give enough interest, so we decided to break them up again, which happens generally to be every 20 to 22 feet, with another motif, which we enlarged. This we broke up in a way and placed our basic rhythm above it. It is a sort of fluting motif.... So, what we actually have on the face of our walls is two rhythms, one imposed upon the other. We believe that the building is going to show, as a matter of fact, the influence of this rhythmic design.[18]

Walker's rhythmic "fluting motif," with an angled pitch of 1:9, echoed the syncopated window series and vertical "reeding" of the landmark Woolworth Building, Irving Trust's quarters before One Wall Street.[19] At One Wall Street the fluting motif dominates all the exterior surfaces, including the flared portals and splayed window frames (which cost an extra $40,000 to install), knitting the skyscraper's skin into one integral rippled whole (*Fig. 97*). Inside, too, angled walls line One Wall Street's reception room, tenants' lobby, and penthouse directors' observation lounge.

One Wall Street's complex fluted rhythms were motivated by Walker's belief that architecture should meet people's "demand for beauty" and that "advanced" civilizations require more beauty than "pioneering" civilizations.[20] In the fast-paced modern financial district "we figured out, roughly, that the building we are doing at 1 Wall Street would in one year have 200 thousand people looking at it from all sides," Walker recalled; "we have got to give them mental relief and pleasure."[21]

For Walker architecture provided the best "mental escape" and "recreation for the mind" when its surfaces composed "a pattern that is not easily read at a glance...a unity not easily comprehended."[22] Intricacy stimulated the attention and imagination and provided mental relief because, in Walker's mind, it mimicked nature's own "ever-changing light and pattern."[23] Like a dappled landscape scene, One Wall Street's angled walls would catch "sunlight and flitting shadows through the day," promised an Irving Trust press release.[24] One Wall Street's rhythmic facade also expressed the character of the modern age, Walker believed. "The time is one of movement," he insisted.[25] "To my mind [One Wall Street's rhythmic design] is quite sophisticated and quite in line with our machine age in which precision as well as motion is necessary."[26]

One Wall Street's exterior integrated Art Deco's jazzy rhythms into a comprehensive fluted verticality governed by disciplined wholeness, expressive seriousness, and theoretical insight. In effect, Walker rediscovered in new forms the assurance and conviction that architects had lost with the abridgement of tradition.

To the modernist critic Lewis Mumford, however, Walker's idea of modernity missed the mark entirely.

> By creating a scalloped facade of concave stone, the architects succeeded in making a steel-frame building with a curtain wall look like a solid pile of stone; but why? Chaste though that exterior is, it is mere swank, and unconvincing swank at that. The Irving Trust Company Building is only a more refined and subtle version of the notion that modern domestic life can be happily encased in Ye Olde Tudor Manor House—and if we believe this, where are we?[27]

Fundamentally, Mumford believed that a wall's primary expressive purpose lay in its representation of a building's *internal* structural condition. On the contrary Walker believed that a wall's primary expressive purpose should be directed *externally* toward its ameliorative effect on beholders. Between the two views there could be little common ground. Mumford based his ideas on contemporary avant-garde European tendencies. His misunderstanding and disappointment with much of New York's and especially Wall Street's architectural production in the 1930s was profound. About the Cities Service Building, for example, all Mumford could say in 1932 was that "the new tower is little more than a sad, admonitory finger, reminding us of the past."[28]

CITIES SERVICE BUILDING: VERTICAL ASPIRATION
Mumford's modernist ideology blinded him to the qualities of the Cities Service Building. Monumental in scale and integrated in effect, Clinton & Russell, Holton & George's 952-foot structure surpassed all local skyscrapers in quantitative height and qualitative vertical expression, its separate stages sculpted together into one unified rising mass (*Fig. 98*).

At one level the Cities Service Building's architecture conformed to the owner's workmanlike image of itself. Company leader Henry L. Doherty "insisted on dignity with beauty, to the absolute avoidance of the garish, the flamboyant and the over-colorful," wrote the publicist Edwin Hill. To attract tenants, too, the architecture should appear "exclusive, rich, yet simple and even a little severe," representing "good taste, artistic reticence...obvious strength and grace."[29]

At sidewalk level the Cities Service Building's luxurious oriental Minnesota granite podium, in warm rose and black, appears as a sophisticated thin veneer sliding up through the sidewalk, sliced through by low frameless windows and cut back at the building's roll-molded corners and entrances along Pine and Cedar streets (*Fig. 99*). Here the lofty portals received a rich patterning of low-relief Art Deco sunflowers, curling acanthus scrolls, sunbursts, chevrons, and stepped-pyramidal mountains that continued along the base's spandrels (*Fig. 100*). At numerous points the stylized ornament framed the official Cities Service delta and expanding circle logo, intertwining corporate identity with modern symbolization of natural vitality and optimism.

In the piers dividing the paired bays of the Pine and Cedar street portals, scale models of the skyscraper rest atop the granite podium. Seeming to grow out of their hewn limestone blocks, these models underscore the organicism of the surrounding ornament. The models also present to visitors and inhabitants of the Cities Service Building the only complete image of the monumental skyscraper they would ever likely have in the cramped financial district, thus advertising and ennobling Cities Service's architectural achievement.

Above the lower three stories of gray Indiana limestone, the Cities Service Building's buff-gray brick exterior was only modestly adorned. Projecting vertical piers alternate with thinner mullions to create a varied lateral syncopation. The brick subtly darkens in four stages so that the upper part of the skyscraper shaft, above the 47th floor, stands out most against the sky. Limestone coping accents the set-back rhythms while recessed spandrels, textured with woven brick cross-patterns, enliven the looming walls. Above the level of the set-backs, the tower's vertical piers and mullions recede into one plane with the horizontal spandrels, while the angled corners emphasize the shaft's verticality. More than in traditional or Art Deco facades the overall sculpted form dominates particular details.

The most original section of the Cities Service Building exterior is the skyscraper's crest where the architects created "a new style of roof architecture which is almost sensational in its 'differentness,'" enthused the New York chronicler W. Parker Chase (*Fig. 101*).[30] Commencing at the 54th floor's corners with a staggered series of light-toned limestone set-backs and terraces, the crest's tapering rhythm quickens at the 61st floor, then retracts back into a compact rectangular pinnacle at the 65th floor (housing Cities Service's oval boardroom), before culminating with the 66th-floor metal and glass observation gallery, itself surmounted by a 27-foot metal lantern and 97-foot stainless steel

SKYSCRAPER RIVALS

OPPOSITE PAGE: FIG. 98. *The steeply ascending stages of the Cities Service Building (1930–32, Clinton & Russell, Holton & George) rise from a base nearly identical to neighboring One Cedar Street (1930), built by the same architects under similar zoning restrictions. In the background, left to right, are the prominent spires of One Wall Street, 40 Wall Street, and the Woolworth Building.* Western History Collections, University of Oklahoma Libraries

ABOVE RIGHT: FIG. 99. *At the Cities Service Building's Pine and Pearl streets corner, swirling rose and black Minnesota granite rises flush from the sidewalk, its veneer quality accentuated by the windows cut cleanly into the flat surfaces.* Norman McGrath

ABOVE LEFT: FIG. 100. *The Cities Service Building's main Pine Street entrance portal uses limestone and metal Art Deco ornament, entwined with the Cities Service expanding circle logo, to frame, in the pier between the doors, a large-scale model of the skyscraper itself.* Norman McGrath

mast. The crest's stages blend into each other and with the tower below, unlike traditional caps where borrowed historical motifs rest separately atop the skyscraper mass.

At night the Cities Service Building's pinnacle stood out in the floodlit glow of powerful 400-watt Lucalox arc lamps, a profligacy of energy and light advertising the skyscraper on the metropolitan skyline, celebrating the modern 24-hour city, and honoring Cities Service's identity as an energy conglomerate (*Fig. 102*). In the 1930s the skyscraper's construction and floodlighting helped fix the corporation's image in the public consciousness, like the Cities Service Radio Hour and Orchestra on NBC. Atop the skyscraper's mast burned a hot, cathode-tube, red "neon light for the guidance of aviators" out of Roosevelt Field and Newark Airport.[31] Supposedly visible for two hundred miles on land and sea—"And, on some very clear nights, they say, can

be seen in Boston"—the Cities Service Building beacon light's stupendous luminosity embodied the essential skyscraper fantasy of territorial omnipresence and self-importance, casting the building's domain, in legend, over tens of thousands of square miles deep into New England.[32]

Isolated at the northeast corner of the financial district skyline, the Cities Service Building stood out for its forceful, unrelenting verticality. Its overall style conformed to the sobriety of late Art Deco's monochrome brick walls, minimal exterior ornamentation, and avoidance of historical motifs and associations. Symbolized as a force of organic nature in the portal models, the Cities Service Building rose as one integrated form that looked like it could go on forever. Looking upwards from its base, the tower section seems to hover without support above the set-backs, the terminating crest disappearing from view (*Fig. 103*). At a distance the monolithic spire springs upwards in unified vertical aspiration, its mast pointing the building like a rocket to the heavens.

MODERNIST RESTRAINT AND VOLUME

The unified verticality of the Cities Service Building as well as the self-conscious control of One Wall Street represented emerging sensibilities within the financial district's architecture. Skyscrapers built mainly in the first years of the 1930s presented similar mono-tone facades, denuded of ornament and horizontal projections. Walls flattened back.

FIG. 103. *The Cities Service Building's brick-and-glass shaft seems to rise to infinity from Pearl Street, the tower levitated above the base and ascending without visible end.*
Norman McGrath

Sculptural decoration disappeared on both bases and shafts. Verticality received its emphasis in barely projecting vertical strips framing banks of slightly recessed windows and spandrels. Striping like this featured on the 38-story Chase National Bank Building (1928) at 20 Pine Street for the country's largest financial company, designed by the Chicago firm of Graham, Anderson, Probst & White (*Fig. 104*). Other vertically striped area buildings include Sloan & Robertson's 38-story Maritime Exchange Building (1931) at 80 Broad Street and the 48-story Continental Bank Building (1929–32) at 30 Broad Street, by Benjamin Wistar Morris and Robert O'Connor, whose flat vertical striping and frameless windows earned it the designation "contemporary" (*Fig. 105*).[33] Vertical striping also featured on two modest buildings by Empire State Building architects Shreve, Lamb & Harmon: the 26-story Bankers Trust Company addition (c. 1932) at Wall and Nassau Street and the 28-story Insurance Company of North America Building (1933) at 99 John Street (*Fig. 106*). The latter's aluminum and stainless steel spandrels, chrome nickel stripping, and dark windows running up in high bands between light Rockwood stone piers made a striking impression, which Mumford praised as a "resolute design.... The beautiful directness of the structure...is both honest and handsome: there is nothing left to be done in the design of business buildings but repeat this fundamental pattern."[34] A few years earlier in 1930 Arthur Loomis Harmon had described a

FIG. 104. *Looking up Broad Street, the vertically-striped Chase National Bank Building (1928, Graham, Anderson, Probst & White) looms above the 1840s Sub-Treasury in a typical view by Anton Schutz, who etched numerous similar midair perspectives of financial district scenes.* Collection of The New-York Historical Society

skyscraper "wall as a series of vertical piers," and he cautioned against too frank expression of the skyscraper steel frame's actual stacked horizontal articulation, which "would not now, at least, please the eye nor satisfy the mind; later perhaps it will."[35] By the early 1930s some architects were willing to push forward the expression of the skyscraper's underlying grid.

In 1931 at the Stone & Webster Building at 90 Broad Street, Cross & Cross, while finishing the City Bank Farmers Trust Building, produced a facade of very different effect, which featured simple frameless windows punched into a flat stone facade articulated by a syncopated grid of low-relief horizontal and vertical strips without directional emphasis. In similar fashion Ely Jacques Kahn designed 120 Wall

BELOW: FIG. 105. *The Continental Bank Building (1929–32) towers forty-eight stories above Broad Street, the austerity of its facade departing from the architect Benjamin Wistar Morris' earlier historicist designs for the Cunard, Seamen's Bank, and Bank of New York buildings.* Sixty-Five Years of Progress

RIGHT: FIG. 106. *The disciplined vertical grid of Shreve, Lamb & Harmon's Insurance Company of North America Building at 99 John Street (1933) earned the praise of modernist critic Lewis Mumford: "There is nothing left to be done in the design of business buildings but repeat this fundamental pattern."* Architectural Record

Street (1929–31) at the financial district's far eastern end along the East River at South Street (*Fig. 107*). The massive 36-story building filled the zoning envelope to the maximum with a series of steep set-backs, and abandoned the jazzy textures of Kahn's earlier John Street skyscrapers (*Figs. 92 and 93*). At 120 Wall Street Kahn experimented with European avant-garde modernism's flat tonality and horizontality, producing the visual effect of a volumetric box with neutral cladding thinly wrapping the internal structural grid.

The skyscraper in the financial district proceeding farthest down the path of tectonic representation was a small building at 99 Wall Street (1930–31), just across the street from Kahn's 120 Wall Street (*Fig. 108*). Designed by Schwartz & Gross, the 29-story loftlike office building features wide four-window bays framed by plain gray brick piers and deep lintels, rising up in a regular rhythm through the shaft and set-back stories, starkly expressing the horizontal structural steel frame. While Schwartz & Gross had produced somewhat similar plain facades at 55 Central Park West (1930), the Bricken Building on Broadway (1926), and the Mercantile Building on 39th Street (c. 1926), the radical austerity of 99 Wall Street's open frame expression far exceeded in stacked tectonic articulation the firm's other work, as well as practically anything else built in the financial district until Skidmore, Owings & Merrill's U. S. Steel Building (1974) at One Liberty Plaza.

Besides 99 Wall Street the other early 1930s skyscraper anticipating Wall Street's post-World War II architectural future was 21 West Street (1930–31) by Starrett & Van Vleck (*Fig. 95*). Next door to the same firm's Downtown Athletic Club Building, the architects articulated the 31-story tower vertically with thin mullions and fluted piers, and horizontally with windows strikingly wrapping each floor's corners. From inside, the wrapped corner windows provided sweeping views of New York harbor. From outside, the wrapped windows dematerialized the skyscraper's corners, dramatically expressing the fact that the building's walls and particularly its corners, always in earlier skyscrapers visually reinforced, no longer did any structural work, which was now entrusted to the internal steel frame. In Europe wrapped corner windows signified avant-garde modernism. In this company 21 West Street was "probably the first commercial [office] building in America to be so designed" with all-glass corner windows.[36] Around Wall Street such expression of horizontal glass voids and thin vertical solids would not be achieved so spectacularly again for a generation, until Skidmore, Owings & Merrill's Chase Manhattan Bank Building (1961).

In the early 1930s, as the economic recession deepened, these last plain financial district buildings, on the drawing boards and built before the full depression hit, seemed to symbolize a chastened capitalism. Coming late in time they reflected the evolution of American architectural taste toward European abstraction. As an ensemble the late skyscrapers also filled in the open spaces and low valleys of the financial district skyline, putting finishing touches on the iconic tableau until the 1960s when new tall skyscrapers would again remake Lower Manhattan's skyline.

OPPOSITE: FIG. 107. *In Berenice Abbott's 1936* Downtown Skyport, Foot of Wall Street, *commuter seaplanes by the East River accentuate the modernity of the flat facade of 120 Wall Street (1930, Ely Jacques Kahn), right, and of the Cities Service Building's cropped tower, left.* Museum of the City of New York

ABOVE: FIG. 108. *99 Wall Street (1930–31, Schwartz & Gross) represented the financial district's starkest visual expression of the skyscraper's underlying structural frame. Near the East River the building housed firms specializing in commodity brokerage.* Norman McGrath

Chapter Eight

INTERIOR
DISTINCTION

The public observation gallery on the Cities Service Building's 66th floor.

SKYSCRAPER EXTERIORS AND INTERIORS ARE TWO DISTINCT ENTITIES: one fixed, the other transient. Fixed skyscraper facades make historical associations, express verticality and structure, and advertise the building on the street and skyline. What skyscraper facades do not do is represent the ever-changing divisions and diversity of the life inside. Behind the immutable brick and stone lie shifting constellations of tenants and functions, offices and halls, suites and boardrooms, lobbies and corridors.

GENERAL AND PARTITIONED OFFICES

The overwhelming majority of any Wall Street area skyscraper's interior is devoted to office work, in spaces large and small, subdivided and open. On skyscrapers' broad lower stories, corporations located their large accounting and clerical departments in open areas (*Fig. 109*). In what were called general offices no corridors separated elevators from working areas. Regular rows of identical desks and chairs ranged without partition or privacy on cement floors covered with economical linoleum, beneath overhead lights and plain plastered ceilings with beam shapes exposed. This collective uniformity the architectural writer John Taylor Boyd, Jr., interpreted as a sign that "business architecture is becoming more democratic."[1] In reality a general office's open planning and utilitarian finish was designed to accommodate flexibly the routinized labor of the maximum numbers of workers in conditions of material economy and easy supervision.

A skyscraper's more compact set-back and tower stories, with better light and air, usually rented to smaller tenants, such as law firms, accountants, insurance agencies, and individual businessmen. These businesses rented combinations of basic office units to lay out, partition, and finish as needed for their interrelated executive, clerical, and reception functions (*Figs. 63, 64, and 110*). Partitions came in prefabricated wood, steel, and glass; or for prestige, more traditional, permanent looking plastered walls, perhaps elaborated with arched doorways and faux columns. In partitioned offices executives, managers, and senior partners typically occupied decorated private rooms with windows, while reception, clerical, and storage space lay inside the building without natural light. Besides this segregation, clear glass partitions created "solidarity of the corps" and allowed managers "to see that the occupant of no desk is idle," noted the critic Royal Cortissoz in 1921 about the Cunard Building.[2]

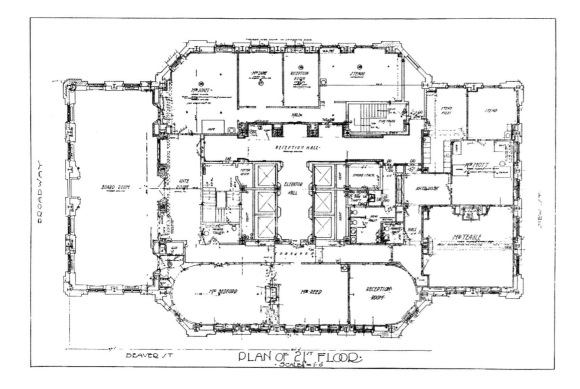

CORPORATE SUITES

In skyscrapers occupied by major banks or corporations, the most lavishly decorated office interiors always belonged to company directors, executives, and upper-level managers. In plan corporate suites generally consisted of an outer enfilade of well-lit and privately interconnected boardrooms, conference rooms, executive offices, and personal toilets. The corporate suite was guarded from visitors and serviced by an interior ring of windowless corridors, anterooms, reception, and secretarial spaces (*Fig. 111*).

In 1920s Wall Street many companies kept to the tradition of locating corporate suites on ground or lower floors to maintain intimacy with customers and staff and, from pre-elevator days, to save executive time and exertion. The Cunard and Manhattan Company corporate suites overlooked their buildings' main entrances. The City Bank Farmers Trust executive offices lay behind the ground floor senior officers' hall. The Irving Trust Company's fifth-floor executive suite lay amid the bank's other departments, which ran up through One Wall Street's ninth floor. Companies less bound to habit situated corporate suites in skyscrapers' upper stories to take advantage of better light and air. Standard Oil Company of New Jersey's executives worked in a lavish suite of 21st-floor rooms in their 31-story skyscraper on Broadway. Cities Service Company executives occupied penthouse aeries with rooftop terraces on their skyscraper's 62nd through 64th floors. In locating corporate suites atop skyscraper towers, companies took advantage of modern communications and high-speed elevators. They sacrificed valuable tower rental space for executive prestige. Tower corporate suites also embodied spatially the impersonal relations in big companies between upper-floor executives and lower-floor workers.

FIG. 111. *Clinton & Russell, Holton & George laid out a 21st-floor annular corporate suite in Carrère & Hastings' Standard Oil Building (1922–26), with president's and chairman's offices at the bottom and a large boardroom overlooking Broadway to the left.* American Architect

EXECUTIVE OFFICES

The decorator and industrial designer Henry Dreyfuss wrote in 1932 that company executives' offices should convey "an atmosphere of mental ease, business-like but

LEFT: FIG. 112. *The wood-paneled office of City Bank Farmers Trust president James H. Perkins typified domestic executive decor: a comfortable arrangement of carpets, curtains, chairs, lamps, desk, fireplace, picture, and other furnishings.* Getty Research Library, 940010

RIGHT: FIG. 113. *On the 61st floor of the Cities Service Building this large executive office may have belonged to company chairman Henry L. Doherty, judging from its size, fine furnishings, and proximity to Doherty's planned 63rd-floor penthouse apartment.* Western History Collections, University of Oklahoma Libraries

comfortable," in order to do the "work of soothing [visitors] into the undisturbed, pleasant and receptive state of mind."[3] Informal arrangements of soft chairs, patterned carpets, individualized desks, and curtains and valences expressed luxury and orderliness in "pleasingly striking contrast to the modern severity of the usual treatment of financial district structures," noted The Manhattan Company magazine of 40 Wall Street's American colonial style executive rooms.[4] The librarylike executive offices of the Equitable Trust and Cunard companies possessed the "dignity and comfort of old England,"[5] while City Bank Farmers Trust president James Perkins' oak-paneled office "combines dignity with warm friendliness" (*Fig. 112*).[6] In the Cities Service Building, a large 61st-floor, light-colored and curtained office (which may have belonged to Cities Service president Henry L. Doherty) resembled a living room with clusters of chairs, couches, and side tables (*Fig. 113*). "Particularly if the man be married, his office is more castle than his home," declared *Fortune* magazine about intimate, personal executive offices. [7] These also embodied a sense of "family" corporate cultures which executives promoted for humane as well as business reasons.[8]

In 1930, however, architect Arthur Loomis Harmon argued against an executive decorating his private office with books, picture, and other "feminine influences which go to make his home."[9] "If [the executive] used all these things he would be exposing himself to every stranger who came to see him on business." Harmon's phrasing points to the executive private office's ambiguous construction of identity,

divided between feminized personalism and domesticity on one hand, and masculinized reserve, authority, and competition on the other. More in line with Harmon's views the Irving Trust's austere "conservative modern"[10] executive offices in One Wall Street had as their primary decoration veneer paneling, with different woods for different offices (African teak, English oak, Australian yuba, birch, koa, blackwood, walnut, and holly), plus pigskin for the vice chairman's room (*Fig. 114*). This exoticism symbolized modern banking's global reach, while the decor's plainness corrected some of the deficiencies of historicist, domestic offices, as Harmon saw it. Either choice of decoration, though, embodied the executive's power: either to domesticate his surroundings, which average workers could not do, or to mystify his adversaries, through architectural impersonality.

FIG. 114. *The modern veneer-paneled offices in various exotic woods of the Irving Trust Company at One Wall Street represented a sophisticated and impersonal alternative to traditional domestic executive office decor.* © HLW International LLP

BOARD OF DIRECTORS ROOMS

In any executive suite the board of directors room is the single most important space: the site of ultimate corporate control and authority. Its decor represents the character of the corporation to itself. On the fourth floor of 40 Wall Street, Morrell Smith designed The Manhattan Company's windowless boardroom in imitation of the Declaration of Independence signers' room in Independence Hall, Philadelphia, with Doric orders, Chippendale chairs, colonial blue rug, and fireplace. Thus the room "recaptured the artistic spirit of the days of the institution's founding,"

ABOVE: FIG. 115. *Morrell Smith designed The Manhattan Company's boardroom on 40 Wall Street's fourth floor, imitating the architecture and furnishings of the Declaration of Independence signers' room in Philadelphia to honor the bank's Revolutionary-era roots.* Courtesy Chase Manhattan Archives

BELOW: FIG. 116. *The Standard Oil Company of New Jersey's boardroom, on its Broadway skyscraper's 21st floor, re-creates an English baronial great hall, designed by Clinton & Russell, Holton & George, replete with oak beams, stone fireplace, and swirled plaster ceiling.* American Architect

explained the company magazine (*Fig. 115*).[11] Clinton & Russell, Holton & George designed a baronial great hall for the Standard Oil Company of New Jersey's board of directors, featuring massive oak beams and thick stone walls within the steel frame of the Carrère & Hastings designed skyscraper (*Fig. 116*). "With such settings does the twentieth century attempt to stage again the old romance of commerce," observed John Taylor Boyd.[12]

In the late 1920s, as tradition's hold loosened in architecture generally, some corporations opted for more up-to-date boardroom identities, dispensing with faux attachments of columns, cornices, beams, and brackets. Cities Service directors met in a sleek 64th-floor, high-ceilinged, leather-paneled oval boardroom (*Fig. 117*). Irving Trust's directors met in a spacious, "ultra-new, ultra-smart" 47th-floor, teak-paneled boardroom beneath a gold-leaf ceiling and metal light fixtures (*Fig. 118*).[13] The flat surfaces expressed the decor's "true character as a mere lining or veneer upon the walls."[14] In contrast to historical imitations, these modern boardrooms conveyed an air of efficiency, directness, contemporaneity, and sophistication.

EXECUTIVE AMENITIES

Besides boardrooms and private offices corporations provided directors, executives, and managers with the amenities of dining rooms, luncheon clubs, and penthouse

FIG. 119. *Atop One Wall Street the three-story-high directors' observation (or great) lounge ensconced Irving Trust executives in a luxurious living room space, whose dynamically angled walls were decorated in an abstract Native American war-bonnet pattern.* Architecture and Building

lounges. The Cities Service Company, on its skyscraper's 61st and 62nd penthouse floors, planned an employee cafeteria, officers' luncheon room, and club space for the Doherty men's fraternity. The Manhattan Company's officers' lounge on 40 Wall Street's 55th floor included sitting and dining rooms decorated in the corporation's favored American colonial theme made to look like an old New York inn with fake wood-beamed ceilings, fireplace, and Windsor chairs. In One Wall Street's penthouse floors, the Irving Trust Company had a 48th-floor officers' dressing room and a 46th-floor officers' luncheon club with a fluted pier supporting a polygonal scalloped ceiling. Most spectacularly, atop One Wall Street, lay Irving Trust's 49th-floor directors' observation lounge (also known as the great lounge), a soaring three-story room with ceiling-high windows, teak flooring, red marble fireplace, angled walls that mimicked the building's facade, and an informal array of living room couches, easy chairs, and tables (*Figs. 97 and 119*). Thousands of iridescent Philippine kappa seashells

sparkled on the ceiling (*Fig. 120*), while a woven red tapestry patterned the walls with a stylized Native American war-bonnet motif. This decor alluded to modern imperial America's westward push across the Great Plains and the Pacific Ocean, as opposed to older European and early American colonial decorative identities.

Corporate spaces were architectural fantasies within steel-frame skyscrapers that did important social work, too. Homey, historically imitative offices expressed tradition, personal ownership, and executive individuality. More austere modern offices conveyed competitive, masculinized detachment and impersonality. Gradations in office size and sumptuousness underscored corporate hierarchies, while stylistic consistency created collective identities among directors, executives, and managers. Above all corporate luxury divided its privileged inhabitants from the rest of the corporate workforce and other skyscraper tenants who labored away in quotidian general and partitioned offices.

FIG. 120. *An angled canopy of iridescent kappa seashells from the Philippines sparkles on the ceiling of the directors' observation lounge atop One Wall Street.* Norman McGrath

FIG. 121. *The Cunard Building great hall (1919–21) by Benjamin Wistar Morris ennobled the act of travel with its Roman monumental piers, arches, and vaults, lavishly ornamented by Ezra Winter with classical motifs and nautical themes.* Architectural Forum

PUBLIC HALLS

The one area of interior luxury which a Wall Street skyscraper shared with the general community was its public hall, usually located on an accessible first or second floor. Invariably a building's grandest interior, public halls functioned as mediating thresholds between corporations and their customers and general public.

Wall Street's grandest public hall was the first one built after World War I: the Cunard Building's great hall (1919–21), designed by Benjamin Wistar Morris, at 25 Broadway (*Fig. 121*). Morris applied his classical Beaux-Arts training to a vast, biaxial vaulted hall, centered on a central octagonal dome, altogether measuring 187 feet long and 74 feet wide, the "size of a six-story building covering nearly six city lots," marveled a contemporary report (*Fig. 32*).[15] Passengers bought their tickets at travertine-clad counters and relaxed in corner, wood-paneled lounges. Overhead, vines, seashells, tritons, and mermaids were painted on the ceiling by muralist Ezra Winter, along with frescoes of the voyager ships of Ericson, Columbus, Cabot, and Drake. Maps of the Cunard Company's ship routes, painted by Barry Faulkner, adorned the

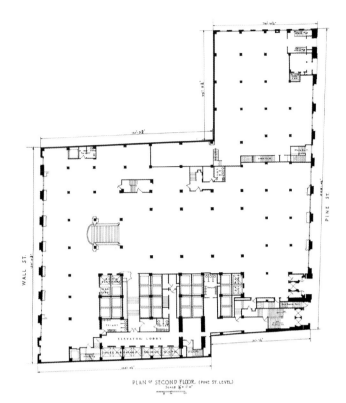

PLAN OF SECOND FLOOR. (PINE ST. LEVEL)

ABOVE: FIG. 122. *40 Wall Street's second floor accommodated The Manhattan Company's main bank hall which was accessed from Wall Street via a grand staircase rising into the hall's central aisle, or via rear doors directly from Pine Street.* Architecture and Building

LEFT: FIG. 123. *The Manhattan Company's "Georgian" bank hall on the second floor of 40 Wall Street, designed by Morrell Smith, looking north toward Pine Street, with glimpses to the right of Ezra Winter's mural scenes of the company's early history.* Architecture and Building

niches. The great hall's theme, in Winter's words, was "the age-old romance of the sea or the lure of travel." Indeed the Cunard great hall ranks among New York's finest monuments to travel, along with the old Pennsylvania Station's main waiting room (1906–10) and Grand Central Terminal's grand concourse (1903–13).

Most often a Wall Street area skyscraper's public hall was used for banking. Notable examples include the hall at Morris' Seamen's Bank for Savings Building at 74 Wall Street, in a romanesque style with nautical murals by Ernest Peixotto, and the same architect's Georgian hall for the Bank of New York at 48 Wall Street, with murals of commercial scenes by James Monroe Hewlett. These murals in typical self-

FIG. 124. *At the Wall Street end of 40 Wall Street's main banking hall, the officers' platform of the Bank of Manhattan Trust Company accommodated semiprivate meetings between bankers and clients in a carpeted, wood-paneled area.* Courtesy Chase Manhattan Archives; Edward Ozern, photographer

congratulatory fashion "portray the progress of the institution along with important epochs of national history," wrote the chronicler W. Parker Chase.[16] Other prominent financial district bank halls include the romanesque public rooms of Trowbridge & Livingston's Equitable Trust Company Building, the Greek Doric hall of Cross & Cross' Lee, Higginson & Company Building, and the soaring Art Deco spaces of 14–16 Wall Street by Shreve, Lamb & Harmon.

The grandest historically styled bank hall in the financial district belonged to The Manhattan Company affiliates occupying the first and second floors of 40 Wall Street (*Figs. 122 and 123*). On the first floor a set of utilitarian rooms for the Bank of Manhattan Trust Company accommodated brokerage house messenger traffic. Up a wide flight of marble stairs lay The Manhattan Company's main banking room, filling the whole 195-foot depth of the site from Wall to Pine streets. The central hall featured a wide travertine aisle flanked by limestone arcades and marble tellers' counters. At either end, separated from the tellers' hall by black marble columns toward Pine Street and veined octagonal piers toward Wall Street, lay the officers' platforms for the

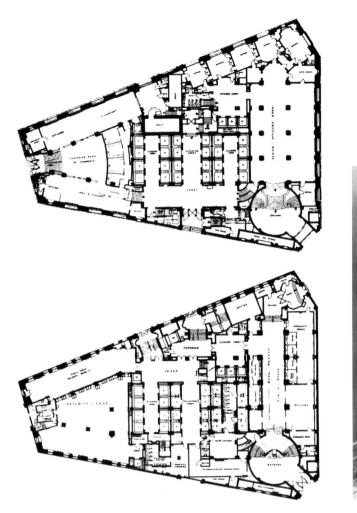

International Acceptance Bank and the Bank of Manhattan Trust Company, respectively (*Fig. 124*). Here officials at their desks met individually with customers in areas decorated with wood paneling and light ivory paint, "to give these spaces a more intimate character suited to their purpose," explained building architect Yasuo Matsui.[17]

The Manhattan Company main banking room's light-toned and classical "Georgian" decor, designed by the bank's architect Morrell Smith (with Walker & Gillette as consultants), honored the corporation's 1799 foundation.[18] To underscore the theme of federal era venerability, Ezra Winter was hired for $40,500 to paint six murals (now lost) behind the tellers' counters. These murals illustrated events from the corporation's early history, when it began as a water company and evolved into a bank, and so claimed for The Manhattan Company a public service identity within the financial district's history.[19]

Like 40 Wall Street, the City Bank Farmers Trust Building, designed by Cross & Cross, accommodated several separate bank halls on its first two stories (*Fig. 125*). Along the narrow eastern Hanover Street end, ground and first-floor halls served the Canadian Bank of Commerce, which had occupied this site prior to the skyscraper's construction. City Bank Farmers Trust's own bank halls occupied the site's broad western edge along William Street, including a long low ground-floor branch office for the National City Bank (the commercial and retail banking affiliate). Upstairs on the first floor lay the main City Bank Farmers Trust senior officers' room (the functional equivalent of The Manhattan Company's officers' platforms) where trust

LEFT: FIG. 125. *The ground and first floors of the City Bank Farmers Trust Building (1930–31, Cross & Cross) accommodated, at the narrow eastern end, rooms for the Canadian Bank of Commerce; at the wide William Street end, quarters of City Bank Farmers Trust; and, in the middle, lobbies and elevators.* Architectural Forum

RIGHT: FIG. 126. *In the City Bank Farmers Trust Building's first-floor senior officers' room, the vaulted central reception aisle is flanked by more intimate areas for meetings with clients. The hall's overall monumentality is softened by wood paneling, carpets, and casual furniture.* Getty Research Library, 940010

FIG. 127. *The Irving Trust Company's One Wall Street reception room, here seen from its Broadway end, was not a conventional bank teller hall, but rather "where we shall meet our friends and customers," explained bank chairman Lewis Pierson.*
© HLW International LLP

OPPOSITE: FIG. 128. *The Irving Trust reception room was designed by Ralph Walker and his colleagues with a sparkling lining of red and orange glass mosaic upon its angled walls, veined in gold and silver with blue and black mortar.* Norman McGrath

officers sat at individual desks in the lower side aisles flanking a 20-foot-high, barrel-vaulted nave (*Fig. 126*). The room's basilican plan focused on a polygonal niche preceding the executive office suite, thus ennobling and organizing the bank's customer service and management functions. Oak paneling and comfortable leather sofas and chairs in the center aisle created an intimate gentlemanly air appropriate to close client consultation and the bank's trust operations. In this understated space small overhead wood carvings by the English sculptor David Evans depicted wheat, airplanes, and ships.

IRVING TRUST'S RECEPTION ROOM

At One Wall Street the Irving Trust Company's ground-floor reception room, like the City Bank Farmers Trust senior officers' room, varied from the conventional bank hall type in having no tellers' counters (*Figs. 127 and 128*). As a 1928 press release explained, Irving Trust's "self-sufficient" branch network and its headquarter's "purely coordinative and administrative" functions meant that "in a very important sense the Company possesses no main banking office."[20] Instead of a bank teller hall, One Wall Street's main public place was "where we shall meet our

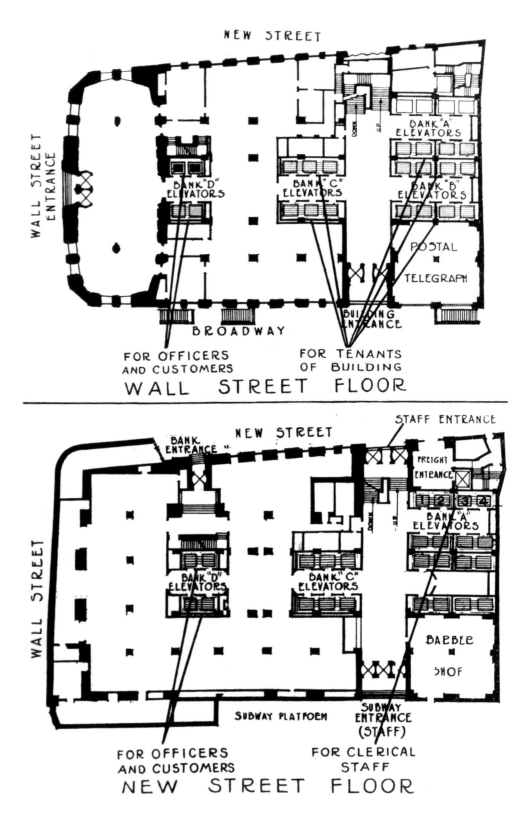

NEW STREET

WALL STREET ENTRANCE

BANK "A" ELEVATORS

BANK "D" ELEVATORS

BANK "C" ELEVATORS

BANK "B" ELEVATORS

POSTAL TELEGRAPH

BUILDING ENTRANCE

BROADWAY

FOR OFFICERS AND CUSTOMERS

FOR TENANTS OF BUILDING

WALL STREET FLOOR

STAFF ENTRANCE

NEW STREET

BANK ENTRANCE

FREIGHT ENTRANCE

BANK "A" ELEVATORS

WALL STREET

BANK "D" ELEVATORS

BANK "C" ELEVATORS

BARBER SHOP

SUBWAY PLATFORM

SUBWAY ENTRANCE (STAFF)

FOR OFFICERS AND CUSTOMERS

FOR CLERICAL STAFF

NEW STREET FLOOR

FIG. 129. *The upper Wall Street entrance level of One Wall Street features the Irving Trust reception room at its north end and a long axis of elevators designated for different classes of inhabitants. The tenants' lobby runs from Broadway to the lower level New Street.* The Bank of New York Archives

friends and customers," explained Irving Trust chairman Lewis Pierson.[21] Architecturally this meant making "the place seem as little like a bank as possible," explained *Fortune*.[22] The reception room was designed by Ralph Walker and his assistant Perry Coke Smith, with muralist Hildreth Meiere serving as "color consultant" and Yale art school dean Everett Meeks as the skyscraper's overall design consultant.[23] Filling the northern edge of the site, between Broadway and New Street, the 110-by-40-foot reception room possessed in plan a classical Beaux-Arts biaxiality, with the short entrance axis from Wall Street bisected by a lateral axis aligned with a pair of polygonal piers (*Fig. 129*). At the eastern New Street end of the room lay desks for brokers loan officers; at the western Broadway end were desks for city office officials.

Walker and his collaborators elaborated vertically the Irving Trust reception room's underlying symmetrical order in a more fantastical Gothic, expressionistic spirit. They undulated the three-story-high walls and flared the window recesses in echo of the angled exterior facade. The reception room's walls, piers, and ceiling were completely covered with a shimmering skin of glass mosaic tiles specially picked out by Walker and Smith from the stock of the Ravenna Mosaic Company of Berlin and New York.[24] At the walls' base, above a burgundy marble dado, dull flame red tesserae, pressed into cement and held in place by dark blue and black mortar, rose up and shaded into brilliant orange and golden yellow tiles that sparkled along the ceiling overhead. Veining the vibrant surface, jagged gold and silver lines drew together up the walls and across the shimmering ceiling, the chaotic skeins forming matching patterns in each of the room's corner quadrants, enforcing a subtle order upon the walls' overriding movement.

The stunning red and bronze walls of the Irving Trust reception room resemble a veined foliate forest or perhaps a rising ranges of crystalline mountains. "What a room should do is to lose its walls for your mind's sake," Walker wrote in 1930, believing that movement, texture, and pattern provided "recreation for the mind" and "mental escape."[25] The subtle blending in color and angle created a "rich, free-hanging fabric," in *Metal Arts* editor Eugene Clute's phrasing, "a cage set within the frame of the building and finished with a lining that has no more structural significance than the lining of my lady's work basket."[26] The Irving Trust reception room weaves around the visitor a space of fantasy and imagination—feminized in Clute's phrasing—that transcends its mundane function. Like the Cunard great hall, the Irving Trust reception room is a civic gift, a private commercial property bestowed upon the metropolis' citizenry. Like New York's great train stations and Art Deco movie palaces and theaters, the financial district's public halls provided a measure of architectural beauty and emotion in the midst of modern urban life.

LOBBIES

In terms of use lobbies are a skyscraper's most public interior, functioning as extensions of city streets. From a practical point of view lobbies are meant to "get the public from the street to the elevators with as little delay as possible," explained architect William Frederick Lamb.[27] At the same time they offered opportunities to dazzle tenants and visitors, "when one may polish up the harness and drive one's thoroughbreds in the ring," Lamb put it.[28]

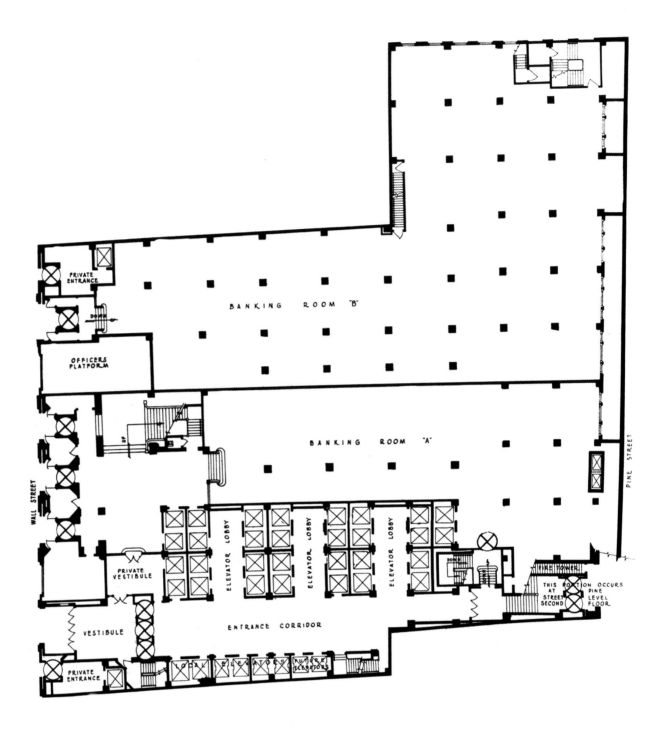

FIG. 130. 40 *Wall Street's ground-floor plan shows a three-part division into two bank halls and a main lobby, plus seven separate doorways from Wall Street that include private entrances at the flanks for tenants with their own elevators.* Architecture and Building

To move thousands of hurried people in and out of a skyscraper and its elevators, architects planned lobbies with multiple entrances to different streets and levels, and with revolving doors to maintain steady traffic flows (and as insulating air locks). The Cities Service Building, for example, possessed five entrances at two levels along Pearl, Pine, and Cedar streets. Multiple entrances could also be a function of tenant demands, as at 40 Wall Street, where several prestige-minded financial firms, like the 11th-floor investment bankers J. A. Sisto & Company, negotiated for their own private elevators and street entrances. This forced the architects to place no fewer than seven separate doorways and various sized vestibules along the Wall Street frontage, creating a fragmented and spatially uncoordinated ground floor (*Fig. 130*).

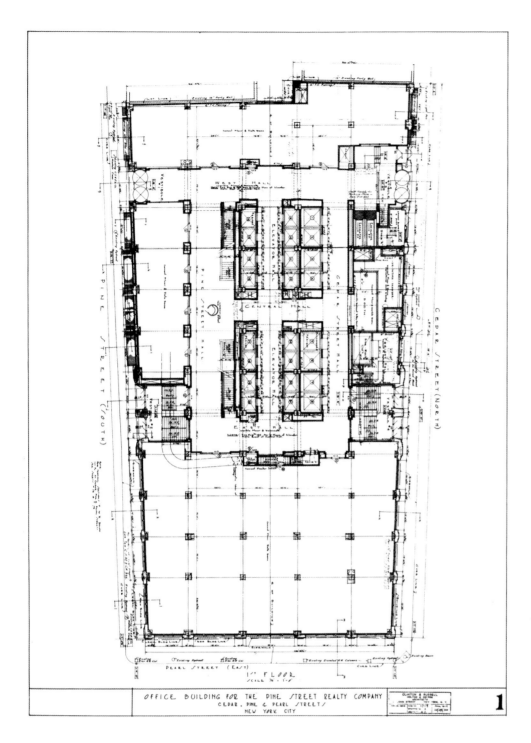

OFFICE BUILDING FOR THE PINE STREET REALTY COMPANY
CEDAR, PINE & PEARL STREETS
NEW YORK CITY

1

FIG. 131. *Cities Service Building's first-floor plan shows pairs of entrances from Cedar and Pine streets leading clear through the building into right-angled circulation and elevator halls, which are lined with open space for stores and other facilities.* American International Realty Corporation

Inside, skyscraper entrance floors were often subdivided into one lobby for the main corporate or banking occupant, and a separate lobby for the rest of the building's tenants. This provided architectural prestige and freer circulation to the primary corporate tenant and marked social distinctions. At One Wall Street, Irving Trust's officers and customers used one set of elevators near the Wall Street reception room, while clerical staff and tenants were directed to other elevators accessed via Broadway, New Street, and a staff subway entrance (*Fig. 129*).

Generally in skyscraper lobbies, elevator banks were arranged as dead-end pockets out of the way of the pedestrian traffic flow. The Cities Service Building represented an exception to this pattern. Its elevator banks lined through passages at

OPPOSITE: FIG. 132. *The long east–west spine of the Cities Service Building's main elevator hall served as the "main street" of the lobby's circulatory system, where tenants crossed paths before ascending to their offices.* Western History Collections, University of Oklahoma Libraries

LEFT: FIG. 133. *The Pine Street hall of the Cities Service Building lobby focuses on the information desk, marble-clad like nearly all the rest of the brilliant surfaces, save the ceiling that features vaguely Mesoamerican painted corbel brackets.* Norman McGrath

right angles, in a Beaux-Arts manner, between the lobby's east and west circulation halls (*Figs. 131 and 132*). An information desk at the intersection of the Pine Street and central halls became the lobby plan's focus (*Fig. 133*). In effect, the open passages between Cedar and Pine streets made it possible for pedestrians to use the Cities Service Building's interior as a throughway, turning the skyscraper's lobby into an extension of the city's streets. And like city streets the lobby's passages were lined with a drugstore, bookstore, stationer, tobacconist, and telegraph office, providing rental income to the owners and amenities for the tenants.

Stores and through passages in skyscraper lobbies were a common phenomenon in New York and Chicago especially, and made private buildings appear to be genuine public spaces, kin to metropolitan retail streets and descended from Europe's nineteenth-century covered arcades. Not all skyscrapers, however, commercialized their lobbies. A report on the Cunard Building emphasized that "the entrance halls will not be covered up with newsstands, cigar booths, bootblacks, and other miscellaneous minor business adventures which have been tolerated in many of the bigger New York buildings."[29] At One Wall Street, the architects cautioned the Irving Trust Company building committee that placing stores along the Broadway front might "detract from the prestige of the bank...[and] make the bank appear to be a second class institution."[30]

The inclusion or exclusion of shops in a skyscraper lobby could speak to a building owner's self-identity, as too could the manner of a lobby's decoration. Up through the late 1920s around Wall Street the dominant tendency was toward classicism. The Standard Oil Building, the Bank of New York Building, the Equitable Trust Building, and 40 Wall Street all had rusticated lobbies accented by pilasters, columns, classical moldings, and heavy door frames and staircases. The effect was of a princely palace or merchant's mansion, lending an air of permanence and venerability to modern business.

The financial district's most monumental skyscraper lobby belonged to the City Bank Farmers Trust Building (*Fig. 134*). At the intersection of Exchange Place and William Street, the architects Cross & Cross placed a cylindrical domed rotunda, 36 feet across, whose round plan mediated the odd angle between the corner entrance and interior bank halls (*Fig. 125*). A grand marble staircase in three parts led down to the National City branch office and up in the center, between thick marble balustrades, to the City Bank Farmers Trust senior officers' room. Along the rotunda's frieze and embedded in the floor were emblems of the bank's character, including a telephone and stock ticker, plus, for its architecture, a T-square, triangle, and bas relief of the building itself (*Fig. 135*). Rising some thirty feet on all sides, the rotunda's stone walls varied only in the hues of their massive stone blocks. Six giant marble pylons accented the austere surfaces and were articulated as bundled rods like Roman fasces, representing strength and authority. These were surmounted by American eagles instead of traditional axe blades. Up in the stepped-dome ceiling Cross & Cross applied bands of flat Art Deco silver and gray stenciling in blocks of abstractly classical wave and fret patterns, synthesizing tradition and modernity. Overall, the austere, stripped classical City Bank Farmers Trust rotunda combined traditional mass with modern simplicity, creating a space of great clarity, power, intensity, and solidity at an imperial scale and in a mood of solemn grandeur.

One of the key elements of the character of the City Bank Farmers Trust rotunda and other Wall Street area lobbies was the use of marble as the primary facing and decorative material. Besides its associations with classicism, luxury, and permanence, marble was a popular Art Deco material when used as a colorful, patterned veneer. The marbles used around Wall Street came from all over the world, as was frequently publicized, and so symbolized corporate America's global reach. The City Bank Farmers Trust Building contained some 300,000 square feet of marble from forty-five different sources.[31] More moderately, the Cities Service Building's Art Deco lobby featured Roman and Golden travertine, plus Tinos, Levanto, Belgian Black, Belgian Grand Antique, and Champville marbles.[32]

ABOVE: FIG. 134. *Cross & Cross' monumental cylindrical rotunda at the City Bank Farmers Trust Building blends traditional and modern styles. Its stone walls are articulated by marble Roman fasces and American eagles, capped by an Art Deco stenciled dome.* Norman McGrath

BELOW: FIG. 135. *At the base of the grand stairs leading from the City Bank Farmers Trust rotunda into the senior officers' room lie emblems of the institution's commercial identity, including a telephone, stock ticker, and T-square and triangle to symbolize the skyscraper's architecture.* Norman McGrath

FIG. 136. *The Art Deco lobby of Shreve, Lamb & Harmon's Insurance Company of North American Building at 99 John Street (1933) features an amoebic marble veneer finish and a realistic mural of modern industry, including a pair of riveters.* Architectural Record

In the early 1930s, Art Deco superceded traditionalism in financial district lobbies, as in the streamlined metal and marble entrance corridor of Shreve, Lamb & Harmon's Insurance Company of North America Building (1933) (*Fig. 136*); the oceanic green vestibule and streaked paneled entrance lobby of Sloan & Robertson's 29 Broadway (1930–31); and the interior of 14–16 Wall Street. The area's most extensive Art Deco lobby belongs to Clinton & Russell, Holton & George's Cities Service Building. Here, all the vestibules and passages are completely lined with flat polished panels of golden-yellow, sand-tan, and rose-tinted marbles. At frieze level the harmonizing colors and angled planes create a continuous rippling surface, splashing light and texturing shadows across the scalloped veneer. The Cities Service Building's machine-age polish, cladding, and precision received additional emphasis in the aluminum paneling and grillwork for radiator covers, door and window frames, light fixtures, stairway railings, mail boxes, directory board, elevator hatches, and shopfronts. The patterns followed conventional Art Deco zigzag, chevron, sunburst, and fluted geometric arrangements as well as typical flowering stalk, reed, leaf, sunflower, and butterfly designs. These lent an organic and, for a skyscraper, appropriately vertical exuberance to the mechanistic style.

Particular to the Cities Service Building's decoration the architects emblazoned the Cities Service expanding circle logo on the elevator hatchways (*Fig. 137*). The aluminum elevator doors also received zigzag, sunburst, and diagonal motifs that appear vaguely southwestern Native American. This regional connotation was underscored

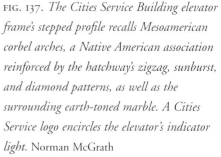

FIG. 137. *The Cities Service Building elevator frame's stepped profile recalls Mesoamerican corbel arches, a Native American association reinforced by the hatchway's zigzag, sunburst, and diamond patterns, as well as the surrounding earth-toned marble. A Cities Service logo encircles the elevator's indicator light.* Norman McGrath

by the elevator frames' corbel profiles that evoked Mesoamerican stepped-pyramid outlines and corbel vaulting. Indeed, the architects conspicuously lined the lobby's passages with prominent corbel brackets whose geometrical patterning and swelled moldings seem even more literally Mesoamerican. Following this associative line the lobby's earth-toned marbles seem to reinforce an overall Indian tone, as do the stepped parapets in the entrance vestibules.

Native American associations were not unusual in the late 1920s and early 1930s, as could be felt in the polychromatic zigzag ornament of Ely Jacques Kahn's John Street skyscrapers and in the radial ceiling patterns, eagle motifs, and earth tones of the City Bank Farmers Trust tenants' lobby (*Fig. 90*). Designers valued Mesoamerican abstract decorative patterning and the linkage with New World architecture versus tired European references. At the Cities Service Building these associations could also connote the conglomerate's national reach and concentration in western oil fields. At the very least the Cities Service Building's glimmering marble and vaguely Mesoamerican finish endowed the lobby with a distinctive (and thus more marketable) appearance.

On an economic level lobbies helped commodify a skyscraper's architecture, exciting tenants' desires for the building's rentable office space. Viewed more broadly lobbies functioned as a daily threshold between skyscraper occupants' worlds of home and community and their lives as office workers: a kind of a public town square, providing an interval of beauty amid ordinary workaday and urban environments.

MURALS

Traditionally styled and Art Deco skyscraper lobbies ennobled office work and provided moments of beauty at the threshold between work and private lives. In both styles architecture produced its effects abstractly, through combinations of scale, color, texture, and architectural motifs. On occasion designers chose more explicit means to comment on Wall Street's work.

Lobby murals, like those in bank halls, literally communicated the character of modern capitalist enterprise. A typical example, like that in the elevator lobby of Shreve, Lamb & Harmon's Insurance Company of North America Building, celebrates in realistic fashion the achievements of New York's skyscraper builders and the marvels of modern air and rail transportation. In One Wall Street's tenants' lobby, a more complex mural entitled *Allegory of Wealth and Beauty* (now destroyed or covered up) was created by the muralist Hildreth Meiere (*Fig. 138*) in collaboration with the sculptor Kimon Nicolaïdes as a pendent to the nearby Irving Trust reception room.[33] Upon the tenants' lobby's 66-foot-long ceiling Meiere and Nicolaïdes airbrushed browns, oranges, and blues over a reflective silver leaf background, composing balletic ranks of fragmented figures unified by sweeping curves and slashing diagonals (*Fig. 139*).

Meiere meant to tell a particular story in *Allegory of Wealth and Beauty,* as her artist's statement details. The mural begins at the western Broadway entrance with a "great army of workers" out of whose struggles emerge the "Big Men" of finance raised by "Ambition" to become "Possessors of Wealth . . . the men who are weighted down with their riches, and those who through wealth, are given power to rise above their fellows, and riding on their shoulders, to direct them."[34] Importantly, Meiere did not end the allegory here, with capital triumphant, but "bends [the composition] back on itself, and rushing through the Pursuit of Money, symbolizes that evolution into Beauty which money can have." Concluding back at the Broadway entrance, where it began, Meiere's mural offers an allegory of capitalism's moral and aesthetic vindication. It instructs One Wall Street's brokers, lawyers, and bankers that their workaday pursuit of money bears meaning only if transfigured into beauty. "Money is what it buys, and unless it buys Beauty in some form, it has no lasting form. . . . Without an evolution into Beauty, Money has no ultimate reason and existence." This beauty is undefined but it could, of course, be in the form of an artistic building such as One Wall Street itself, which thus becomes the site of both wealth's accumulation and its redemption.

OBSERVATION GALLERIES

Of all the interiors discussed so far—offices, corporate suites, public halls, and lobbies—none exist exclusively in skyscrapers. Just one kind of skyscraper interior belongs solely to the type: the observation gallery. Around Wall Street the observa-

FIG. 139. *At the far Broadway end of One Wall Street's tenants' lobby, Hildreth Meiere's* Allegory of Wealth and Beauty *commences with a scrum of striving workers, leading to the lucky few who grasp the disc of wealth, left foreground, before the composition turns back on itself to symbolize "that evolution into Beauty which money can have."* Through the Ages

tion galleries were much more intimate than the famous midtown Empire State Building's spacious decks for mass tourism. Smaller financial district lots limited floor areas and owners saw little advantage in accommodating the public atop their office spires. Plans of the City Bank Farmers Trust Building indicate a 57th-story "observation floor." 40 Wall Street's pyramidal cap housed 69th- and 70th-floor "observation rooms" that, according to *The New York Times*, could accommodate a hundred people.[35] The everyday uses, however, are unknown for these private spaces (which are now inaccessible and presumably altered). One Wall Street's 49th-story directors' observation lounge was not an observation gallery in practice since it offered limited views; it focused instead on the interior space and decor.

The Wall Street area's most spectacular observation gallery rests atop the Cities Service Building at the skyscraper's ultimate 66th floor (*Figs. 140 and 141*). No bigger than a large living room, measuring some 23 by 33 feet, the Cities Service Building's observation gallery was originally planned as the private "watch tower" for the penthouse apartment of Cities Service's founder, Henry L. Doherty.[36] (There were also

FIG. 140. *The intimate observation gallery atop the Cities Service Building's 66th floor, looking north over the staircase and lowered elevator hatch toward a panorama of midtown Manhattan.* Norman McGrath

residential penthouse apartments atop 40 Wall Street and 19 Rector Street.[37]) Having lived in the early 1920s atop 24 State Street, Doherty wanted to create at the Cities Service Building the perfect skytop abode, with bedroom, library, office, living room and fireplace, suffused with healthful light and air and commanding views of the metropolis. Illness and marriage, however, prevented the eccentric millionaire bachelor from residing in his skyscraper aerie. The apartment became corporate offices and the observation gallery opened to the public in the summer of 1932, visitable from 10 A.M. to 6 P.M. at a price of fifty cents—half that for Cities Service employees and building tenants (*Fig. 142*).

Visitors ascended into Doherty's "watch tower" observation gallery either up narrow stairs on the north side or by an adjacent small elevator running from the 60th floor. The metal-clad cab rose through the observation gallery floor—then amazingly descended back beneath hinged hatches. The observation gallery's deck now lay completely unobstructed in every direction through continuous banks of

windows, from knee level up, and around the chamfered glass corners. Across the terrazzo floor lay sleek modern tubular steel furniture. Phones plugged into the floor. At the center a compass pointed out the cardinal directions and enclosed the Cities Service emblem. Glass doors at the corners and north and south sides led out onto six small slate terraces, enclosed only by chest-high aluminum railings, that felt like crow's nests pitched out into the harbor air (*Fig. 143*). Below was the city. South across New York harbor lay Staten Island and the New Jersey coast. West across the Hudson shimmered New Jersey's inland mountains. To the north appeared glimpses of Westchester County and to the east, Babylon and Huntington on Long Island.

At its opening in the summer of 1932 the Cities Service Building's observation gallery received considerable publicity. If you couldn't travel to the countryside, advised Dr. Scott Edwards, visit the Cities Service Building's observation gallery: "The roof of every high building is a potential sanitarium."[38] "Special glass in win-

FIG. 141. *The Cities Service Building's observation gallery, now a private room, looking south over the sweep of New York harbor, with the Cities Service trefoil logo peaking out beneath the globe at the center of the compass in the floor.* Norman McGrath

FIG. 142. *The Cities Service observation gallery as a public space in the early 1930s, with modern tubular steel furniture, phones plugged into the floor, and the raised metal-clad elevator attended by a female operator.*
Museum of the City of New York

dows and doors admits the health-giving ultra-violet rays of the sun," advertised the visitors' brochure (in the days before skin cancer worries).[39] "It does pep you up," an official attendant, Martha Midboe, told the *Evening Post.*[40] Visiting the Cities Service Building's observation gallery was mentally rejuvenating. "Above the sordid chitchat of the Street," one man explained to a newspaper reporter. "Where I can watch my ship come in," mused a bond seller.[41]

In the history of architecture the Cities Service Building's observation gallery fulfilled centuries-old desires for interior expansion into nature (from the seventeenth-century French château Vaux-le-Vicomte's swelling oval garden salon to Frank Lloyd Wright's Fallingwater terraces cantilevered over Bear Run). The Cities Service living room-like observation gallery lifted visitors up into the clear air, out into space from its terrace overlooks, and visually in a 360-degree arc away from the city across rivers, harbors, and mountains. At this height, in the eerie skytop quiet, the city loses its human definition, becomes abstracted and itself seemingly naturalized. "No one can imagine it who has not seen it," wrote the astonished European modernist architect Le Corbusier about the Manhattan nighttime view from a similar skyscraper vantage. "It is a titanic mineral display, a prismatic stratification shot through with an infinite number of lights, from top to bottom, in depth, in a violent silhouette like a fever chart beside a sick bed. A diamond, incalculable diamonds."[42]

Atop the Cities Service Building, architecture dwindles to its starkest essence: a cloud-capped primitive hut. The corners dissolve, walls are reduced to thin piers, the roof to nearly nothing. From the terraces one can hardly see the supporting skyscraper below. In the small space, with the elevator sunk in the floor, one can imagine being all alone, as Doherty must have dreamed, magically levitated, master in vision of the

FIG. 143. *From the south terrace of the Cities Service Building's observation gallery, nearly a thousand feet in the air, an elevator attendant gazes over the Hudson River and New Jersey, with 40 Wall Street's nearby pinnacle at eye level.* Western History Collections, University of Oklahoma Libraries

metropolis' great sweep, standing at the center of the marble compass on the pivot of the universe. The bracing bodily experience intensifies physical self-awareness, as if one has ascended a man-made mountain in transcendence of the reality below.

Still, in the end, one must turn away from verticality's dangerous solipsism (mythologized in the Tower of Babel story). The elevator rises up through the floor to bring one back to earth, city, and community. The redemptive turn in the experience of the Cities Service Building's observation gallery in fact echoes the structure of Meiere's *Allegory of Wealth and Beauty* in One Wall Street's tenants' lobby. There the mural turns back on itself to redeem wealth through a beauty that may be architectural. Both interiors in effect speak to skyscrapers' moral meanings—*Allegory of Wealth and Beauty* in relation to capitalist wealth; the Cities Service Building's observation gallery in relation to human aspiration.

Chapter Nine

SKYSCRAPER LIVES

The Cities Service Building's female elevator attendants and male starters pose on the skyscraper's innovative escalators.

FIG. 144. *A steel-armored and chemical-infused door to one of One Wall Street's basement vaults protected Irving Trust's multibillion dollar treasure of cash, gold, securities, and depositors' valuables.*
The Bank of New York Archives

O N SUNDAY MORNING, MARCH 22, 1931, A BLOCKADE APPEARED ON lower Broadway of "armored trucks, manned like fortresses with squads of men armed with rapid-fire rifles and chemicals guns," reported *The New York Times*.[1] Between these lines sped trucks carrying $3 billion in gold, securities, and currency from the Woolworth Building office of the Irving Trust Company to the bank's new headquarters at One Wall Street. Here the treasure was lowered into basement security vaults guarded by watchmen, alarms, and 30-inch-thick doors, the *Times* reported, "lined with protective armor consisting of layers of chrome steel and infusite and a sheet of solidified chemicals which, under the heat of a cracksman's torch, would give off paralyzing fumes, against which it is said even gas masks do not give protection."[2] (*Fig. 144*) A month earlier the City Bank Farmers Trust's $5 billion hoard had been similarly transferred, over a 48-hour period, into its new skyscraper's subterranean vaults, guarded by electric sentinels "developed from the ones used during the war to detect the approach of enemy submarines," plus for the guards' use a "three-man shooting gallery for pistol practice . . . with movable targets and special shields to trap ricocheting bullets."[3]

The publicized, sensational vault moves of Irving Trust and City Bank Farmers Trust momentarily revealed Wall Street's hidden treasures and displayed the banks' organizational, technological, and security acumen. Symbolically, vault moves also marked the passage of the new skyscrapers from empty shells to occupied entities. Vault moves were rituals in the lives of Wall Street area skyscrapers, one of a number of ceremonies marking their stages of development.

RITUALS

A building's first moment of public introduction was its cornerstone laying when owners entrusted the skyscrapers' realization to the architects and builders. At the Irving Trust Company's carefully staged ceremony on January 14, 1930, the traditional silver trowel accompanied the encapsulation of historical and contemporary objects plus speeches by the building committee chairman, architects, and builders.[4] The ceremony was filmed and the movie screened that night during dinner.

To inaugurate 40 Wall Street's steel framing, a "Golden Rivet" ceremony was held on July 10, 1929, marking the first column's first rivet.[5] In July 1930 steelworkers at One Wall Street performed another characteristic ritual: the topping-out ceremony commemorating the steel frame's completion. "As customary on such occasions," an Irving Trust official remembered, "the steel workers celebrated the completion of their labors by erecting a pole surmounted by a broom. It is said that their usual ceremony included the opening of a barrel of beer, but as these were prohibition times, this was omitted."[6] Modern topping-out ceremonies echoed the ancient carpenter's ritual of placing a young conifer atop a completed wooden frame in gratitude for the workers' safety, nature's bounty, and continued good luck.

The most glamorous Wall Street skyscraper rituals were the opening ceremonies, celebrating the delivery of the building from its constructors to the owner and public. At the City Bank Farmers Trust Building, on February 24–25, 1931, an estimated 25,000 visitors toured the new skyscraper.[7] At 40 Wall Street's opening, on May 26, 1930, Ezra Winter's bank hall murals were "easily the center of attention."[8] The Irving Trust Company opted for "a simple, dignified event" rather than "something theatrical," in early Depression days, staging a ceremony on March 20, 1931, with speeches by the owners and architects and by descendents of both the bank's namesake, Washington Irving, and the site's colonial inhabitants.[9] In contrast with Irving Trust's heritage-oriented ceremony, the Cities Service Company adopted a more technological theme, in keeping with the company's engineering identity, for its skyscraper opening on May 13, 1932. Company founder Henry L. Doherty returned from a six-year sick leave to throw the switch on a "moonbeam condenser," activating the rooftop floodlights and powering Doherty's voice nationwide on NBC radio.[10]

Rituals brought honor and recognition, personalizing the skyscraper and turning private property momentarily into public event. Skyscraper rituals also point to the "lives" of buildings beyond design and form. Outside the facts of their making, the motivations of their builders, and the chronologies of their construction, Wall Street area skyscrapers "lived" as microcosmic cities within the metropolis and as symbols within the wider culture.

"CITY IN A TOWER"

By the 1920s perceiving Wall Street area skyscrapers as self-contained cities had become a cliché. "It is not a building but a city," Ralph Walker, the designer of One Wall Street, called the skyscraper form.[11] "A modern vertical city . . . virtually a city within a city," *The New York Times* intoned about Manhattan's great towers.[12] A "City in Itself, housing 16,000 souls," described the pre-World War I Equitable Building whose population exceeded those of all the largest, later, interwar period skyscrapers, including 40 Wall Street and the Equitable Trust Building (both with populations of 10,000), the Cunard Building (pop. 9000), the Cities Service Building (pop. 7500), the City Bank Farmers Trust Building (pop. 6500), 120 Wall Street (pop. 6000), and One Wall Street (pop. 5000).[13]

Manhattan's skyscrapers seemed microcosmic cities not just quantitatively but qualitatively too. The variety of interior life enthralled contemporaries like the photographer Weegee who portrayed the Cities Service Building's inhabitants in a 1946 photo essay titled "City in a Tower." Weegee "was fascinated by this city within a city, its swift transportation, its towering height and subterranean depth, its busy thousands of tenants and visitors, and the unobtrusive, night-and-day efficiency of its service staff."[14]

Among his subjects Weegee photographed the Cities Service Building's 29th-floor law library, whose 16,000 volumes and bar-certified librarian distinguished the building from its Wall Street area rivals (*Fig. 145*).[15] Another special service Weegee photographed was the "world's largest private gymnasium" operated by Artie McGovern, "America's Greatest Trainer," whose "mission is keeping executives in top shape."[16] (*Figs. 146 and 147*) To that end McGovern's "Twenty-Five Thousand Square Feet of 'Healthland'" filled the Cities Service Building's seventh floor with squash courts, golf apparatuses, massage rooms, electric ray cabinets, high-powered Scotch douches, and a gymnasium bathed by an ultra-violet ray system "which suntans as it lights."

The Cities Service Building's law library and gymnasium were unusual features among Wall Street area skyscrapers. Other facilities that made the skyscraper feel like a small city were more common. In the Cities Service Building's basement was the 400-seat Tower Restaurant. On the same floor could be found, as in many skyscrapers, a barber shop, chiropodist, manicurist, beauty salon, sandwich shop, florist, photostat store, and hat cleaning and shoe shining establishment. On the main entrance floor were located a typical mix of drug, book, and stationery stores, a Western Union telegraph office with pneumatic tube links to the Broad Street main branch, and, special to this skyscraper, the "Cities Service Exposition" displaying an "interesting free exhibition of the national Cities Service oil, gas and electric facilities."[17] Upstairs on the seventh floor, alongside McGovern's Gymnasium, was a conference room for tenants' use. On the fourth floor was a "medical section" staffed by two reg-

FIG. 145. *The Cities Service Building's 29th-floor tenants-only law library, as photographed by Weegee for his 1946 study of the microcosmic skyscraper city.* Weegee's People

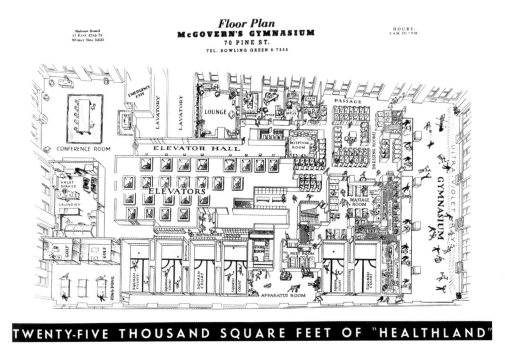

Floor Plan
McGOVERN'S GYMNASIUM
70 PINE ST.
TEL. BOWLING GREEN 9-7555

TWENTY-FIVE THOUSAND SQUARE FEET OF "HEALTHLAND"

istered nurses. This was a common skyscraper feature to be found also at 40 Wall Street where "we try to keep the human machinery of your organization functioning smoothly," explained the building's publicity book.[18]

Private luncheon clubs were another common facility in microcosmic skyscraper cities. At 40 Wall Street, besides The Manhattan Company's 55th-floor Officers' Luncheon Club, there were two membership-only establishments: the 58th-floor Rookery Club and the Luncheon Club of Wall Street, which occupied the skyscraper's 26th and 27th floors and was designed by one of the building's architects, Yasuo Matsui, in collaboration with the decorator Robert L. Powell (*Fig. 148*). Club members alighted from elevators to enter "a haven of restful, Colonial atmosphere and charm," described the club brochure, replete with an "Early Colonial Farmhouse" knotty pine entrance great hall, a wood-beamed main dining chamber, and daintily wallpapered private banquet rooms.[19]

The retail businesses and services that made skyscrapers seem like microcosmic cities brought direct rental income to the building owners and, more important, attracted tenants seeking time-saving efficiencies. "This affords the American executive a tremendous advantage over the European business man, who is forced to leave his office building and often must travel considerable distance to obtain these services," explained *The New York Times*.[20] Besides formal facilities many financial district offices were also served by "skyscraper peddlers" who went office to office selling food, magazines, candy, shirts, jewelry, stationery, office furniture, shoeshines, manicures, and haircuts. "At first I was afraid of interrupting them in business hours," explained one skyscraper peddler, "but I soon found that they welcomed me. It saved time for them and they knew it."[21]

Weegee, in portraying the microcosmic Cities Service Building, was especially drawn to the people who kept the skyscrapers running: elevator operators, cleaners, carpenters, plumbers, electricians, engineers, scrubwomen, janitors, porters, night-

LEFT: FIG. 146. *McGovern's Gymnasium filled nearly the whole seventh floor of the Cities Service Building, providing everything from an ultraviolet-ray hot room to golf driving cages to personal trainers working with clients in the gymnasium.* Western History Collections, University of Oklahoma Libraries

RIGHT: FIG. 147. *Earnest exercisers ride the "Everlast Gym-Cycle" at McGovern's Gymnasium in the Cities Service Building, captured in an unflattering but typically human moment by Weegee's idiosyncratic camera eye.* Weegee's People

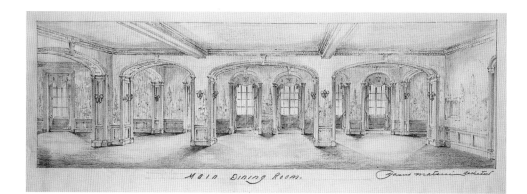

RIGHT: FIG. 148. *On 40 Wall Street's 26th floor architect Yasuo Matsui designed the fantasy American colonial decor of the Luncheon Club of Wall Street, featuring an oak-beamed lounge and pastel-colored dining room.* Avery Library

LEFT: FIG. 149. *Weegee's candid photograph of Cities Service Building maintenance men on break in their basement locker room represents just a fraction of the staff at work in modern skyscrapers.* Western History Collections, University of Oklahoma Libraries

watchmen, and plainclothes detectives (*Fig. 149*). The Cities Service Building's staff numbered over 200 people, supervised by the building manager Edgar J. Smith who functioned in effect as the skyscraper-city's mayor, serving as rental agent and financial officer, administering all services, responding to tenant requests, and adjudicating disputes.[22]

TENANTS

If the building manager was the skyscraper-city's mayor—and his staff its workers, and its stores its merchants—then tenants represented the microcosmic city's citizens. The Cities Service Building's tenantry was dominated by the Cities Service Company and its affiliates (for example, Henry L. Doherty & Company and Federal Light and Traction Company), which housed some 3000 workers in the skyscraper's lower seven floors.[23] Next, law firms represented over half of the rest of the Cities Service Building's tenantry, drawn to the building's prestigious tower floors and the useful law library. After lawyers, many insurance, investment, and brokerage firms took space in the building, as did mining, engineering, and transport companies (who likely did business with the Cities Service energy conglomerate) such as the Mobile & Ohio Railroad Company, the American Potash & Chemical Corporation, and Etco Engineering. There was also a smattering of other types of businesses and associations drawn to Wall Street's capital markets and services, such as the Hudson's Bay Company, Economics Statistics, Inc., the Sillcox Radio & Television Corporation, the American Bleached Shellac Manufacturers Association, the Consulate General of Mexico, the Sanborn Map Company, the Thomas Jefferson Memorial Foundation, and, uniquely for the financial district's major skyscrapers, the architecture firm that had designed the building, Clinton & Russell, Holton & George, which occupied 20th-floor offices.

Every Wall Street area skyscraper had its own particular mix of tenants.[24] Two blocks south and one block west of the Cities Service Building, the City Bank Farmers Trust Building, above the bank's lower eight floors, possessed a similar majority of lawyers and also a fair number of investment, bond, and brokerage firms, including Lehman Brothers. Often the proportion of one type of firm to another was a function of location. 40 Wall Street was also about half-filled with lawyers, but because of its proximity to the New York Stock Exchange it catered particularly to banking and brokerage houses. The Manhattan Company banking group occupied the skyscraper's first seven floors, joined on the upper floors by companies such as Merrill Lynch, the Bank of China, and the offices of the tower's financial backers, George L. Ohrstrom & Company, Starrett Brothers & Eken, and A. Iselin Company. 40 Wall Street also possessed a fair number of industrial companies, including the Phelps Dodge copper company, which rented three floors, and the submarine manufacturer, Electric Boat. Unfortunately, in the early 1930s many of 40 Wall Street's large securities firm tenants failed (such as J. A. Sisto & Company in 1930) or had to move to cheaper quarters (like Ohrstrom himself), depressing the building's finances and leading to its eventual sale.[25]

One Wall Street possessed a prestigious site close to the district's heart, and so besides the Irving Trust Company itself, which took the first nine stories and penthouse, the building was populated by investment service and stock brokerage firms (such as Bear Stearns & Company on the 10th floor) whose numbers equaled those of the lawyers. As in other central financial district skyscrapers the predominant population of law and financial firms was leavened by industrial and commercial interests: Phillips Petroleum (37th floor), Brooks Brothers (13th floor), and the J. Walter Thompson advertising agency (12th floor).[26]

A few blocks away from the financial district's core, mixes of tenants shifted perceptibly. 19 Rector Street, between Greenwich and Washington streets, just two blocks west of One Wall Street, possessed a much lower proportion of lawyers, insurance companies, accountants, and brokers, but a much higher number of import-export, engineering, and industrial concerns, such as the Emsco Derrick & Equipment Company and the Coronet Phosphate Company. This likely reflected 19 Rector Street's proximity to the Hudson River wharves. On the other side of the financial district, along the East River, the tenantry of 99 Wall Street and 120 Wall Street reflected this area's particular mercantile character. The starkly modernistic 99 Wall Street had more commodities firms than lawyers, with sixteen separate sugar specialists, plus lesser numbers of dealers in lumber, rubber, tobacco, burlap, coffee, tea, coal, and olive oil. 120 Wall Street's tenantry was especially strong in transportation companies, such as the Atlantic and Caribbean Steam Navigation Company, and also included anomalous tenants such as the Young Israel social welfare agency and an artist named Robert Ball. Along John Street, at the financial district's northern extreme, insurance companies dominated tenant rosters. Clinton & Russell, Holton & George's 60 John Street, for example, possessed nearly twice as many insurance concerns as lawyers, including offices for the Massachusetts Mutual Life Insurance Company and the New Amsterdam Casualty Company, whose name graced the 31-story skyscraper.

Tenant listings for Wall Street area skyscrapers reveal the variety of businesses and the tendency for types of firms to congregate within certain areas. Lawyers were ubiquitous, as to a lesser extent were brokers, investment advisors, accountants, and insurers. These services were everywhere in demand. Brokerage and other financial firms predominated in the district's heart around the New York Stock Exchange at Broad and Wall streets. To the west, east, and north could be found concentrations of transportation, commodities, and insurance firms. Geographic patterns of business echoed the diversity of occupations within each building.

"HALF A MILLION PENMEN" (AND WOMEN)

Through the tapestry of financial district businesses ran the common thread of workers' daily lives. In December 1929, just after the jolt of the October market crash, *Business Week* described the frantic pace of the "half a million penmen [who] slave in the giant fortress of finance." Remarking on the vastness of firms like the Cities Service Company, *Business Week* noted, "the clerical employee is no longer an intimate as he used to be. He is anybody at all, a worker, almost a number, like a mill hand."[27]

The old intimate office world was by the 1920s a hazy reminiscence of small familial Victorian organizations housed in the cozy architectural surroundings of low-rise brick buildings where a handful of male clerks and office boys worked closely with their bosses amid a clutter of high stools, overflowing rolltop desks, dark wooden cabinets, and flickering gas lights. The growth of corporate America in the late nineteenth and early twentieth centuries changed much of this. Enterprises grew and merged. Torrents of paperwork flooded administrative headquarters. New business technologies were invented to harness and feed the flow: addressographs, duplicators, and tabulators; billing, stenotype, and stamping machines. Corporate clerical staffs mushroomed into the hundreds and then thousands. Women entered the workforce in unprecedented numbers, from less than three percent of office workers in 1870 to over fifty-two percent in 1930.[28] "The offices of our grandfathers were without steel frames and files, without elevators and radiators, without telephones,—and without skirts," observed architect Charles Loring (*Fig. 150*).[29]

A new class of managers, taking over day-to-day control of corporations from their capitalist owners, rationalized work systems and subdivided jobs for greater efficiency and profit.[30] Where once all-purpose clerks, office boys, and bookkeepers performed numerous tasks, now much of Wall Street's workforce was specialized and

stratified, from high-paid, generally male accountants (earning up to $700/month), secretaries, auditors, and payroll clerks, to lower-paid, generally female, typists, stenographers, receptionists, machine operators, and file clerks (down to $60/month). Women were seen as more compliant than men and therefore more suitable to the low-paid routine tasks of the modern office.

FIG. 150. *A heavily female clerical staff at work on the machinery of modern business in a view typical of the regimented open lower floors of many Wall Street area skyscrapers.* Courtesy Chase Manhattan Archives

Automation and specialization increased profits and paid back capital investment in machinery and architecture—and took their toll on workers. "Standardized jobs meant less initiative. Larger offices meant less personal contact with the employer. Repetitive machine work meant speeding and monotony," reported a 1928 YWCA study by Grace Coyle.[31] Wall Street area office workers were becoming like "mill hands" and offices like factories: "the function of each is to turn out certain things in a given time," noted a 1931 article on modern offices.[32] As recession deepened into depression, unions tried unsuccessfully to organize Wall Street's office workers, stymied in part by unions' working class connotations.[33]

In this situation skyscraper architecture played its part in the industrialization of office work. Wall Street area skyscrapers' broad lower floors provided open areas for large banks, brokerage houses, corporations, and insurance companies to arrange flexibly their clerks and machines for better efficiency, accountability, and surveillance. Gone for these office workers were personal rolltop desks and individual table lamps, replaced instead by modern overhead lighting, which they could not control, and standardized furniture and machines, over which they had no personal ownership. Large group restrooms provided "electric refrigerators for stimulating and

FIG. 151. *The Cities Service Building's famous all-female corps of young elevator attendants pose in their brown-and-yellow uniforms on the building's escalator, flanked by the male starters who actually controlled the elevators' movements from lobby operator panels.*
Western History Collections, University of Oklahoma Libraries

refreshing drinking water."[34] Clear glass partitions allowed supervisors to keep an eye on "every last little cell . . . to see that the occupant of no desk is idle."[35]

In contrast with general clerical workspaces, which were heavily female, corporate managers and executives, mainly male, now usually worked on separate floors thanks to modern elevators and communications systems. Gender segregation coincided with occupational segregation. Those in leadership positions had their own walled offices, more personally decorated with rugs, furniture, and pictures. Modern executive office decor symbolized efficiency and rationality. "A junky office nowadays indicates a junky mind," intoned designer Henry Dreyfuss.[36] By 1930 executives also often had private toilets, to avoid embarrassment and improve efficiency.

Architecture helped proletarianize Wall Street's office workers in isolation from their bosses' personalized domains. The buildings may also have played a subtle part in workers' resistance to unionization. Skyscrapers were middle class in tone, with their elegant lobbies, high-speed elevators, and emphatic cleanliness. The buildings isolated workers from each other, in separate floors and departments, while at the same time solidifying identification with corporate employers and their landmark skyscrapers, which often provided loyalty-inducing amenities such as lunchrooms, clubrooms, and other services and facilities.

Even in the smaller businesses, firms, and law offices filling Wall Street area skyscrapers' tower floors—where people generally worked closer together—there existed social and architectural segregation. Mainly male managers, partners, and executives occupied private windowed offices. Interior areas without natural light were reserved for mainly female receptionists, clerks, stenographers, and typists who worked without privacy in general view of visitors and each other.

In certain skyscraper occupations women were openly equated with the architecture and objectified as decorative adornments. A 1926 *New York Times* article, after praising the architectural "charms" of modern office building lobby materials and fixtures, took note of the new plethora of female receptionists, attendants, elevator operators, and information desk hostesses. "Women are finding a very definite place in these new arrangements and settings, their part in the scheme being based on attractive appearance, intelligence and efficiency, voices and varied individual requirements. Their simple, attractive uniforms add to the general harmony."[37]

At the Cities Service Building an all-female corps of elevator operators attracted considerable publicity in their matching brown-and-yellow outfits emblazoned with the Cities Service logo (*Fig. 151*). Legendarily they were all young redheads and during the Depression "recruited largely from the ranks of unemployed showgirls."[38] "With her sisters of the central information desk, she gives to every visitor an important first impression of courtesy, efficiency, smartness and dignity," noted the Cities Service magazine.[39] "Girls, they say, are more attentive to their work and more courteous than men operators," declared the publicist Edwin Hill.[40]

Not surprisingly there were problems of sexual tension and etiquette in tight-packed skyscraper elevators, where before the 1920s women and men had not encountered each other with such regularity. Cities Service building manager E. J. Smith warned against undisciplined operators becoming "too familiar with tenants and other employees of the building," and observed that "it will be necessary for [the operators] to expend some of their excess energy harmlessly in the locker room."[41] A committee of women building managers in 1926 identified another issue: whether or not in elevators men should remove their hats in the presence of women. The committee recommended that "courtesy does not require such a sign of deference in the commercial elevator" on the grounds, first, that "no exceptional courtesies not extended in other parts of the building need be extended in the elevator" and, second, that "the modern business woman not only considers herself, but in fact is, on a parity with men."[42]

Like a distorted mirror Wall Street's microcosmic skyscrapers reflected and contorted the features of metropolitan society. The buildings' size, populations, facilities, and technological systems made them seem like self-sufficient entities—utopias, even, in their order and efficiency, a notion propagated unconsciously perhaps to promote the skyscraper's particular social system as a more perfect form of urban life. In fact, life in Wall Street area skyscrapers was more rationalized, mechanized, and fragmented than in the city around it. The skyscraper citizenry was overwhelmingly white and the female clerical workers mainly single. Business society was profoundly stratified in terms of occupation, gender, and authority. These social divisions were enforced by the architecture's spatial segregations and rationing of access to natural light, privacy, and individual control. The apparent self-sufficiency of the microcosmic cities was an illusion. Wall Street area skyscrapers were linked at every level to the surrounding metropolis, in function, scale, values, and meaning.

ABOVE: FIG. 152. *In the mid-1930s, the New York City metropolitan region was centered geographically, economically, and symbolically around the Wall Street financial district and its cluster of skyscraper towers.* Library of Congress

RIGHT: FIG. 153. *Berenice Abbott's 1936* Willow and Poplar Streets *presents the Cities Service Building and 40 Wall Street as dominant modern presences in a Brooklyn Heights neighborhood of pre-Civil War townhouses.* Museum of the City of New York, Gift of the Metropolitan Museum of Art

FIG. 154. *40 Wall Street architect Yasuo Matsui rendered his pyramid-capped skyscraper rising above shaded East River wharves and the John Street power station. The watery sky and clouds echo the visual style of Matsui's native Japan.* Avery Library

CHANGING NEW YORK

The years between 1890 and 1940 have been described as New York's Golden Age.[43] Consolidation of Manhattan with the four neighboring boroughs between 1874 and 1898 paved the way for New York's emergence as a great world capital. Even as Manhattan's population itself dropped from 2.3 to 1.9 million between 1910 and 1940, an extensive subway, bridge, and tunnel network linked the financial district to the boroughs, neighborhoods, and suburban homes of its workers. "The real process now under way is not urbanization, but suburbanization," declared *The New York Times* in 1929.[44]

Within the New York region the Wall Street area and its skyscrapers occupied a place of undisputed physical and economic primacy (*Fig. 152*). No fewer than six subway lines converged around Wall Street. The financial district's dominance over the city was vividly symbolized in a 1936 photograph by Berenice Abbott in which the Cities Service Building and 40 Wall Street rise up in foreshortened perspective behind Brooklyn Heights row houses (*Fig. 153*).

At the turn of the century the financial district's crowds and tall buildings had typically left observers, like the writer Henry James, with a "sense of baffled curiosity . . . with the confusion carried to chaos for any intelligence, any perception; a welter of objects and sounds in which relief, detachment, dignity, meaning, perished utterly and lost all rights."[45] In the wake of James' incomprehension, artists' quests for meaning in the financial district's architecture became part of the skyscrapers' lives.

Already in James' time the printmaker Joseph Pennell had produced a small 1905 book of Lower Manhattan skyscraper vignettes, whose documentary agenda was continued in the 1920s and 1930s by commercial illustrators such as Chester B. Price, Chesley Bonestell, and Anton Schutz. In the years around 1930 the German-born printmaker Schutz, educated as an architect and a colleague of Pennell's, was the most prolific producer of portrait views of Wall Street area landmarks for newspapers, magazines, and building owners. Schutz worked in a quick chiaroscuro style, like Pennell's, and often chose a mid-air perspective that emphasized the buildings' monumentality (*Fig. 104*). Following Pennell's more impressionistic leanings were the illustrator James Irza Arnold, the architect Yasuo Matsui, and the watercolorist Norman Guthrie Rudolph, all of whom produced misted images of Wall Street area skyscrapers that softened their hard edges and modernity in a haze of scenic beauty (*Figs. 154 and 155*).

Berenice Abbott, on the other hand, embraced the jarring juxtapositions of the financial district, the "dramatic contrasts of the old and the new and the bold foreshadowing of the future . . . the past jostling the present," she said; "the skyscraper in relation to the less colossal edifices which preceded it."[46] Abbott's 1939 book *Changing New York* is perhaps the single best contemporary visual chronicle of the financial district's architecture. A favorite device of Abbott's, to symbolize the financial district's changing character, was to place old statues in front of modern skyscrapers: for example, in front of Trinity Church, the Revolutionary War hero John Watts, whose rippling robes harmonize with the verticality of One Wall Street's facade (*Fig. 156*). Up the East River, the wharves along South Street offered picturesque contrasts between old maritime New York, with its few remaining houseboats, schooners, and the Fulton Fish Market, juxtaposed against the rising towers of the Cities Service Building and its neighbors, embodying the metropolis' modern corporate and financial economy (*Fig. 157*). To contrast tradition and modernity around Wall Street, few scenes matched the dramatic juxtaposition between the dark spiky mass of Richard Upjohn's 1840s Gothic Trinity Church tower and, across Broadway, the soaring white limestone facade of One Wall Street (*Fig. 158*). In a twist on the trope of old and new contrasted, Wiacheslav K. Oltar-Jevsky, an expatriate Russian architect, depicted the 1840s Sub-Treasury Building as a sleek precursor to neighboring 40 Wall Street, showing the present reinterpreting the past instead of departing from it (*Fig. 159*).

OPPOSITE PAGE: FIG. 155. *Illustrator Norman Guthrie Rudolph produced this watercolor nocturne of the Cities Service Building for a 1940 publicity brochure.* Western History Collections, University of Oklahoma Libraries

LEFT: FIG. 156. *Berenice Abbott contrasted and blended old and new New York in 1938, juxtaposing the John Watts statue's hanging drapery in Trinity Church's courtyard with the vertical fluting of One Wall Street's limestone facade.* Museum of the City of New York

RIGHT: FIG. 157. *In Hugh Pearce Botts' rendering, the financial district skyline makes the East River waterfront seem picturesquely cozy, the area still being home in the 1930s to a few remaining houseboats, schooners, and fishing vessels.* Library of Congress

Documentation of architectural contrasts also symbolized Lower Manhattan's uneven economic development and social conditions. Images by Abbott and others show the Cities Service Building looming above foreground scenes, along South, DePeyster, and Cliff streets, of abandoned old buildings, tenements, cobblestone streets, horse-drawn carts, and idle men (*Figs. 47, 160, and 161*). Even before the Great Depression the neighborhoods north of the financial district were wracked by property abandonment, mortgage foreclosures, and tax delinquencies. Land and building use was in a constant state of flux. Between 1910 and 1930 the overcrowded immigrant Lower East Side lost over half its population and possessed the metropolis' lowest land values. To the west the industrial "valley" of low loft buildings between Chambers Street and Times Square emptied of business. The visual contrast between miles of broken down dereliction and Wall Street's shining towers symbolized the inequities of the age (*Fig. 162*).

SKYSCRAPER DEBATE

Some observers blamed skyscrapers directly for Manhattan's swaths of poverty and abandonment. According to this argument unrestricted tall building at the island's tip and in midtown sucked up investment and left Manhattan's center "dismal," "forlorn," and full of "dead and deserted houses and unimproved properties," in the words of Thomas Hastings, architect of the Standard Oil Building.[47] In the late 1920s architects and the public engaged in loud debate over the social value and proper heights of skyscrapers, as they had done during the century's earlier skyscraper boom. "Probably no question before the public today is of more interest and importance," declared the skyscraper analysts W. C. Clark and J. L. Kingston in 1930 at the height of the controversy.[48]

On one side were those who blamed unlimited skyscraper growth for urban congestion, high land values, strained public services, disease, and blocked views and air. "The greatest enemy of New York is the skyscraper," thundered the architect Clarence Stein.[49] "They are Molochs raised for commercial greatness," judged Frank Lloyd Wright, and should be taxed out of existence.[50] Even New York City's health commissioner blamed skyscrapers for urban illnesses.

On the other side, the New York City tax commissioner was firmly pro-skyscraper and the analysts Clark and Kingston argued that skyscrapers were "a new and powerful economic idea. . . . If, therefore, the skyscraper results in 'blighted districts,' we are inclined to accept these deteriorated neighborhoods as part of the cost of progress."[51] Others suggested that skyscraper building campaigns, like that of the City Bank Farmers Trust Building in 1930–31, provided "unemployment relief, a matter of much moment at this writing."[52] Skyscraper proponents argued that skyscrapers' densities and mixes of services actually kept street congestion down during office hours. Low-rise cities like London, it was pointed out, were even more gridlocked than New York.

LEFT: FIG. 158. *Illustrator Chester B. Price's chiaroscuro variation of the oft-repeated contrast of dark and brooding old Gothic Trinity Church overshadowed by One Wall Street's symbolization of modern capitalism.* The Bank of New York Archives

RIGHT: FIG. 159. *Russian expatriate architect W. K. Oltar-Jevsky rendered the foreground 1840s Greek Revival Sub-Treasury Building as a streamlined mechanistic precursor to the soaring abstract mass of nearby 40 Wall Street in a 1931 composition called* Temples of Commerce. Library of Congress

BELOW LEFT: FIG. 160. *A caretaker's shack at East River Pier 5 shelters a group of idle men in Berenice Abbott's 1938 photograph, setting up a contrast with Wall Street's skyline spires that is both architectural and social.* Museum of the City of New York

RIGHT: FIG. 161. *North of the Cities Service Building and the financial district, Berenice Abbott relished the contrast along Cliff and Ferry streets of a horse-drawn cart and the "Mac Lac Shellac" sign, symbolizing in 1935 Manhattan's old declining commercial economy.* Museum of the City of New York

At heart the debate about skyscrapers was political, between private property and the public good, between the rights of individual skyscraper owners and architects to do what they pleased versus community efforts to maintain control of the environment. The tension between private and public interests was tellingly evident at the base of One Wall Street where the building angled back from its legal plot line for aesthetic effect. This created an ostensibly public right-of-way along the sidewalk, which was, however, marked by an inlaid brass boundary line and plaque establishing the bank's private ownership of that patch of paving: "Crossing and Use Subject to Revocable Permission of Owner at Risk of User."[53]

FIG. 162. *Even as Wall Street's skyline attained its skyscraper climax in 1932, neighborhoods to the north, such as the Lower East Side, lost population and business and fell further into decay.* New York Public Library

SYMBOLIZING NEW YORK

As troublesome as tall buildings could be in "changing New York," by the late 1920s skyscrapers had also come to be seen as the city's quintessential image. "To arriving visitors, the skyline of lower Manhattan as seen from the harbor encapsulated the city's character," wrote the architect and historian Robert A. M. Stern (*Fig. 163*).[54] Distant perspectives of the financial district skyline produced coherent silhouetted images of an otherwise unrepresentable metropolis (*Figs. 1 and 2*). Crowded, concentrated, aspiring, superhuman in scale, rapidly changing, heterogeneous, technologically marvelous—the financial district's skyline stood for metropolitan New York as a whole. The view of the skyscraper skyline from arriving steamships, with the Statue of Liberty in the foreground, came to symbolize New York's identity as a gateway to freedom, opportunity, and the New World.

FIG. 163. *The financial district skyline from Governor's Island represented metropolitan modernity and American promise and prosperity to ship passengers arriving in New York harbor.* Library of Congress, Gottscho-Schleisner Collection

Up-close Wall Street's skyscrapers could symbolize other aspects of New York life—the shattering alienation of the modern city, what Lewis Mumford called the "sinister beauty" of Lower Manhattan's "silhouettes of old and new constructions, high and low buildings."[55] In this vein the illustrator and printmaker Howard Cook's wood engraving *The Dictator* (1928) shows a mountainous Equitable Trust Building crushing its foothill neighbors and the elevated subway at Coenties Slip (*Fig. 164*). Oltar-Jevsky's *A New York Canyon* (1932) looks east down a shadowed Pine Street toward a ghostly Cities Service Building (*Fig. 165*). "Masses of steel, concrete, and stone rise on both sides of narrow streets to make atoms of human beings," intones Oltar-Jevsky's caption.[56]

Manhattan's skyscrapers also came to be associated with jazz, one of New York's most characteristic art forms. Charles Phelps Cushing in 1929 imagined "the steps on the top of the Bankers Trust Building, New York, as the meeting place for the midnight frolics of modern jazz sprites."[57] Three years later Cushing described the Equitable Trust Building "as our Jazz age challenge to the Pre-War Era's Banker's Trust Pyramid."[58] "The American spirit expresses itself most eloquently in jazz music and in the skyscrapers," wrote the theorist Claude Bragdon in 1925.[59] In 1927 the Viennese architect Adolf Loos observed, "The black bottom and the Charleston typify the new rhythm of modern life," referring to two fashionable dances. "An architect of today to be successful must be able to translate that rhythm into something of beauty in brick and stone."[60] That same year Mumford described Ralph Walker's Barclay-Vesey Building as being "like jazz, it interrupts and relieves the tedium of too

strenuous mechanical activity."[61] Around the financial district, other jazz architecture includes Ely Jacques Kahn's polychromatic Art Deco John Street skyscrapers, the rhythmic undulations of One Wall Street's facade, and the steel-and-glass crest of the Cities Service Building, which Paul Goldberger has called "an echo of the jazz age life."[62] Whether or not architects consciously mimicked jazz's aesthetic in their designs, the metaphor conveyed a sense of the skyscrapers' unconventional youthful excitement. The simile also tied these downtown skyscrapers to the uptown music scene of New York's Harlem nightclubs. Perhaps for the only time in the history of American architecture, African-American popular culture makes an appearance as a point of comparison and possible inspiration for a mainstream European-American architectural movement.

FIG. 166. *The naval airship* Akron *sails over the Cities Service Building and nearby 63 Wall Street in November 1931, accenting the modernity of the spired skyscraper whose observation gallery is still under construction.* New York Public Library

Jazz metaphors underscored the perception of Wall Street skyscrapers' modernity, and by extension New York's. Images of the Cities Service Building juxtaposed with an overhead blimp and the seaplanes of the nearby East River Downtown Skyport (serving commuters from Long Island, Boston, and Philadelphia) conveyed comparable meanings (*Figs. 107 and 166*). To artists pursuing modernist aesthetic agendas Manhattan's skyscrapers possessed a magnetic appeal. Abstract shapes, dynamic compositions, oblique angles, illegible fragments, repetitive patterns, and cropped views characterize the well-known skyscraper pictures of Georgia O'Keeffe, Charles Sheeler, John Marin, and Abraham Walkowitz. Photographer Berenice Abbott was particularly attentive to the compositional opportunities presented by the financial district's architecture. In *City Arabesque* (1938) Abbott shot north through the Cities Service Building penthouse terrace's intersecting curved aluminum railings, juxtaposing this curved shallow foreground against a patterned rectilinear background to create an abstract view of Lower Manhattan's packed cityscape (*Fig. 167*). Abbott and other modernists aimed to capture the vertiginous dynamism of the claustrophobic metropolis, rather than a traditional legible image of a single landmark building. A similar cubist aesthetic echoed in the forms of the skyscrapers themselves, as with the torqued towers of 19 Rector Street and the City Bank Farmers Trust Building. The modernity of Wall Street area skyscrapers embodied the character of New York and the possibilities for artistic innovation.[63]

"YOU ARE AMERICA!"

Lower Manhattan skyscrapers' symbolization of New York's modernity could be applied to urbanizing American culture generally in the 1920s. More particularly, Wall Street area skyscrapers seemed both the center of world finance and the built embodiment of American capitalism, "the result of the operation of economic laws rather than due to the fancy of architects or the whim of property owners," declared Paul Robertson in *Architectural Forum* (*Fig. 168*).[64] The critic Douglas Haskell saw office building massings as "the effort to convert [rental] cubage into a noble monument of business," and New York's skyscraper boom as an index of capitalist competition. "The headquarters of large national firms will outdo one another in the effort to proclaim dignity, conservatism, and a suave elegance."[65]

The particular race for height among New York skyscrapers heated up in 1930–32, between downtown's 40 Wall Street and Cities Service Building, and midtown's Chrysler Building and Empire State Building. The competition was avidly followed in New York newspapers and illustrated by Yasuo Matsui's published diagram, "Comparative Height of Skyscrapers" (*Fig. 169*).[66] The most sensational moment came in fall 1929 when William Van Alen bested ex-partner H. Craig Severance's 40 Wall Street by raising for "publicity value" the Chrysler Building's secretly fabricated 185-foot spire from within the completed dome. "The signal was given," Van Alen wrote, "and the spire gradually emerged from the top of the dome

FIG. 167. *Berenice Abbott framed the abstract crazy-quilt of skyscrapers north of Wall Street behind the curved aluminum railings of the Cities Service Building's rooftop terrace, in a composition she titled* City Arabesque *(1938)*. Museum of the City of New York

like a butterfly from its cocoon, and in about 90 minutes was securely riveted in position, the highest piece of stationary steel in the world."[67] The 927-foot 40 Wall Street was also topped by the nearby 952-foot Cities Service Building. "Henry Doherty, the utility magnate, gained more accurate information and his new building exceeded our seventy stories by a few feet—or, perhaps, it was inches," recounted builder Paul Starrett.[68] (Actually, it was 25 feet.) Publicly Starrett denied that any deliberate competition existed and the architect Matsui agreed: "There was no disposition to build the highest building in the world, but the most economic and sound investment."[69] In any event the skyscraper competition effectively ended with the spring 1931 completion of the 1250-foot-high Empire State Building. "Rivalry for Height Is Seen as Ended...Practical Limit Reached," read *The New York Times* headlines.[70] The Great Depression saw to the rest.

RIGHT: FIG. 168. *In a view captioned "The Financial Center of the World" a 1930s postcard's distorted perspective shows, from right to left, the Cities Service Building, 40 Wall Street, One Wall Street, and the City Bank Farmers Trust Building.* Courtesy of AIG Archives Department

BELOW: FIG. 169. *40 Wall Street architect Yasuo Matsui published this graphic illustration, "Comparative Height of Skyscrapers," in 1930, with his own building occupying third place, before its imminent supercession by both the Cities Service and Empire State buildings.* Avery Library

185:—DOWNTOWN SKYSCRAPERS, NEW YORK.

THE FINANCIAL CENTER OF THE WORLD.   44253

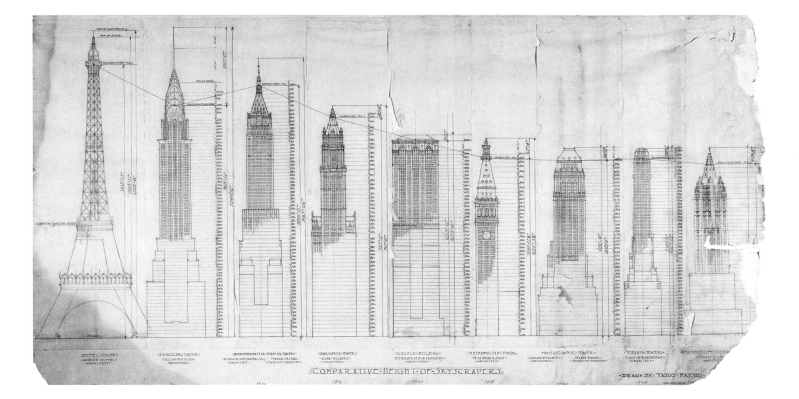

FIG. 170. *Socialist artist Louis Lozowick produced the lithograph* Manhattan Skyline *(1936) as part of a WPA post office mural project. Lozowick conceived the ordered composition, focused on the Cities Service Building, to be symbolic of America's industrial rationality.* Library of Congress

Height competition made good news, provided skyscraper owners with advertising, and seemed to reflect the inherent competitiveness of American business. From another point of view, however, the real struggle in America was not the intramural one among corporate skyscraper contestants, but between the capitalist system itself, symbolized and accommodated in Wall Street area skyscrapers, and those left outside the system's benefits. The socialist printmaker Louis Lozowick implied as much in a dozen images of Lower Manhattan's skyscrapers, including the lithograph *Manhattan Skyline* (1936; *Fig. 170*). This picture was produced in relation to a mural for New York's main post office on Eighth Avenue. It shows a darkly outlined prismatic Cities Service Building as the central apex of a composed pyramid of chugging East River barges, wharves, and neighboring skyscrapers.[71] Lozowick wrote in 1927: "The history of America is a history of gigantic engineering feats and colossal mechanical constructions. The skyscrapers of New York, the grain elevators of Minneapolis, the steel mills of Pittsburgh, the oil wells of Oklahoma, the copper mines of Butte, the lumber yards of Seattle give the American industrial epic its diapason." The artist's goal, as in *Manhattan Skyline*, was to "objectify the dominant experience of our epoch.... Industrialization and standardization ... order and organization which find their outward sign and symbol in the rigid geometry of the American city."[72] "I always believed, then and now," Lozowick said in 1972 about his American imagery, "that this does not necessarily represent capitalism; it represents something that will ultimately be the property of the worker."[73] In Lozowick's conception *Manhattan Skyline* was an abstracted symbol of America: orderly, gigantic, rational, and only for the moment capitalist.

At the same time that New York's skyscrapers appeared to epitomize modern American business, the towering forms also seemed connected to ancient Meso-american architectural culture. "The skyscraper is as indigenous as the Red Indian," announced English architect Alfred Bossom, taking note of the resemblance between, on the one hand, New York skyscrapers' terraced masses, pyramidal caps, polychromatic fretwork, and Art Deco zigzag and floral ornament and, on the other hand, the stepped profiles and geometric decoration of the Mayan pyramids of Tikal, the temple complex at Uxmal, and other buildings at Chichén Itzá and Palenque.[74] "Such is the force of destiny, that the structural form the skyscraper has come to adopt is next of kin to our Indian pyramids," declared the Chilean architect Francisco Mujica who promoted what he called "Neo-American" architecture.[75] In general Indian sources were more noted by Europeans, who saw skyscrapers as exotic and were perhaps less freighted with racist baggage than their American counterparts.

When Americans looked for native national references to authenticate skyscrapers they often thought of the western landscape. "The masses of the Grand Canyon and the peaks and spaces of southern California," the architectural illustrator Hugh Ferriss declared, "they are ... truly American."[76] Mountain imagery suffused renderings by Ferriss and Howard Cook of skyscrapers as dark tapered masses devoid of detail, including Ferriss' view of 40 Wall Street looming above rain-slicked Wall and Broad streets (*Fig. 51*).[77] Canyons were another common metaphor. "Serrated rooflines [that] create a pattern like that of the West's vast canyons, in which soil erosion has carved out abstract sculptures of earth and stone," reads the caption for an Abbott photograph shot from the roof of One Wall Street, and written by Abbott's companion, the art critic Elizabeth McCausland (*Fig. 171*).[78] The European modernist architect Le Corbusier looked around Wall Street and wrote: "One sees canyons surging up, deep and violent fissures, streets such as no one had ever seen before. Not ugly either!"[79]

The identification of skyscrapers with America fired contemporary rhetoric. "You are more than an inanimate giant," Edwin Hill addressed the Cities Service

FIG. 171. *From atop One Wall Street appear in the foreground the Bankers Trust Building pyramid, in the middle 40 Wall Street's cropped shaft, and in the background 120 Wall Street along the East River. Berenice Abbott's 1938 image made the* Wall Street District *look like "the West's vast canyons."* Museum of the City of New York

Building, "You are the visible symbol of integrity and brains and ceaseless aspiration. You are America!" "The skyscraper bespeaks the power and glory of the American people," declared building owners association executive Paul Robertson. "Seldom has architecture so accurately portrayed the characteristics of a nation as does the skyscraper," wrote Alfred Bossom in 1928.[80] Le Corbusier in a talk at the Museum of Modern Art characterized the scene looking up Broad Street toward the Greek Revival Sub-Treasury Building and the looming Chase National Bank skyscraper behind (*Fig. 104*). "For those who are able to see, New York, projected violently into the sky, an outcry that you hate and love at the same time, hides in the bottom of its canyons of banks the architectural composition which is most expressive of the soul of the country."[81]

FIG. 172. *At the 1931 Beaux-Arts ball at the Astor Hotel, William Van Alen poses in the center as his Chrysler Building, flanked to his right by mustached Ely Jacques Kahn (Squibb Building) and to his left by Ralph Walker (One Wall Street). The other costumed architects are, left to right, A. Stewart Walker (Fuller Building), Leonard Schultze (New Waldorf-Astoria), and Joseph Freedlander (Museum of the City of New York).*
Pencil Points/Corbis ©

BEAUTIFUL IRONY

Le Corbusier voiced the paradox of the skyscraper "outcry that you hate and love at the same time." Similarly, the architect Harvey Wiley Corbett described New York's skyscrapers as "a mixture of the splendid and the sordid."[82] Indeed, the skyscraper as a symbol of America absorbed a whole series of contradictory meanings: epitome of capitalism, reincarnation of Mesoamerican architecture, embodiment of western landscape: human and natural, ancient and modern, rational and fantastic.

From one perspective these inconsistencies reflect the multiplicity of American identities (and the problem of trying to make exceptional New York stand for the country as a whole). On another level the skyscraper's ubiquity in visual culture had earned it iconic status—a sign emptied of intrinsic qualities—so that its image was capable of taking on nearly any meaning. From a third view the paradoxes projected onto New York's skyscrapers echo ironies, dualities, and contradictions within the buildings themselves.

Wall Street area skyscrapers were products of owners' rational calculations of profit; and also of emotional desires for distinction and meaning, as evidenced most directly in the Cities Service Building's mechanical fetishes and One Wall Street's self-conscious beauty.[83] From the architects' perspective skyscrapers offered opportunities to design buildings larger than any others in history, firing creative imaginations and creating strong personal identifications, as witnessed by the well-known photograph of Ely Jacques Kahn, Ralph Walker, and William Van Alen dressed up in costumes of their skyscrapers for a 1931 Society of Beaux-Arts Architects ball (*Fig. 172*).[84] Yet, ironically, the romantic myth of the singular architect genius met its demise precisely under the pressures of modern skyscraper production, whose complexities demanded that architects surrender traditional autonomy to work in large practices and collaborate with technical specialists.

Skyscraper buildings themselves contained their own inherent contradictions. While exteriors were designed as fixed, monumental objects, the interiors were conceived of as absolutely flexible, the provisional forms dependent upon tenants' fluid desires and needs. Indispensable and innovative technologies made skyscrapers livable and famous. Yet these systems always remained invisible. And while the latest environmental technology deliberately sealed off inhabitants from their surroundings, skyscraper terraces and observation galleries provided the exact opposite experience of bracing natural air and panoramic views. At the social level skyscrapers were produced and conceived as objects of masculine authority; yet they were increasingly inhabited by female office workers. Within New York's metropolitan context the skyscraper financial district became ever more congested. At the same time the centrifugal forces of suburbanization were decentralizing the region.

At one moment Wall Street's skyscrapers appear as frank expressions of economic rationality, architects' initiative, monumental structure, and masculine authority. And at the same moment they represent owners' emotions, collaborative production, indefinite form, and feminine labor. Ultimately, the beauty and interest of Wall Street's skyscrapers lies not just in their aesthetic character and skyline image, but also in the complex ironies of their forms, histories, and lives.

Chapter Ten

POSTSCRIPT

Wall Street's skyscrapers in 1999, left to right,
Chase Manhattan Bank Building, 40 Wall
Street, 60 Wall Street, and the City Bank
Farmers Trust Building. Norman McGrath

WALL STREET'S SKYSCRAPERS FROM THE 1920S AND 1930S continue to live full if altered lives as the district around them evolves. 40 Wall Street's is the most dramatic story since the skyscraper's completion. It barely survived the Great Depression financially. In 1946 the tower was struck on its 58th floor by an Air Force transport plane lost in the fog, killing five people on the plane but none in the building. Major tenants and owners have come and gone. The Manhattan Company merged with Chase National Bank, and vacated the building in 1960, to be followed in 1990 by the skyscraper's other major banking tenant, Manufacturers Hanover. 40 Wall Street's series of owners have included Webb & Knapp (the real estate firm founded by Eliot Cross), the Philippine dictator Ferdinand Marcos (in the 1980s), and, most recently, Donald Trump, who renamed the building after himself. Architecturally, 40 Wall Street lost its grand main banking hall and Ezra Winter murals, as well as Elie Nadelman's *Oceanus* during an early 1960s renovation of the tower's base. The remaining exterior received city landmark designation in 1995.

The City Bank Farmers Trust Building remains more or less unaltered on its exterior and interior, though the monumental lobby rotunda and the senior officers' hall are now inaccessible to the public. City Bank Farmers Trust became part of Citibank, which moved its headquarters to midtown in 1956 while staying a tenant until 1989, the same year that the Canadian Bank of Commerce also moved out of its banking quarters. The building is now known as 20 Exchange Place and received landmark designation in 1996.

One Wall Street remained in Irving Trust's hands until the late 1980s when the institution merged with The Bank of New York, which now occupies the building as its headquarters. In 1965 a southern annex in similar style was designed by Smith, Smith, Haines, Lundberg & Waehler (the successor firm to Voorhees, Gmelin & Walker). At this time the tenants' lobby was altered and Hildreth Meiere's mural, *Allegory of Wealth and Beauty*, was either covered up or destroyed. Happily, the glass mosaic reception room has been restored and remains open to visitors. The building's penthouse directors' observation lounge still exists, but much altered in decor.

After the Cities Service Company became Citgo and moved to Tulsa, Oklahoma, its skyscraper was sold in 1976 to the American International Group insurance company. AIG's global operations are headquartered in the building and the company has carefully restored the Art Deco lobby and glass observation gallery (both areas are now private). The AIG Building, also known as 70 Pine Street, remains one of the financial district's tallest spires, surpassed only by the twin towers of the World Trade Center (1973–74, Minoru Yamasaki and Emery Roth & Sons). Though still among the financial district's tallest buildings, the AIG Building and its skyscraper rivals are now largely lost in a thicket of postwar towers (*Fig. 173*).

The World Trade Center peaks (1362 and 1368 feet) were part of a northwesterly march of boxy glass and metal skyscrapers in the financial district that commenced with the 60-story Chase Manhattan Bank Building on Pine Street (1960–61, Skidmore, Owings & Merrill) and then continued with the same firm's 51-story Marine Midland Bank Building at 140 Broadway (1967; Gordon Bunshaft, lead designer) and U. S. Steel Building (now One Liberty Plaza, 1974; Roy Allen, lead designer). This last skyscraper's construction led to the demolition of the landmark 612-foot Singer Tower, the tallest building ever torn down. The line of skyscraper development westward toward the Hudson River has culminated with the four towers of the World Financial Center (1985–92), each designed by the architect Cesar Pelli with a distinctive skyscraper cap (pyramid, dome, stepped-pyramid, and mastaba). This return to traditional skyscraper forms has been part of the last generation's postmodernist tendency, and in the financial district also includes Philip Johnson's 33 Maiden Lane (1986) whose rounded towers echo the Federal Reserve Bank Building across the street.

The postwar buildings north and west of the financial district's heart shifted the skyline's visual focus away from the pyramid of skyscrapers around Wall Street. Similarly, a parade of boxy buildings east of the Battery and north along Water Street at the East River has overshadowed the interwar spires from the south and east (*Fig. 174*). While the waterfront margins of the financial district have seen the bulk of skyscraper development, the core remains more or less unchanged. One notable exception is the 52-story 60 Wall Street (1985–88, Roche Dinkeloo & Associates), a pyramid-capped behemoth that replaced Clinton & Russell's old building at the same address.

FIG. 173. *The Hudson River skyline is now focused north of Wall Street on the World Trade Center's twin towers and the quartet of World Financial Center blocks, each with its own distinctive cap.* Norman McGrath

FIG. 174. *From across the East River, 120 Wall Street and the Cities Service (now AIG) Building remain visible along with the crests of 40 Wall Street and the City Bank Farmers Trust Building, sandwiched now between foreground modernist boxes, the new 60 Wall Street behemoth in the center, and the background Chase Manhattan Bank Building and World Trade Center towers.* Norman McGrath

Since the completion of the World Trade Center, and the Sears and Hancock towers in Chicago, the lead in skyscraper architecture has shifted away from America and to Southeast Asia, where the world's tallest and most ambitious skyscrapers now rise in Kuala Lumpur and Shanghai. For economic and cultural reasons it is doubtful that a future Lower Manhattan skyscraper boom will ever match the intensity of the late 1920s and early 1930s. Now the focus is on preservation and adaptation.

The 1990s have seen an upsurge in landmark designations for Lower Manhattan skyscrapers as well as the founding of The Skyscraper Museum by Carol Willis, plus important documentary work by Andrew Dolkart, including his *Forging a Metropolis: Walking Tours of Lower Manhattan* (1990). Columbia architecture school students have also produced the study *Reviving Lower Manhattan: Preserving the Past to Ensure the Future* (1995). The area's architectural heritage is now seen as a valuable asset and, remarkably, as a draw to full-time residents.

FIG. 175. *The financial district around 1950.*
Courtesy of AIG Archives Department

In the 1990s several Wall Street area office skyscrapers were converted to residential use, including 25 Broad Street, 45 Wall Street, and several buildings along John Street. Along with the string of new Battery Park City apartment houses along the Hudson River, these conversions reverse, even if just slightly, the centuries-long trend of the district toward exclusive commercial purposes. The establishment of the National Museum of the American Indian, in the old Custom House, and the new building for the Museum of the Jewish Heritage near the Battery, add culture to the mixed-use strategy.

The full story of the Wall Street area's post-1945 architecture remains to be told. Whatever form that story takes, however, it will grow from the history of the financial district's 1920s and 1930s skyscraper explosion, when the Wall Street skyline came most fully to embody New York City's identity as the capital of the twentieth century (*Fig. 175*).

The weary architect rests after his skyscraper labors, from a radiator grille at the City Bank Farmers Trust Building. Getty Research Library, 940010

CHAPTER ONE: INTRODUCTION

1. "How a Great New Skyscraper Rents Space," *Buildings and Building Management*, 33 (November 1933), 24.

2. Weegee, *Weegee's People* (New York: Duell, Sloan & Pearce, 1946), n. p.

3. "Wall Street Building to Top All in World," *New York Times*, 10 April 1929, 21.

4. "71-Story Skyscraper to Rise in Wall St. Area," *New York Times*, 2 October 1929, 1.

5. "Rising Land Values Mark Expansion of Wall St. Zone," *New York Times*, 23 February 1930, sec. 11, p. 1; "Dearth of Tenants Hits Skyscrapers," *New York Times*, 16 August 1930, 24.

6. Quoted in Carol Willis, "Light, Height, and Site: The Skyscraper in Chicago," in *Chicago Architecture, 1923–1993: Reconfiguration of an American Metropolis*, ed. John Zukowsky (Munich: Prestel-Verlag, 1993), 119.

7. Sarah Bradford Landau and Carl W. Condit, *Rise of the New York Skyscraper, 1865–1913* (New Haven: Yale University Press, 1996), 301.

8. Quoted in Marc A. Weiss, "Density and Intervention: New York's Planning Traditions," in *The Landscape of Modernity: New York City, 1900–1940*, ed. David Ward and Olivier Zunz (Baltimore: Johns Hopkins University Press, 1997), 73.

9. Robert A. M. Stern, Gregory Gilmartin, and Thomas Mellins, *New York 1930: Architecture and Urbanism Between the Two World Wars* (New York: Rizzoli, 1994), 23.

10. Carol Willis, *Form Follows Finance: Skyscrapers and Skylines in New York and Chicago* (New York: Princeton Architectural Press, 1995), 10.

CHAPTER TWO: THE CLIENTS

1. Charles Puckette, "Wall Street's 'Big Little Buildings,'" *New York Times*, 24 August 1930, sec. 5, p. 4.

2. Earle Shultz and Walter Simmons, *Offices in the Sky* (Indianapolis: Bobbs-Merrill, 1959), 13.

3. Quoted in W. C. Clark and J. L. Kingston, *The Skyscraper: A Study in the Economic Height of Modern Office Buildings* (New York: American Institute of Steel Construction, 1930), 78–79.

4. William Donahue Ellis, *On the Oil Lands with Cities Service* (Tulsa: Cities Service Oil and Gas Corporation, 1983), 72. See also W. Alton Jones, *The Cities Service Story* (New York: Newcomen Society, 1955); *Serving a Nation* (New York: Henry L. Doherty & Company, 1923), Cities Service Oil and Gas Corporation Collection (hereafter cited as CSCC), Box 26, Folder 1, Western History Collections, University of Oklahoma Libraries; Adolf A. Berle and Gardiner Means, *The Modern Corporation and Private Property* (New York: Macmillan Company, 1936); *Cities Service Company Annual Reports*, CSCC, Box 18, Folder 2.

5. Jones, *Cities Service*, 27.

6. For the Cities Service Company's financial operations see "Other People's Money," *New Republic*, 6 June 1934, 100–101; Charles R. Geisst, *Wall Street: A History* (New York: Oxford University Press, 1997), 190–192; Frederick Lewis Allen, *The Lords of Creation* (New York: Harper & Brothers, 1935), 257ff; "Doherty: Drops High-Power Sales of Cities Service Stock," *Newsweek*, 5 August 1933, 22.

7. Cities Service real estate subsidiaries were Sixty Wall Street, Inc., 8 State Street Realty Corporation, 66 Pine Street Corporation, South Ferry Realty Company, H. L. D. Realty Corporation, Jay-Eye Realty Corporation, and the Chesebrough Building Company. Besides its 60 Wall Street headquarters (bought in 1923)—behind which would be located the new sky-scraper headquarters—Cities Service owned several blocks of buildings east and north of Battery Park on Greenwich, Bridge, Washington, State, Whitehall, Water, and Pearl streets, and Battery Place, including the Maritime Building, at 8–10 Bridge Street, the Chesebrough Building at 13–20 State Street, the Battery Park Building at 21–24 State Street, the South Ferry Building at State and Whitehall streets, and 8–12 State Street, 22–32 Whitehall Street, 10–12, 19–23, 33–35, and 248–250 Pearl Street, 2–12 and 20 Greenwich Street, 1–13 and 21 Washington Street, and 2–7 Battery Place. For the Cities Service Company's real estate holdings see "Manual of Real Estate Properties, New York, Owned and Controlled by Cities Service Company, Henry L. Doherty Company," 1930–37, CSCC, Box 6, Folder 1; "Real Estate in Greater New York Owned and Operated by Cities Service Company and Subsidiaries," 1937, CSCC, Box 6, Folder 2; *Doherty News*, 15 May 1930, 16, CSCC, Box 9, Folder 4; Norman Klein, "'Sun Deck' Tops 60 Wall Tower," *New York Evening Post*, 7 July 1932; Edwin C. Hill, *Sixty Wall Tower* (New York, 1932), 3.

8. "Doherty: A Locomotive Drive and a Memory Like an Elephant," *Newsweek*, 26 October 1935, 26–7. For Doherty's life see also *Current Biography*; *National Cyclopedia of American Biography*, vol. 34; *Dictionary of American Biography* (1958); David Lawrence, "American Business and Business Men," *Saturday Evening Post*, 26 July 1930, 34; Henry Gibbons, "Cadet Schools of Business," *The Forum*, 58 (December 1917), 741; "Doherty: Drops High-Power Sales of Cities Service Stock," 22; Ellis, *On the Oil Lands*, especially chapter 5.

9. Ellis, *On the Oil Lands*, 158.

10. Floyd W. Parsons, "A Skyscraper Home," *World's Work*, 43 (March 1922), 505–512. See also CSCC, Box 10, Folder 7; "This Millionaire Makes Science a Hobby," *Current Opinion*, 73 (December 1922), 739; "H.L. Doherty Weds Secretly on Dec. 13," *New York Times*, 19 April 1929, 12.

11. Hill, *Sixty Wall Tower*, frontispiece, 8, 13. For Doherty's role in the Cities Service Building see also A. H. Fromm, "Double Deck Elevators and New Equipment," *Proceedings of the Twenty-Fifth Annual Convention of the National Association of Building Owners and Managers*, 1932, 194; "Provides Terraces in Office Building," *New York Times*, 12 July 1931, real estate section, p. 11; "Doherty: A Locomotive Drive and a Memory Like an Elephant," 26–27; Ellis, *On the Oil Lands*, 150.

12. Ellis, *On the Oil Lands*, 150, 177; "Manual of Real Estate Properties, New York, Owned and Controlled by Cities Service Company, Henry L. Doherty Company." For W. Alton Jones see *Who Was Who in America*, vol. 4 (1968).

13. "Hampers Doherty Project," *New York Times*, 22 May 1930, 15.

14. "Address by Lewis E. Pierson, Chairman of the Board of the Irving Trust Company, at Luncheon Prior to the Laying of the Corner Stone of the Irving Trust Company Building, One Wall Street, January 14, 1930," The Bank of New York Archives.

15. Stephen Voorhees, "Remarks at Dedication Ceremony," The Bank of New York Archives.

16. Ralph Walker, "Each Day Anew," 1950s, 47, manuscript, Ralph Walker Papers, Box 19, Syracuse University.

17. Obituary, *New York Times*, 24 September 1960, 23.

18. "Brief Narrative History: Irving Trust Company Building, One Wall Street," 1934, 5, typescript, The Bank of New York Archives.

19. D. G. O'Connor to Robert H. Elmendorf, 14 November 1929, The Bank of New York Archives.

20. CSCC, Box 9, Folder 7.

21. "How a Great New Skyscraper Rents Space," *Buildings and Building Management*, 33 (November 1933), 23–26.

22. One Wall Street construction drawings, E-17A, HLW International, New York.

23. Harold Van B. Cleveland and Thomas F. Huertas, *Citibank, 1812–1970* (Cambridge: Harvard University Press, 1985), 188; *National Cyclopedia of American Biography*, vol. 34; *Dictionary of American Biography* (1958).

24. "71-Story Skyscraper to Rise in Wall St. Area," *New York Times*, 2 October 1929, 1.

25. Other financial companies sponsoring prominent new headquarters included the Equitable Trust Company (30 Broad Street, 1929–32), The Bank of New York and Trust Company (48 Wall Street, 1927–29), the National City Company (52 Wall Street, 1928), Seamen's Bank (74 Wall Street, 1926), the Bank of America (44 Wall Street, 1926), Goldman Sachs (30 Pine Street, 1931), and the nation's largest bank, Chase National (20 Pine Street, 1928). Large transportation and industrial concerns also erected significant headquarters structures, including Cunard (25 Broadway, 1917–21), Munson Steamship (67 Wall Street, 1921), Standard Oil (26 Broadway, 1922–26), and International Telephone & Telegraph (67 Broad Street, 1930).

26. *National Cyclopedia of American Biography*, vol. 46.

27. Jewish developers operated on the fringes of the financial district, marginalized perhaps by anti-Semitism. Elsewhere in Manhattan, Jews and immigrants dominated the real estate industry—men like Fred F. French, Henry Mandel, A. E. Lefcourt, Irwin Chanin, Louis Abrons, Simon William Straus. See Tom Shachtman, *Skyscraper Dreams: The Great Real Estate Dynasties of New York* (Boston: Little, Brown & Company, 1991), chapter 7.

28. The Manhattan Company executive overseeing the design and construction of the bank's interior quarters was the first vice president Raymond E. Jones. *The Manhattan Family*, April 1930, 10, Chase Manhattan Archives, New York.

29. Ohrstrom acknowledged The Manhattan Company's reluctance to promote the developer's scheme when he wrote in January 1929 to the bank's vice chairman, "I appreciate what is in your mind, and realize that if you do enter into a lease with us you do not want us to use it in such a way that we will be leaning on the credit of the Bank. Undoubtedly, you will want the building named after you, but for financing purposes we are perfectly will[ing] to call the building '36 Wall Street' or '40 Wall Street,' and if after the financing you wish to have it called 'The Bank of the Manhattan Building' we will be agreeable." Letter from G. L. Ohrstrom to P. A. Rowley, 14 January 1929, Box 1A8 RG1, "Bank of the Manhattan Company Buildings, 40 Wall Street Corporation, 1929–31" Folder, Chase Manhattan Archives, New York.

30. "How a Great New Skyscraper Rents Space," 23. For the Cities Service Building's financing see also, *Going Up! October Building Campaign*, Henry L. Doherty & Company, 1930, CSCC, Box 9, Folder 7; "200 Star Securities Salesmen Enjoy Half-Million Club Trip," *Doherty News*, 14/22

(1 October 1930), 1, CSCC, Box 6, Folders 1 and 2. In 1936 Sixty Wall Tower, Inc., reported a net income of $500,000 out of a gross of $1.3 million.

31. Quoted in Leonard Louis Levinson, *Wall Street: A Pictorial History* (New York: Ziff & Davis, 1961), 230–231. For 40 Wall Street's financial history see "40 Wall: X-Ray of a Skyscraper," *Fortune*, July 1939, 116–117, 226, 228; Yasuo Matsui, "Skyscraper: Multiple Business Building," 1932, 71, typescript, Chase Manhattan Archives, New York; "Skyscrapers: Pyramids in Steel & Stock," *Fortune*, August 1930, 72–73; *The Manhattan Company Building Forty Wall Street New York City* (New York: Forty Wall Street Corporation, 1929); James Grant, *The Trouble with Prosperity* (New York: Times Books, 1996), chapter 2.

32. *New Republic*, 8 July 1931, 192–193.

33. For the financial district's vacancy rates see Carol Willis, *Form Follows Finance: Skyscrapers and Skylines in New York and Chicago* (New York: Princeton Architectural Press. 1995), fig. 159; "Dearth of Tenants Hits Skyscrapers," *New York Times*, 16 August 1930, 24; C. F. Palmer, "Office Buildings From an Investments Standpoint," *Architectural Forum*, 52 (June 1930), 891–896; *Proceedings of the National Association of Building Owners and Managers*, (1931) 41. "Vacancies in Office Buildings Said to Be Not Abnormal," *New York Times*, 21 June 1931, sec. 11 p. L.

34. "Because escalating land prices drive up the number of stories needed to spread the cost of the lot," explains architectural historian Carol Willis, "the tallest buildings generally appear at the end of the boom cycle." Willis, *Form Follows Finance*, 166.

35. $125 million worth of construction and over a dozen major projects were planned for the Wall Street area in 1930 alone. See Gordon D. MacDonald, *Office Building Construction Manhattan 1901–1953* (New York: Real Estate Board of New York, 1952), 3; "Active Features of City and Suburban Realty Market," *New York Times*, 12 May 1929, sec. 12, p. 1; "Rising Land Values Mark Expansion of Wall St.," *New York Times*, 23 February 1930, sec. 11, p. 1; "73-Story Skyscraper to Rise in Broad St.," *New York Times*, 4 April 1930, 1; "Wall St. Skyscraper May Rise 105 Stories," *New York Times*, 8 May 1930, 1; "Wall Street Deal Big Realty Task," *New York Times*, 11 May 1930, sec.11, p. 2; "Tall Structures Ever Increasing in New York," *New York Times*, 26 October 1930, sec. 11, p. 1.

36. "Wall Street Area to Get Skyscraper Homes," *New York Times*, 7 May 1929, 22; "Rising Land Values Mark Expansion of Wall St. Zone," *New York Times*, 23 February 1930, sec. 11, p. 1.

37. For Doherty's Battery Park area holdings see CSCC, Box 6, Folders 1 and 2, and note 7 above.

38. "Doherty Again on Stand," *New York Times*, 26 June 1935, 2.

39. The bird's-eye view of the Doherty Battery Park scheme, in the AIG Archives, is derived from an earlier 1911/15 topographic view of Lower Manhattan by Louis Dreger (a copy is in the Library of Congress, Prints and Photographs Division, reproduction number LC-D431T01-600009-x). I am thankful to Tom Heard for this information.

40. "Doherty Project Killed by Slump," *New York Times*, 25 June 1935, 9; "Doherty Again on Stand," *New York Times*, 26 June 1935, 2.

41. "$10,000,000 in Wall St. Rentals," *New York Times*, 19 June 1929, sec. 13, p. 2; "Reveals No Overproduction in Office Buildings," *Real Estate Record and Guide*, 24 August 1929, 7–8.

42. "Wall Street District Showing Activity," *New York Times*, 26 October 1930, sec. 11, p. 1; "Stock Conditions Will Aid Building," *New York Times*, 3 November 1929, sec. 12, p. 1; "Readjustment the Keynote of the 1931 Realty Market," *New York Times*, 4 January 1931, sec. 12–13, p. 1.; Charles F. Noyes, "New York Realty on a Sound Basis," *New York Times*, 21 June 1931, sec. 11, p. 1.

CHAPTER THREE: THE ARCHITECTS

1. Le Corbusier, *When the Cathedrals Were White: A Journey to the Country of Timid People* (New York: Reynal and Hitchcock, 1947; first published in French, 1938–39), 61.

2. Ralph Walker, "The Relation of Skyscrapers to Our Life," *Architectural Forum*, 52 (May 1930), 695.

3. William Engle, "Men and Steel: Architect's Pencil Guides Skyscraper," *New York World-Telegram*, 6 April 1931, sec. 2, p. 2.

4. *American Architect*, 130 (20 October 1926), 323–324.

5. "Alfred Holton, 57, Architect, Is Dead," *New York Times*, 7 April 1936, 25; *Architectural Forum*, 64 (May 1936), 68.

6. *National Cyclopedia of American Biography*, vol. 35; "T. J. George Dead; Retired Architect," *New York Times*, 9 February 1947, 61; *Empire State Architect*, 7 (May-June 1947), 22.

7. *Clinton & Russell, Holton & George* (New York: Architectural Catalog Company, 192–).

8. W. Parker Chase, *New York: The Wonder City* (New York: Wonder City Publishing, 1931), 183.

9. Clinton & Russell, Holton & George's offices were in Nassau Street, Maiden Lane, and John Street before the firm moved into the Cities Service Building. By contrast the architects of other Wall Street area skyscrapers were based in midtown, near 42nd Street and along Park and Madison avenues. James Ward, *Architects in Practice: New York City, 1900–1940* (Union, N. J.: J. & D. Associates, 1989).

10. "Ralph T. Walker Is Dead at 83," *New York Times*, 18 January 1973, 44.

11. Meredith Arms Bzdak, "The Architecture of Ralph Thomas Walker: 1919–1939," (Ph. D. dissertation, Rutgers, The State University of New Jersey, 1995), 117.

12. Priscilla Ogden Dalmas, "Simplified Practice for Drafting Room Efficiency," *Architectural Forum*, 56 (May 1932), 515–518; John F. Gone, ed., *American Architects Directory*, 3rd ed. (New York: R. R. Bowker, 1972), 588.

13. Eliot Cross, *Architectural Record*, 105 (March 1949), 18 and *New York Times*, 24 January 1949, 14; John Walter Cross: *National Cyclopedia of American Biography*, vol. 40, 158–159 and "John W. Cross 73, Architect, is Dead," *New York Times*, 7 July 1951, 21. See also *Country Life*, 38 (October 1920), 51.

14. "H. Craig Severance Fined," *New York Times*, 3 August 1931, 4.

15. Matsui's Houston Tower was rendered in a large watercolor perspective that is now part of the Chase Manhattan Archives, New York. The Houston Tower is also noted in the research guide to the Yasuo Matsui Collection of drawings at Avery Library, Columbia University. For Matsui's career see his obituary, *New York Times*, 12 August 1962, 81, and Jay Shockley and Rosita Chalem, "Manhattan Company Building," New York City Landmarks Preservation Commission, Designation List 269, LP-1936, 4. Matsui's Japanese Pavilion is discussed in Akiko Takenaka, "Pan-Asianism vs. Changeless, Timeless Japan: The Construction of a Wartime National Identity," *Thresholds*, 17 (1998), 63–68.

16. Morris' association with the Morgan family commenced in 1910–15 with the design of J. P. Morgan's Glen Cove, Long Island, home (in partnership with Christopher Grant LaFarge) and continued at Hartford's Colt-Morgan Memorial (1909–10) and Wadsworth Atheneum, the Class of '79 Dormitory (c. 1905) and Patton Hall at Princeton University, the American Women's Association Building (New York, 1929–30), and the Pierpont Morgan Library Annex (New York, 1927). See "Benjamin W. Morris, F.A.I.A.," *Michigan Society of Architects*, 19 December 1944, 7; Henry F. Withey and Elsie Rathburn Withey, *Biographical Dictionary of American Architects (Deceased)* (Los Angeles: Hennessey & Ingalls, 1970); *New York Times*, 5 December 1944, 23.

17. "Thomas Hastings: Memoir," in *Thomas Hastings, Architect: Collected Writings*, ed. David Gray (Boston: Houghton Mifflin, 1933), 11 and "Thomas Hastings, 1860–1929," *Architectural Record*, 66 (December 1929), 596.

18. Warren D. Bruner, "Office Layouts for Tenants," *Architectural Forum*, 52 (June 1930), 905.

19. Ely Jacques Kahn, *Ely Jacques Kahn, New York Architect* (New York: McGraw-Hill, 1931; New York: Acanthus Press, 1995), xx; Chase, *Wonder City*, 163; Robert A. M. Stern, Gregory Gilmartin, and Thomas Mellins, *New York 1930: Architecture and Urbanism Between the Two World Wars* (New York: Rizzoli, 1994), 56.

20. Allene Talmey, "Profiles: Man Against the Sky," *New Yorker*, 11 April 1931, 24. Kahn was President of the No. 111 John Street Corporation according to building records in the City of New York Municipal Archives.

21. 19 Rector Street, City of New York Municipal Archives; Aline Lewis Goldstone and Harmon H. Goldstone, *Lafayette A. Goldstone: A Career in Architecture* (New York: privately printed, 1964).

22. Chase, *Wonder City*, 113. For Schwartz & Gross, see also *Schwartz & Gross, Architects* (New York: Architectural Catalog Company, 1927); Stern, *New York 1930*. For Schwartz see *Michigan Society of Architects Bulletin* (June 1956), 19; "Simon I. Schwartz," *New York Times*, 25 April 1956, 35. For Gross see "Arthur Gross," *New York Times*, 27 November 1950, 25. The Jewish names of Kahn, Goldstone, Schwartz, and Gross perhaps handicapped these architects from working in the financial district's geographic and institutional core, in contrast to the socially eminent Christian architects working at Wall Street's heart, such as Livingston and Morris. Wall Street's anti-Semitism was well-known, notwithstanding the presence of leading Jewish financiers such as Bernard Baruch, William Loeb, and Felix and Paul Warburg. "Jewish Renaissance," for example, was a term used, somewhat mysteriously, to deride One Wall Street's unconventional facade. Earl Sparling, "Architect Designed the Irving Trust on Basis of Its 'Biological Appeal,'" *New York World-Telegram*, 11 November 1931.

23. The Wall Street area architects who attended Columbia University included Goodhue Livingston (Class of '92), Arthur Loomis Harmon ('06), Thomas Hastings (c. '82), Benjamin Wistar Morris ('94), Ely Jacques Kahn ('03 and '07), John Walter Cross ('02), Everett V. Meeks ('04), Perry Coke Smith ('23), Robert D. Kohn ('90), W. A. Delano, and C. H. Aldrich.

24. "Arbiter of the Arts," *Architectural Forum*, 86 (June 1947), 76.

25. Ralph Walker, "Architectural Education," *Pencil Points*, 18 (January 1937), 49–50 and Ralph Walker, "Architecture," *North American Review*, 231 (June 1931), 529.

26. E. J. Kahn, "American Office Practice," *Journal of the Royal Institute of British Architects*, 64 (September 1957), 443.

27. R. H. Shreve, "The Economic Design of Office Buildings," *Architectural Record*, 67 (April 1930), 343.

28. E. J. Kahn, "The Office Building Problem in New York," *Architectural Forum*, 41 (September 1924), 94.

29. Cf. Yasuo Matsui, 20 William Street Building analysis, Yasuo Matsui Collection (10000.038, Dr. 343), Drawings and Archives, Avery Library, Columbia University.

30. Walker, "Architecture," 529.

31. Ely J. Kahn, "Economics of the Skyscraper," *Architectural Record*, 63 (April 1928), 300. For calculations of 40 Wall Street's prospective profitability see Yasuo Matsui, "Skyscraper: Multiple Business Building," 1932 typescript, Chase Manhattan Archives, New York, and *The Manhattan Company Building*, album compiled by Yasuo Matsui, Special Collections, Avery Library, Columbia University.

32. Matsui, "Skyscraper," 32.

33. Warren D. Bruner, "The Office Layout Specialist and the Building Manager," *Skyscraper Management*, 16 (September 1931), 28. See also Bruner, "Office Layouts."

34. One Wall Street construction drawings, HLW International, New York. The One Wall Street Corporation laid out most tenant interiors.

35. William Marshall Ellis, "The Architect and the Building Manager," *Architectural Form*, 41 (September 1924), 135–136.

36. "Planning Service on N. Y. Bank: Analyze Plans for Farmers Loan & Trust Co.," *Bulletin of the National Association of Building Owners and Managers*, 133 (February 1929), 145. For NABOM's Building Planning Service and the building manager's point of view on skyscraper architecture generally, see Earle Shultz, "Build for Profit," *Skyscraper Management*, 16 (March 1931), 19–20; Paul Robertson, "The Skyscraper Office Building," *Architectural Forum*, 52 (June 1930), 879–880; Earle Shultz and Walter Simmons, *Offices in the Sky* (Indianapolis: Bobbs-Merrill, 1959), 136–142; George R. Bailey, "Analyzing Alternative Floor Plans," *Bulletin of the National Association of Building Owners and Managers*, 15 (March 1930), 183–184; Clarence T. Coley, "Office Buildings, Past, Present and Future," *Architectural Forum*, 41 (September 1924), 113–114; C. A. Heisterkamp, C. C. Lawrence, and E. J. Smith, "The Technique of Opening an Office Building," *Real Estate Record*, 17 July 1937, 21–34; Ellis, "The Architect and the Building Manager," 135–136.

37. Shultz, *Offices in the Sky*, 137.

38. Shultz, *Offices in the Sky*, 140–141.

39. See building records in City of New York Municipal Archives and individual architects' biographical data, especially obituaries.

40. Quoted in Carol Willis and Donald Friedman, *Building the Empire State* (New York: W. W. Norton, 1998), 26.

41. Arthur Loomis Harmon, "The Design of Office Buildings," *Architectural Forum*, 52 (June 1930), 819. "The design of a modern skyscraper is not primarily a matter of aesthetic expression," declared the Cross brothers. "It is rather a coordinated solution to complex mechanical problems and the strenuous demands of economics, and the aesthetic approach must be made after such major problems have been adequately solved." "The Design of a Bank's Skyscraper: The City Bank Farmer's Trust Company," *Architectural Forum*, 55 (July 1931), 7.

42. R. H. Shreve, "The Empire State Building Organization," *Architectural Forum*, 52 (June 1930), 773.

43. Kahn, "American Office Practice," 443.

44. Shreve, "Empire State Building," 771.

45. Walker, "Architecture," 529, 531. "The architect, in essence, is the conductor of an orchestra that is quite large and is a bit difficult to keep in tune," Kahn opined. "American Office Practice," 447. Expressed more bluntly in the *Architectural Forum*, "it is the architect alone who can correlate the economic with the engineering and aesthetic interests." W. R. Morton Keast and A. B. Randall, "The Minimum Building for Varying Land Values," *Architectural Record*, 67 (April 1930), 376.

46. Dalmas, "Drafting Room Efficiency," 515.

47. Dalmas, "Drafting Room Efficiency," 515.

48. Harmon, "Design of Office Buildings," 819.

49. *Country Life*, 52 (September 1927), 66.

50. Kahn, "On What Is Modern," 1930, in *Ely Jacques Kahn*, 12–13.

51. Ralph Walker, "Architecture of To-Day," *Creative Arts*, 5 (July 1929), 460–465.

52. Ely Jacques Kahn, "Sources of Inspiration," *Architecture*, 60 (November 1929), 251, 255.

53. Harmon, "Design of Office Buildings," 820.

54. Hildreth Meiere, "The Question of Decoration," *Architectural Forum*, 57 (July 1932), 1.

55. Everett V. Meeks, "Return to Functional Architecture," *Yale Review*, 23 (December 1933), 288.

56. Walker, "Relation of Skyscrapers to Our Life," 689 and Kahn, "On New York: Past, Present and Future," 1926, in *Ely Jacques Kahn*, 25.

57. John Taylor Boyd, Jr., "A New Emphasis in Skyscraper Design Exemplified in the Recent Work of Starrett & Van Vleck," *Architectural Record*, 52 (December 1922), 497–509.

58. *Ely Jacques Kahn*, xi.

59. Stern, *New York 1930*, 566.

60. Kahn, "On the Use of Color," 1928, in *Ely Jacques Kahn*, 24 and Kahn, "On Decoration and Ornament," 1929, in *Ely Jacques Kahn*, 21.

61. Ralph Walker, "Color in Architecture," *Architectural Record*, 63 (January 1928), 80.

62. "I think the architect of the future will have to be a psychologist," Walker prophesied, "because it is just as important for the architect to design a building for man to be mentally comfortable in as it is for him to design one in which he will be physically comfortable." Walker, "Relation of Skyscrapers to Our Life," 694. "The demand for beauty increases in ratio to the distance people are removed from the pioneering stage of civilization," Walker further argued in a primitivist vein resembling Kahn's exotic tastes, "and in this country we have reached an advanced stage in the development." Walker, "Architecture," 530.

63. Ralph Walker, "Paper, Romance and the Humble Architect," *American Architect*, 139 (April 1931), 84.

64. Ralph Walker, *Ralph Walker, Architect* (New York: Henahan House, 1957), 35.

CHAPTER FOUR: PLANNING

1. Between 1924 and 1930 expert opinion also showed trends toward better lit, shallower, and less crowded office spaces (from 28-foot depths to an ideal 20-foot, and 75–90 square feet per occupant versus the earlier recommended 100–125), but with also lower, more economical floor heights (from 10 feet to 9 1/2 feet).

2. Quoted in Carol Willis, *Form Follows Finance: Skyscrapers and Skylines in New York and Chicago* (New York: Princeton Architectural Press, 1995), 19.

3. Clark and Kingston arrived at the shape of their ideal economic skyscraper through an analysis of presumed land cost, building expense, rentability, amortization, elevator service, and other variables. W. C. Clark and J. L. Kingston, *The Skyscraper: A Study in the Economic Height of Modern Office Buildings* (New York: American Institute of Steel Construction, 1930).

4. Yasuo Matsui, "Skyscraper: Multiple Business Building," 1932 typescript, 51, Chase Manhattan Archives, New York.

5. A. H. Fromm, "Double Deck Elevators and New Equipment," *Proceedings of the Twenty-Fifth Annual Convention of the National Association of Building Owners and Managers*, 1932, 196.

6. "Questions Raised by the Architects of the New Building (Voorhees, Gmelin & Walker) Concerning Matters of Bank Layout and Arrangements on Which They Will Have Decisions by Sept. 1," 8 August 1928, The Bank of New York Archives. HLW International, New York, possesses slides of several different massing studies for One Wall Street.

7. City of New York Board of Standards and Appeals, Resolution 944-28-BZ, 29 January 1929, One Wall Street records, City of New York Municipal Archives. The zoning variance was granted in part because "all properties immediately affected have filed consents."

8. Yasuo Matsui Collection, Drawings and Archives, Avery Library, Columbia University.

9. Cross & Cross, "City Bank Farmers Trust Building: Vol. 1, A Portfolio of Data Showing Progress of Sketches, Evolution of Models and Final Development of Construction; Vol. 2, Sketch Progress," 1931, (Accession Number 940010*), Special Collections, Getty Research Institute, Los Angeles; Yasuo Matsui, Study of 20 William Street, April 1929, Yasuo Matsui Collection (Dr. 343/1000.038), Drawings and Archives, Avery Library, Columbia University; "The Design of a Bank's Skyscraper: The City Bank Farmer's Trust Company," *Architectural Forum*, 55 (July 1931), 8.

10. *Real Estate Record and Guide*, 12 October 1929, 9.

11. "Design of a Bank's Skyscraper," 7.

12. "At one side of the table he set down a block, a rough model of the Cotton Exchange; near it he set another, the Corn Exchange; close by, another, the Brown Brothers' Building; adjoining, the old National City Bank. The fifth he put down inside the square which the others made. It

was the new skyscraper, still a dream, still a thing of blueprints and miniature plaster, but already, on Maguolo's table, alive." William Engle, "Men and Steel: Architect's Pencil Guides Skyscraper," *New York World-Telegram*, 6 April 1931, sec. 2, p. 1.

13. "Sell Your Building—Not Just Space," *Skyscraper Management*, 18 (April 1933), 4–6. See also Earle Shultz and Walter Simmons, *Offices in the Sky* (Indianapolis: Bobbs-Merrill, 1959), 85–87, and Willis, *Form Follows Finance*, 29–30.

14. Shultz, *Offices in the Sky*, 234.

15. "Income Factors in Office Building," *New York Times*, 1 December 1929, sec. 13, p. 8.

16. For various definitions of the ideal office unit see articles by Albert Kahn, C. F. Palmer, Arthur Loomis Harmon, Paul Robertson, and James Newman in *Architectural Forum*, 52 (June 1930) as well as R. H. Shreve, "The Economic Design of Office Buildings," *Architectural Record*, 67 (April 1930), 340–359; A. Lawrence Kocher and Albert Frey, "Planning Offices for Economy," *Architectural Record*, 72 (September 1932), 197–202; and Willis, *Form Follows Finance*, 27.

17. Harvey Wiley Corbett, "The Planning of Office Buildings," *Architectural Forum*, 41 (September 1924), 93.

18. Frederick S. Tisdale, "City in a Tower," *Service*, January 1946, CSCC, Box 9, Folder 7.

19. Matsui, "Skyscraper," 80.

20. Matsui, "Skyscraper," 89.

CHAPTER FIVE: CONSTRUCTION

1. "Skyscrapers: Builders and Their Tools," *Fortune*, October 1930, 85.

2. "Hampers Doherty Project," *New York Times*, 22 May 1930, 15.

3. "Of all the construction work which I have handled, the Bank of Manhattan was the most complicated and the most difficult and I regard it as the most successful." Paul Starrett, *Changing the Skyline: An Autobiography* (New York: McGraw-Hill, 1938), 283.

4. Yasuo Matsui, "Skyscraper: Multiple Business Building," 1932 typescript, 110, Chase Manhattan Archives, New York.

5. Walter H. Kilham, Jr., "Tower Floor Plans of New York Skyscrapers Compared," *American Architect*, 138 (October 1930), 78.

6. For One Wall Street's special wall system of layered zinc sheets between limestone cladding, see "Brief Narrative History, Irving Trust Company Building, One Wall Street," 1934, 9, The Bank of New York Archives.

7. William A. Starrett, *Skyscrapers and the Men Who Build Them* (New York: Charles Scribner's Sons, 1928), 202, 206.

8. "Skyscrapers: Builders and Their Tools," 85.

9. "Skyscrapers," *Fortune*, July 1930, 37. See also Matsui, "Skyscraper," plate 31.

10. Each building firm administered several projects at a time, but because of the small profits to be made in construction itself, the firms were also often associated with development and financing companies. Starrett Brothers & Eken was a subsidiary of the Starrett Corporation and George A. Fuller was owned by the United States Realty & Improvement Company. "Skyscrapers: Pyramids in Steel & Stock," *Fortune* (August 1930), 60–61, 72–75; Carol Willis and Donald Friedman, *Building the Empire State* (New York: W. W. Norton, 1998), 26.

11. "Contracts & Sub-Contracts Awarded, One Wall Street," 20 November 1930, The Bank of New York Archives.

12. "Skyscrapers: Builders and Their Tools," 85ff.

13. "Stone Work Finished on Bank Skyscraper," *New York Times*, 30 November 1930, sec. 12, p. 1.

14. "Skyscrapers: Builders and Their Tools," 92.

15. Alfred C. Bossom, *Building to the Skies: The Romance of the Skyscraper* (New York: Studio Publications, 1934), 119.

16. "Skyscrapers: Builders and Their Tools," 89, 91.

17. "Skyscrapers: Builders and Their Tools," 94.

18. "Wage Scales in the Building Trades," *Architectural Record*, 74 (August 1933), 22. Total wages at the City Bank Farmers Trust Building of $7.5 million represented about forty percent of the total building cost. "Stone Work Finished on Bank Skyscraper," *New York Times*, 30 November 1930, sec. 12, p. 1.

19. "Banker Lauds Mechanics," *New York Times*, 16 January 1931, 40. Speaking at the ceremony were the bank president James Perkins, the architect John Walter Cross, the building company president Lou Crandall, the Building Congress awards committee chairman Ernest McCullough, and John J. Collins "representing labor."

20. C. H. Fister, "60 Wall Tower," *Building Investment*, June 1932, 28; Edwin C. Hill, *Sixty Wall Tower* (New York, 1932), 6–7; Sixty Wall Tower, Inc., *Sixty Wall Tower: The Aristocrat of Office Buildings* (New York, 1932), CSCC, Box 9, Folder 7.

21. *New York Times*, 11 July 1929: "Golden Rivet in Building," 12 and "California Plane Still Up at 207th Hour," 1.

CHAPTER SIX: TECHNOLOGY

1. Ralph Walker, "Paper, Romance and the Humble Architect," *American Architect*, 139 (April 1931), 84.

2. Louis T. M. Ralston, "The Engineer's Problem in Tall Buildings," *Architectural Forum*, 52 (June 1930), 909.

3. Yasuo Matsui, "Skyscraper: Multiple Business Building," 1932 typescript, chapter 15, Chase Manhattan Archives, New York. In elevator manufacturing the Otis Elevator Company dominated its rivals Westinghouse, General Electric, and Tyler, charging customers about $2500–$5000 per car, with complete building installations running in the $20,000–$40,000 range. For elevator history see also Lutz Hartwig, "Lifts and Architecture—Lift Architecture," in *Vertical: Lift Escalator Paternoster: A Cultural History of Vertical Transport*, ed. Vittoria Magnago Lampugnani et al., trans. Robin Benson and Catherine Kerkhoff-Saxon (Berlin: Ernst & Sohn, 1994), 42–53; "Skyscrapers: Life on the Vertical," *Fortune*, November 1930, 77–80, 105.

4. For comments on ideal skyscraper elevator service see Ely J. Kahn, "Economics of the Skyscraper," *Architectural Record*, 63 (April 1928), 298; "The Design of a Bank's Skyscraper: The City Bank Farmer's Trust Company," *Architectural Forum*, 55 (July 1931), 7; R. H. Shreve, "The Economic Design of Office Buildings," *Architectural Record*, 67 (April 1930), 355.

5. James B. Newman, "Factors in Office Building Planning." *Architectural Forum*, 52 (June 1930), 883.

6. "Double-Deck System for Doherty Lifts," *New York Times*, 15 March 1931, sec. 12, p. 10; "Double-Deck Lifts Ready in City Soon," *New York Times*, 18 October 1931, sec. 2, p. 5; E. J. Smith, "Advantages of the Double Deck Elevator," *Skyscraper Management*, 18 (December 1933), 9.

7. A. H. Fromm, "Double Deck Elevators and New Equipment," *Proceedings of the Twenty-Fifth Annual Convention of the National Association of Building Owners and Managers*, 1932, 194. For the history of escalators see Lampugnani, *Vertical*.

8. Matsui, "Skyscraper," chapter 16 and Clyde R. Place, "The Mechanical Equipment of Office Buildings," *Architectural Forum*, 41 (September 1924), 149–151.

9. W. C. Clark and J. L. Kingston, *The Skyscraper: A Study in the Economic Height of Modern Office Buildings* (New York: American Institute of Steel Construction, 1930), 93.

10. "Temperature Control Is Exact in Sixty Wall Tower," *Buildings and Building Management*, 33 (July 1933), 31–33; J. A. Space, "A Hot Water Heating System for a 67-Story Building," *Heating and Ventilating*, 29 (June 1932), 23–28; "Skyscraper Hot-Water Heating Completes First Season," *Buildings and Building Management*, 33 (July 1933), 28–30; Fromm, "Double Deck Elevators and New Equipment," 191–192. Blown, chilled, and dehumidified air had been used in textile mills, movie houses, and on the New York Stock Exchange's trading floor since the early 1900s. The builders of 40 Wall Street planned to use refrigerated air on its first six floors, while in San Antonio in 1928 the Milan Building became the country's first fully air-conditioned office structure.

11. G. W. Gray, "Every Modern Convenience," *World's Work*, 61 (February 1932), 35.

12. "Bank Opens Biggest Private Phone Exchange," *New York Times*, 22 February 1931, 12.

13. "Design of a Bank's Skyscraper," 107.

14. Matsui, "Skyscraper," 208.

15. B. H. Belknap, "Modern Office Building Appliances," *Architectural Forum*, 41 (September 1924), 155.

16. C. H. Fister, "60 Wall Tower," *Building Investment*, June 1932, 26–28.

17. Edwin C. Hill, *Sixty Wall Tower* (New York, 1932), 10.

18. Clark and Kingston, *Skyscraper*, 92.

19. Frederick S. Tisdale, "City in a Tower," *Service* (January 1946), 2–4, CSCC, Box 9, Folder 7; Sixty Wall Tower, Inc., *Sixty Wall Tower: The Aristocrat of Office Buildings* (New York, 1932), n. p., CSCC, Box 9, Folder 7; Fromm, "Double Deck Elevators," 194.

20. Rem Koolhaas, *Delirious New York: A Retroactive Manifesto for Manhattan*, new ed. (New York: Monacelli Press, 1994), 82.

21. Ralston, "Engineer's Problem in Tall Buildings," 912.

22. Space, "Hot Water Heating System," 28.

CHAPTER SEVEN: EXTERIOR EXPRESSION

1. Royal Cortissoz, "The Cunard Building," *Architectural Forum,* 35 (July 1921), 5.
2. *The Seamen's Bank for Savings in the City of New York, 1829–1926* (New York: Seamen's Bank, 1926), 7.
3. Lewis Mumford, "The Sky Line," *New Yorker,* 3 December 1927, 100.
4. Yasuo Matsui Collection (Folio 1, Drawing No. 1000.038), Drawings and Archives, Avery Library, Columbia University. This study for a westward extension of The Manhattan Company Building deleted the old Assay Office between the skyscraper and the Sub-Treasury Building.
5. Lincoln Kirstein, *Elie Nadelman* (New York: Eakins Press, 1973), 230.
6. "Wall St. Building to Top All in the World," *New York Times,* 10 April 1929, 21.
7. "The Design of a Bank's Skyscraper: The City Bank Farmer's Trust Company," *Architectural Forum,* 55 (July 1931), 8.
8. Cross & Cross, "City Bank Farmers Trust Building: Vol. 1, A Portfolio of Data Showing Progress of Sketches, Evolution of Models and Final Development of Construction," 1931, plates 23ff (Accession Number 940010*), Special Collections, Getty Research Institute, Los Angeles.
9. Cross & Cross, "City Bank Farmers Trust Building," vol. 1, plate 14.
10. "Design of a Bank's Skyscraper," 8.
11. *Real Estate Record and Guide,* 12 October 1929, 9.
12. Francisco Mujica, *History of the Skyscraper* (Paris: Archaeology and Architecture Press, 1929), 67.
13. Ely Jacques Kahn, "On Decoration and Ornament," 1929, in *Ely Jacques Kahn, New York* (New York: McGraw-Hill, 1931; New York: Acanthus Press, 1995), 21.
14. Ralph Walker, "The Relation of Skyscrapers to Our Life," *Architectural Forum,* 52 (May 1930), 689.
15. Walker, "Skyscrapers," 695.
16. Ralph Walker, "Each Day Anew," unpublished manuscript (Box 19), Ralph Walker Papers, Syracuse University.
17. John Shapley, "Architecture in New York," *Parnassus,* 1 (May 1929), 6.
18. Walker, "Skyscrapers," 695.
19. "Arris and Spandrel Motif," One Wall Street construction drawings, 599-174, HLW International, New York; Sarah Bradford Landau and Carl W. Condit, *Rise of the New York Skyscraper, 1865–1913* (New Haven: Yale University Press, 1996), 387.
20. Ralph Walker, "Architecture," *North American Review,* 231 (June 1931), 530.
21. Walker, "Skyscrapers," 694.
22. Ralph Walker, "Color in Architecture," *Architectural Record,* 63 (January 1928), 80.
23. Walker, "Color in Architecture," 80.
24. Irving Trust Company, press release, The Bank of New York Archives.
25. Ralph Walker, "Architecture of To-Day," *Creative Art,* 5 (July 1929), 460.
26. Walker, "Skyscrapers," 695.
27. Lewis Mumford, *Sidewalk Critic: Lewis Mumford's Writings on New York* (New York: Princeton Architectural Press, 1998), 65.
28. Mumford, *Sidewalk Critic,* 81.
29. Edwin C. Hill, *Sixty Wall Tower* (New York, 1932), 8.
30. W. Parker Chase, *New York: The Wonder City* (New York: Wonder City Publishing, 1931), 179.
31. Hill, *Sixty Wall Tower,* 13.
32. Norman Klein, "'Sun Deck' Tops 60 Wall Tower," *New York Evening Post,* 7 July 1932.
33. *Buildings and Building Management,* 30 May 1932, 52.
34. Mumford, *Sidewalk Critic,* 100.
35. Arthur Loomis Harmon, "The Design of Office Buildings," *Architectural Forum,* 52 (June 1930), 820.
36. Warren D. Bruner, "Office Layouts for Tenants," *Architectural Forum,* 52 (June 1930), 905. In New York nascent examples of wrapped glass corners began to appear at the 1930 Majestic Apartments on Central Park West (Irwin Chanin, Jacques Delamarre, and Sloan & Robertson) and the 1931 industrial Starrett-Lehigh Building on Twelfth Avenue (Russell G. and Walter M. Cory with Yasuo Matsui).

CHAPTER EIGHT: INTERIOR DISTINCTION

1. John Taylor Boyd, Jr., "Office Interiors," *Architectural Forum,* 41 (September 1924), 145.
2. Royal Cortissoz, "The Cunard Building," *Architectural Forum,* 35 (July 1921), 8.
3. Henry Dreyfuss, "The Modern Business Address," *Skyscraper Management,* 17 (August 1932), 9, 18.
4. *The Manhattan Family,* May–June 1930, 5, Chase Manhattan Archives, New York; Yasuo Matsui, "Skyscraper: Multiple Business Building," 1932 typescript, 143, Chase Manhattan Archives, New York.

5. Sydney De Brie, "Decorating the Eight-Hour House," *Country Life,* 48 (October 1925), 116.
6. "The Design of a Bank's Skyscraper: The City Bank Farmer's Trust Company," *Architectural Forum,* 55 (July 1931), 26.
7. "The Executive and His Office," *Fortune,* July 1930, 38.
8. Margery W. Davies, *Woman's Place Is at the Typewriter: Office Work and Office Workers, 1870–1930* (Philadelphia: Temple University Press, 1982); Angel Kwolek-Folland, *Engendering Business: Men and Women in the Corporate Office, 1870–1930* (Baltimore: Johns Hopkins University Press, 1994); Elyce J. Rotella, "The Transformation of the American Office: Changes in Employment and Technology," *Journal of Economic History,* 41 (March 1981), 51–57; Sharon Hartman Strom, *Beyond the Typewriter: Gender, Class, and the Origins of Modern American Office Work, 1900–1930* (Urbana: University of Illinois Press, 1992); Olivier Zunz, *Making America Corporate, 1870–1920* (Chicago: University of Chicago Press, 1990).
9. Arthur Loomis Harmon, "The Interior Architecture of Offices," *Architectural Forum,* 52 (June 1930), 864.
10. H. A. Mathews, "At the Head of Wall Street," 2 March 1931, manuscript, The Bank of New York Archives.
11. *The Manhattan Family,* May–June 1930, 5, Chase Manhattan Archives, New York.
12. Boyd, "Office Interiors," 145.
13. "American Board Rooms: Directors and Decorations," *Fortune,* October 1931, 100.
14. Eugene Clute, "Modern Veneer Construction," *American Architect,* 140 (September 1931), 37.
15. *Real Estate Record and Guide,* 2 August 1919, 141; Ezra Winter, "Mural Decorations of the Cunard Building," *Architectural Forum,* 35 (July 1921), 16.
16. W. Parker Chase, *New York: The Wonder City* (New York: Wonder City Publishing, 1931), 158.
17. Matsui, "Skyscraper," 139.
18. *The Manhattan Family,* October 1929, 6, Chase Manhattan Archives, New York.
19. The Manhattan Company murals' other subjects included the company's reservoir on Chambers Street, the Tontine Coffee House where the company's charter was signed, Federal Hall, the Battery wharves, the Buttonwood Tree where the Stock Exchange was founded, and the Reade Street water pump. The seventh and last mural was painted in 1949 by Lumen Winter and Dean Cornwall after Ezra Winter's suicide. *Murals in Main Banking Room of Bank of the Manhattan Company* (New York: Bank of the Manhattan Company, c. 1949), Chase Manhattan Archives, New York.
20. Irving Trust press release, 29 March 1928, The Bank of New York Archives.
21. Lewis B. Pierson, "Address at Luncheon Prior to the Laying of the Corner Stone of One Wall Street," 14 January 1930, 3, typescript, The Bank of New York Archives.
22. "Off the Record," *Fortune,* June 1931, 22.
23. Eugene Clute, "Glass Mosaic," *Architecture,* 64 (September 1931), 142–143.
24. The One Wall Street reception room's decor was apparently inspired by Einar Forseth's glass mosaic Golden Hall in Ragnar Östberg's Stockholm City Hall (1907–23). The reception room's material also bore resemblance to the colored glass tesserae of the lobby of the Woolworth Building, the Irving Trust Company's previous headquarters. *The Irving's New Headquarters* (New York: Irving Trust Company, 1931), 24–25, The Bank of New York Archives; Meredith Arms Bzdak, "The Architecture of Ralph Thomas Walker: 1919–1939," Ph.D. dissertation (Rutgers, The State University of New Jersey 1995), 119–120.
25. Ralph Walker, "Color in Architecture," *Architectural Record,* 63 (January 1928), 80.
26. Clute, "Glass Mosaic," 141.
27. William F. Lamb, "Office Building Vestibules," *Architectural Forum,* 41 (September 1924), 105.
28. Lamb, "Office Building Vestibules," 105.
29. *Real Estate Record and Guide,* 2 August 1919, 141.
30. "Questions Raised by the Architects," 8 August 1928, The Bank of New York Archives. The business allowed on One Wall Street's Broadway side, at the southwest end, was an office of the Postal Telegraph Cable Company. *Irving's New Headquarters,* The Bank of New York Archives and One Wall Street construction drawings, HLW International, New York.
31. "The Home of the Oldest Trust Company in America," *Through the Ages,* 9 (December 1931), 11.
32. Cities Service Building construction drawings, American International Realty Corporation, New York.
33. Meiere had trained in Italy, California, and in New York under the Seamen's bank hall muralist Ernest Peixotto. In the 1920s Meiere had risen to prominence under the patronage of the prominent architect Bertram Goodhue who employed Meiere at his Nebraska State Capitol, National Academy of Science in Washington, and St. Bartholomew's Episcopal Church on Park Avenue. One Wall Street architect Ralph Walker had once worked closely with Goodhue, and it was per-

haps this connection that led to Meiere's employment. Anne Lee, "Hildreth Meiere: Mural Painter," *Architectural Record*, 62 (August 1927), 103–112.

34. Hildreth Meiere, "Symbolism of Lobby Ceiling. Number One Wall Street," draft #1, The Bank of New York Archives. A transfer cartoon for *Allegory of Wealth and Beauty* can be found in a slide owned by HLW International, New York.

35. "Bank of Manhattan Built in Record Time," *New York Times*, 6 May 1930, 49.

36. Norman Klein, "'Sun Deck' Tops 60 Wall Tower," *New York Evening Post*, 7 July 1932.

37. Lafayette A. Goldstone Collection, microfilm, Drawings and Archives, Avery Library, Columbia University, and 19 Rector Street building records, City of New York Municipal Archives. The Philadelphia investment counselor William Stix Wasserman lived in a three-room apartment on 40 Wall Street's 66th floor. "40 Wall: X-Ray of a Skyscraper," *Fortune*, July 1939, 117.

38. *New York World Telegram*, 30 June 1932, 1.

39. CSCC, Box 9, Folder 7.

40. Klein, "Sun Deck."

41. Klein, "Sun Deck."

42. Le Corbusier, *When the Cathedrals Were White: A Journey to the Country of Timid People* (New York: Reynal and Hitchcock, 1947), 42.

CHAPTER NINE: SKYSCRAPER LIVES

1. "200 in Armed Guard Move Bank Billions," *New York Times*, 23 March 1931, 5.

2. "200 in Armed Guard," 5 and "Vault Below Water Level," *New York Times*, 3 February 1929, sec. 2, p. 11. See also "The Head of Wall Street in 1930," promotional brochure, The Bank of New York Archives.

3. *Number Eight*, 26 (February 1931), 1, Citibank, New York; "Another Tower in Lower Manhattan: City Bank-Farmers Trust Building," *Architecture and Building*, 63 (February 1931), 31–39.

4. "Cornerstone Is Laid for the Irving Trust," *New York Times*, 15 January 1930, 14.

5. "Gold Rivet in Building," *New York Times*, 11 July 1929, 12.

6. "Brief Narrative History, Irving Trust Company Building, One Wall Street," 31 August 1934, The Bank of New York Archives. For topping-out ceremonies see William Collins, "Our Queerest Building Custom," *Pencil Points*, 21 (March 1931), 179–182 and Michael Pollan, *A Place of My Own: The Education of an Amateur Builder* (New York: Delta, 1997), 171–175. For building rituals generally see Neil Harris, *Building Lives: Constructing Rites and Passages* (New Haven: Yale University Press, 1999).

7. *Number Eight*, 26 (February 1931), 1ff, Citibank; "City Bank Farmers Trust Company Visited by 3,851 an Hour to Inspect Its New Home," *New York Times*, 25 February 1931, 37.

8. *The Manhattan Family*, May–June 1930, 3, Chase Manhattan Archives, New York.

9. Publicity outline, 12 January 1931, and L. E. Pierson to R. H. Elmendorf, 11 February 1931, The Bank of New York Archives; "Irving Trust Takes Fifty-Story Home," *New York Times*, 21 March 1931, 29.

10. "'Dancing' Moonbeam Carries Human Voice," *New York Times*, 14 May 1932, 17. Two decades earlier the Woolworth Building opened with a floodlit display activated by President Woodrow Wilson in Washington. Sarah Bradford Landau and Carl W. Condit, *Rise of the New York Skyscraper, 1865–1913* (New Haven: Yale University Press, 1996), 390.

11. Ralph Walker, "The Relation of Skyscrapers to Our Life," *Architectural Forum*, 52 (May 1930), 692.

12. "The Skyscraper Community in a Modern Vertical City," *New York Times*, 6 April 1928, sec. 10, p. 2.

13. For Wall Street skyscraper population figures see W. Parker Chase, *New York: The Wonder City* (New York: Wonder City Publishing, 1931).

14. Frederick S. Tisdale, "City in a Tower," *Service*, January 1946, 31, CSCC, Box 9, Folder 7. Weegee's photographs of the Cities Service Building were also published in his book *Weegee's People* (New York: Duell, Sloan & Pearce, 1946).

15. "How a Great New Skyscraper Rents Space," *Buildings and Building Management*, 33 (November 1933), 25. For skyscraper law libraries generally see *Bulletin of the National Association of Building Owners and Managers*, 129 (October 1928), 71.

16. *Sixty Wall Tower at 70 Pine Street*, 1937 building directory, CSCC, Box 9, Folder 7; promotional literature, CSCC, Box 9, Folder 7.

17. *Sixty Wall Tower at 70 Pine Street.*

18. *40 Wall Street: Designed for Working* (New York: William E. Rudge's Sons, n. d.), Chase Manhattan Archives, New York.

19. *The Luncheon Club of Wall Street* (New York: Forty Wall Street, n.d.), Museum of the City of New York. See also *The Luncheon Club of Wall Street* (n.p., n.d.) (C111r) Archives and Drawings, Avery Library, Columbia University. An inspiration apparently of the skyscraper's builder, William A. Starrett, the Luncheon Club of Wall Street was directed by a Belgian manager and admitted members for fees ranging from $75 to $200, depending on whether or not one resided within a 60-mile radius of the city.

20. "The Skyscraper Community in a Modern Vertical City," *New York Times*, 6 May 1928, sec. 10, p. 2 and "Big Building Efficiency," *New York Times*, 18 August 1929, sec. 11, p. 16.

21. "Packmen Who Use the Skyscraper Route," *New York Times*, 30 September 1928, sec. 5, p. 16 and "Office Buildings Are Like Bazaars," *New York Times*, 16 October 1927, sec. 10, p. 13.

22. C. A. Heisterkamp, C. C. Lawrence, and E. J. Smith, "The Technique of Opening an Office Building," *Real Estate Record*, 17 July 1937, 21–34. For building management see also Harris, *Building Lives*, 102–113.

23. Originally the Cities Service Company planned to occupy the first nineteen floors of the skyscraper. *Doherty News*, 15 May 1930, 16, CSCC, Box 9, Folder 4. For the Cities Service Building tenantry see A. H. Fromm, "Double Deck Elevators and New Equipment," *Proceedings of the Twenty-Fifth Annual Convention of the National Association of Building Owners and Managers*, 1932, 189–197; *Manhattan Address Telephone Directory* (New York: New York Telephone Company, 1935); *Classified Directory…Sixty Wall Tower and Sixty Wall Street*, 1940, CSCC, Box 9, Folder 7; *Sixty Wall Tower at 70 Pine Street*, 1937 building directory, CSCC, Box 9, Folder 7.

24. Most of the following information about Wall Street's skyscraper tenants is taken from the *Manhattan Address Telephone Directory* (New York: New York Telephone Company, 1933).

25. "40 Wall: X-Ray of a Skyscraper," *Fortune*, July 1939, 116–117, 226, 228.

26. One Wall Street construction drawings, HLW International, New York.

27. "When Wall Street Calls Out the Reserves," *Business Week*, 11 December 1929, 36.

28. Elyce J. Rotella, "The Transformation of the American Office: Changes in Employment and Technology," *Journal of Economic History*, 41 (March 1981), 51–57.

29. Angel Kwolek-Folland, *Engendering Business: Men and Women in the Corporate Office, 1870–1930* (Baltimore: Johns Hopkins University Press, 1994), 94.

30. John Urry, "The Growth of Scientific Management: Transformation in Class Structure and Class Struggle," in *Class and Space: The Making of Urban Society*, ed. Nigel Thrift and Peter Williams (London: Routledge & Kegan Paul, 1987), 255 and Kwolek-Folland, *Engendering Business*, chapter 3.

31. Grace L. Coyle, "The Clerical Worker and Her Job," *Survey*, 15 December 1928, 361.

32. "Modernizing the Office," *Review of Reviews*, 83 (February 1931), 84.

33. "The Plight of the White-Collar Army," *Literary Digest*, 7 June 1930, 70. For unionization efforts by the Bookkeepers, Stenographers, and Accountants Union see *New York Times*, 22 July 1933, 2; 31 July 1933, 15; 1 August 1933, 32. For the union's failure see Ruth Shonle Cavan, "The Girl Who Writes Your Letters," *Survey*, 15 July 1929, 438–439.

34. "Modernizing the Office," 84.

35. Royal Cortissoz, "The Cunard Building," *Architectural Forum*, 35 (July 1921), 8.

36. Henry Dreyfuss, "The Modern Business Address," *Skyscraper Management*, 17 (August 1932), 9–10, 18.

37. "City's Offices Gain Charm in New Order of Business," *New York Times*, 10 October 1926, sec. 8, p. 5.

38. Clinton Field, "How to Get an Aching Neck," *Western Electric GHQ*, September 1947.

39. Frederick S. Tisdale, "City in a Tower," *Service*, January 1946, 2, CSCC, Box 9, Folder 7.

40. Edwin C. Hill, *Sixty Wall Tower* (New York, 1932), 9.

41. Heisterkamp, "The Technique of Opening an Office Building," 26, 33. For female elevator operators' presumed interest in male riders as future husbands see the excerpt from a letter from Kaarlo Urpelainen to Cities Service, 29 June 1948, translating into English a 1948 article from the Finnish women's magazine *Viuhka* mentioning the Cities Service Building. CSCC, Box 9, Folder 7.

42. Report of Women's Committee, "Elevator Etiquette," *Proceedings of the Annual Convention of the National Association of Building Owners and Managers*, 1926, 441–442.

43. Kenneth T. Jackson, "The Capital of Capitalism: the New York Metropolitan Region, 1890–1940," in *Metropolis, 1890–1940*, ed. Anthony Sutcliffe (Chicago: University of Chicago Press, 1984); Emanuel Tobier, "Manhattan's Business District in the Industrial Age," in *Power, Culture & Place: Essays on New York City*, ed. John Hull Mollenkopf (New York: Russell Sage Foundation, 1988); David Ward and Olivier Zunz, "Between Rationalism and Pluralism: Creating the Modern City," in *The Landscape of Modernity: New York City, 1900–1940* (Baltimore: Johns Hopkins University Press, 1997).

44. "High Life in Babel," *New York Times*, 21 February 1929, 26.

45. Henry James, *The American Scene*, in *Collected Travel Writings: Great Britain and America*, ed. Richard Howard (New York: Library of America, 1993), 422, 425.

46. Quoted in Hank O'Neal, *Berenice Abbott: American Photographer* (New York: McGraw-Hill Book Company, 1982), 16–17.

47. Thomas Hastings, "The City of Dreadful Heights," *Forum*, 77 (April 1927), 575.

48. W. C. Clark and J. L. Kingston, *The Skyscraper: A Study in the Economic Height of Modern Office Buildings* (New York: American Institute of Steel Construction, 1930), 1. Numerous articles, editorials, and letters appeared in *The New York Times* especially between 1929 and 1931. See, for example, "The Future of the Skyscraper" cover story in *The New York Times Magazine* with essays by Ralph Walker, Raymond Hood, Harvey Wiley Corbett, William Lamb, and Edwin Lutyens (13 September 1931), and also an earlier *New York Times Magazine* cover article, "The Limits of Our Sky-Scraping," by Corbett (17 November 1929).

49. "Predicts Skyscrapers Will Destroy New York City," *Bulletin of the National Association of Building Owners and Managers*, 142 (December 1929), 115.

50. "Skyscraper Passing, Says Frank Lloyd Wright," *New York Times*, 14 November 1931, 14.

51. Clark and Kingston, *The Skyscraper*, 149.

52. "The Home of the Oldest Trust Company in America," *Through the Ages*, 9 (December 1931), 11.

53. Ralph Walker, *Ralph Walker, Architect* (New York: Henahan House, 1957), 35–36. For the general conflict between public and private interest in skyscraper building see Manfredo Tafuri, "The Disenchanted Mountain: The Skyscraper and the City," in *The American City: From the Civil War to the New Deal* (London: Granada, 1980).

54. Robert A. M. Stern, Gregory Gilmartin, and Thomas Mellins, *New York 1930: Architecture and Urbanism Between the Two World Wars* (New York: Rizzoli, 1994), 18.

55. "The Sky Line," *New Yorker*, 3 December 1927, 99.

56. W. K. Oltar-Jevsky, *Contemporary Babylon* (New York: Architectural Book Publishing Company, 1933), n. p.

57. Charles Phelps Cushing, "Frozen Jazz," *World's Work*, 58 (May 1929), 50–51.

58. Stern, *New York 1930*, 335.

59. Quoted in Anna C. Chave, "'Who Will Paint New York?': 'The World's New Art Center' and the Skyscraper Paintings of Georgia O'Keeffe," *American Art*, 5 (Winter/Spring 1991), 88.

60. Quoted in David Gebhard, *The National Trust Guide to Art Deco in America* (New York: John Wiley & Sons, 1996), 1.

61. Quoted in Stern, *New York 1930*, 566.

62. Paul Goldberger, *The Skyscraper* (New York: Alfred A. Knopf, 1985), 83.

63. The art historian Erica Hirshler has recently noted that "the architecture of New York provided American artists with a way to domesticate the French Cubist style, to redefine it through American eyes." Erica E. Hirshler, "The New New York and the Park Row Building: American Artists View an Icon of the Modern Age," *American Art Journal*, 21/4 (1989), 43.

64. Paul Robertson, "The Skyscraper Office Building," *Architectural Forum*, 52 (June 1930), 879. The opinion that skyscrapers are economic objects remains prevalent. "Perhaps no other major building type in world history was less the product of architects and more that of lawyers, developers, and politicians." Michael J. Lewis, "The Idea of American Building," in G. E. Kidder Smith, *Source Book of American Architecture*, updated ed. (New York: Princeton Architectural Press, 1996), 15.

65. Douglas Haskell, "Building or Sculpture? The Architecture of 'Mass,'" *Architectural Record*, 67 (April 1930), 366-367. For skyscrapers as symbols of American business and capitalist competition, see also Mona Domosh, "The Symbolism of the Skyscraper," in *Re-reading Cultural Geography*, ed. Kenneth E. Foote (Austin: University of Texas, 1994); Kenneth Turney Gibbs, *Business Architectural Imagery in America, 1870–1930* (Ann Arbor: UMI Research Press, 1984), chapter 9; William R. Taylor, *In Pursuit of Gotham: Culture and Commerce in New York* (New York: Oxford University Press, 1992), 67; Ann Douglas, *Terrible Honesty: Mongrel Manhattan in the 1920s* (New York: Farrar, Straus & Giroux, 1995), 434, 439; Landau and Condit, *Rise of the New York Skyscraper*, 187; Gail Fenske and Deryck Holdsworth, "Corporate Identity and the New York Office Building: 1895–1915," in Ward and Zunz, *The Landscape of Modernity*.

66. Versions of Matsui's diagram appeared in "New York's Skyscraper Contest for Height Supremacy," *New York Times*, 2 March 1930, sec. 12, p. 2 and *Fortune*, September 1930, 56–57. Matsui's original drawing is in the Yasuo Matsui Collection (1000.038, Dr. 342, fol. 12 [00022]), Drawings and Archives, Avery Library, Columbia University.

67. William Van Alen, "The Structure and Metal Work of the Chrysler Building," *Architectural Forum*, 53 (October 1930), 494.

68. Paul Starrett, *Changing the Skyline: An Autobiography* (New York: McGraw-Hill, 1938), 283.

69. "Denies Altering Plans for Tallest Building," *New York Times*, 20 October 1929, 14; Yasuo Matsui, "Skyscraper: Multiple Business Building," 1932 typescript, 61, Chase Manhattan Archives, New York.

70. "Rivalry for Height Is Seen as Ended," *New York Times*, 2 May 1931, 7.

71. Janet Flint, *The Prints of Louis Lozowick, A Catalogue Raisonné* (New York: Hudson Hills Press, 1982), 119. Lozowick's mural, *Manhattan Skyline* (1935), is still in the northeast vestibule of the James A. Farley Building at 33rd Street and 8th Avenue.

72. Louis Lozowick, *Survivor From a Dead Age: The Memoirs of Louis Lozowick* (Washington: Smithsonian Institution Press, 1997), 281–282.

73. Lozowick, *Memoirs*, 268.

74. Alfred C. Bossom, *Building to the Skies: The Romance of the Skyscraper* (New York: Studio Publications, 1934), 9.

75. Francisco Mujica, *History of the Skyscraper* (Paris: Archaeology and Architecture Press, 1929), 18. See also Harvey Wiley Corbett in Introduction to Oltar-Jevsky, *Contemporary Babylon*, n. p. and the Lower Manhattan photographs of Drahomir Joseph Ruzicka.

76. Ferriss quoted in Chave, "'Who Will Paint New York?'" 96.

77. Ferriss' rendering of 40 Wall Street was produced for American Institute of Steel Construction publicity and published in Hugh Ferriss, *The Metropolis of Tomorrow* (1929; reprint, Princeton: Princeton Architectural Press, 1986), 54–55, 192.

78. Berenice Abbott and Elizabeth McCausland, *Changing New York* (New York: E. P. Dutton & Company, 1939), 28.

79. Le Corbusier, *When the Cathedrals Were White: A Journey to the Country of Timid People* (New York: Reynal and Hitchcock, 1947), 55.

80. Hill, *Sixty Wall Tower*, 14; Robertson, "Skyscraper Office Building," 880; Alfred C. Bossom, *New York Herald Tribune*, 22 July 1928.

81. Le Corbusier, *When the Cathedrals Were White*, 73–74.

82. Oltar-Jevsky, *Contemporary Babylon*, n. p.

83. The architect and theorist Rem Koolhaas, in his book *Delirious New York*, constructs an argument for New York skyscrapers' essentially fantastical and utopian impulses, suggesting that economics was merely an alibi to "lend the Skyscraper the legitimacy of being inevitable." New ed. (New York: Monacelli Press, 1994), 87. The historian Thomas Van Leeuwen argues that modern skyscrapers are incarnations of humanity's "perennial dream" for tower cities. Thomas A. P. Van Leeuwen, *The Skyward Trend of Thought: The Metaphysics of the American Skyscraper* (Cambridge: MIT Press, 1988), 36.

84. Rem Koolhaas, "The Architect's Ball—A Vignette, 1931," in *Oppositions Reader*, ed. K. Michael Hays (New York: Princeton Architectural Press, 1998).

ARCHIVE AND PHOTOGRAPH COLLECTIONS

American International Group (AIG) Archives, New York

American International Realty Corporation, New York

Avery Architectural and Fine Arts Library, Columbia University, New York

The Bank of New York Archives, New York

Buildings Owners and Managers Association International, Washington

Chase Manhattan Archives, New York

Citibank, New York

Cities Service Oil and Gas Corporation Collection (CSCC), Western History Collections, University of Oklahoma, Norman

City of New York Municipal Archives, New York

Getty Research Institute, Los Angeles

HLW International, New York

Landmark Society of Western New York, Rochester

Library of Congress (Prints and Photographs Division), Washington

Museum of the City of New York, New York

New-York Historical Society, New York

New York Public Library, New York

SERIALS

Architectural:

American Architect

The Architect

Architectural Forum

Architectural Record

Architecture

Architecture and Building

Buildings and Building Management

Bulletin of the National Association of Building Owners and Managers

Country Life (New York)

Metal Arts

Proceedings of the Annual Convention of the National Association of Building Owners and Managers

Real Estate Record and Guide

Skyscraper Management

Through the Ages

General:

Current Biography

Dictionary of American Biography

Doherty News (Cities Service Company)

Fortune

Literary Digest

Manhattan Family (Bank of the Manhattan Company)

National Cyclopedia of American Biography

New Republic

New York Times

Newsweek

Number Eight (City Bank Farmers Trust)

Review of Reviews

Saturday Evening Post

Survey

Who Was Who in America

Who Was Who in American Art

World's Work

CITIES SERVICE (NOW AIG) BUILDING

Cities Service Building construction drawings. American International Realty Corporation, New York.

Classified Directory… Sixty Wall Tower and Sixty Wall Street. 1940. CSCC, Box 9, Folder 7.

Fister, C. H. "60 Wall Tower." *Building Investment*. June 1932, 26–28.

Fromm, A. H. "Double Deck Elevators and New Equipment." *Proceedings of the Twenty-Fifth Annual Convention of the National Association of Building Owners and Managers*. 1932, 189–197.

Gray, Christopher. "An Art Deco Tower with Double-Deck Elevators." *New York Times*. 8 March 1998, sec. 11, p. 7.

Heisterkamp, C. A., C. C. Lawrence, and E. J. Smith. "The Technique of Opening an Office Building." *Real Estate Record*. 17 July 1937, 21–34.

Henry L. Doherty & Company. *Going Up! October Building Campaign*. 1930. CSCC, Box 9, Folder 7.

Hill, Edwin C. *Sixty Wall Tower*. New York, 1932.

"How a Great New Skyscraper Rents Space." *Buildings and Building Management*. 33 (November 1933), 23–26.

Klein, Norman. "'Sun Deck' Tops 60 Wall Tower." *New York Evening Post*. 7 July 1932.

"Manual of Real Estate Properties, New York, Owned and Controlled by Cities Service Company, Henry L. Doherty Company." 1930–37. CSCC, Box 6, Folder 1.

Mruk, Frank. "The American International Building." American International Realty Corporation, New York.

"Organization for Service." CSCC, Box 9, Folder 7.

Otis Elevator Company. *Detailed Description of Double-Deck Elevators*. CSCC, Box 9, Folder 7.

"Real Estate in Greater New York Owned and Operated by Cities Service Company and Subsidiaries." 1937. CSCC, Box 6, Folder 2.

Sixty Wall Tower, Inc. *Sixty Wall Tower: The Aristocrat of Office Buildings*. 1932. CSCC, Box 9, Folder 7.

Sixty Wall Tower at 70 Pine Street. 1937. Building directory. CSCC, Box 9, Folder 7.

"Skyscraper Hot-Water Heating Completes First Season." *Buildings and Building Management*. 33 (July 1933), 28–30.

Smith, E. J. "Advantages of the Double Deck Elevator." *Skyscraper Management*. 18 (December 1933), 9.

Smith, E. J. "Sixty Wall Tower." *Service*. April 1952, 14–17.

Smith, E. J. "Special Tenant Services as a Factor in Lease Renewals." *Real Estate Record*. 7 May 1938, n. p.

"Some Facts About Sixty Wall Tower." 1972. CSCC, Box 9, Folder 7.

Space, J. A. "A Hot Water Heating System for a 67-Story Building." *Heating and Ventilating*. 29 (June 1932), 23–28.

"Temperature Control Is Exact in Sixty Wall Tower." *Buildings and Building Management*. 33 (July 1933), 31–33.

Tisdale, Frederick S. "City in a Tower." *Service*. January 1946, 2–4. CSCC, Box 9, Folder 7.

CITY BANK FARMERS TRUST BUILDING

"Another Tower in Lower Manhattan: City Bank-Farmers Trust Building." *Architecture and Building*. 63 (February 1931), 31–39.

Aspegren, Joakim. "The City Bank Farmers Trust Company Building." 1994? Unpublished student paper. Witkoff Group, New York.

Citibank. *Trust in America: The Story of the First Trust Company*. New York: Citibank, 1993.

City Bank Club. *Number Eight*. 1929–31. Citibank Archives, New York.

Cross & Cross. "City Bank Farmers Trust Building: Vol. 1, A Portfolio of Data Showing Progress of Sketches, Evolution of Models and Final Development of Construction; Vol. 2, Sketch Progress." 1931. Accession Number 940010*. Special Collections, Getty Research Institute, Los Angeles.

"The Design of a Bank's Skyscraper: The City Bank Farmer's Trust Company." *Architectural Forum*. 55 (July 1931), 7–26, 94–108.

[Hofmann, Arnold]. *The Oldest Trust Company and Its Newest Home*. New York: City Bank Farmers Trust, 1931.

"The Home of the Oldest Trust Company in America." *Through the Ages*. 9 (December 1931), 8–15.

Robins, Anthony, and Joanna Oltman. "City Bank–Farmers Trust Company Building." Designation List 273, LP-1941. New York City Landmarks Preservation Commission, 1996.

"Some Recent Sculpture by David Evans." *Architecture*. 63 (May 1931), 277–279.

"Structure and Equipment of the City Bank Farmers Trust Company." *Architectural Forum*. 55 (July 1931), 94–108.

40 WALL STREET

Bank of The Manhattan Company. *The Manhattan Family*. 1928–. Chase Manhattan Archives, New York.

Fortune, skyscraper series on 40 Wall Street, July–December 1930.

"40 Wall: X-Ray of a Skyscraper." *Fortune*. July 1939, 116–117, 226, 228.

40 Wall Street: Designed for Working. New York: William E. Rudge's Sons, n.d.

Grant, James. *The Trouble with Prosperity: The Loss of Fear, the Rise of Speculation, and the Risk to American Savings*. New York: Times Books, 1996.

Gray, Christopher. "40 Wall St.: A Race for the Skies, Lost by a Spire." *New York Times*. 15 November 1992, sec. 10, p. 7.

Kirstein, Lincoln. *Elie Nadelman*. New York: Eakins Press, 1973.

Kirstein, Lincoln. *The Sculpture of Elie Nadelman*. New York: Museum of Modern Art, 1948.

Levin, Gail, and John B. Van Sickle. "Elie Nadelman's New Classicism." *Sculpture Review*. 46 (Spring 1998), 8–15.

The Luncheon Club of Wall Street. New York: William E. Rudge's Sons.

"The Manhattan Company Building, New York City." *Architecture and Building*. 62 (July 1930), 193–204.

"The Manhattan Company Building and the Bank of Manhattan Trust Company." *The Metal Arts*. 3 (July–August 1930), 281–286, 314.

The Manhattan Company Building Forty Wall Street New York City. New York: Forty Wall Street Corporation, 1929.

Matsui, Yasuo. *The Manhattan Company Building*. Album. Special Collections, Avery Architectural and Fine Arts Library, Columbia University.

Matsui, Yasuo. "Skyscraper: Multiple Business Building." 1932 . Typescript. Chase Manhattan Archives, New York.

Murals in Main Banking Room of Bank of the Manhattan Company. New York: Bank of The Manhattan Company, c. 1949. Chase Manhattan Archives, New York

Nadelman, E. Jan. "Carving Out a Life: A Son's Memories of a Sculptor." *Art & Antiques*. 7 (April 1990), 94–100.

Shockley, Jay, and Rosita Chalem. "Manhattan Company Building." Designation List 269, LP-1936. New York City Landmarks Preservation Commission, 1995.

Van Alen, William. "The Structure and Metal Work of the Chrysler Building." *Architectural Forum*. 53 (October 1930), 493–498.

Yasuo Matsui Collection, Drawings and Archives, Avery Architectural and Fine Arts Library, Columbia University.

ONE WALL STREET

"Brief Narrative History: Irving Trust Company Building, One Wall Street." 1934. Typescript. The Bank of New York Archives.

Clute, Eugene. "Glass Mosaic." *Architecture*. 64 (September 1931), 141–146.

Clute, Eugene. "How Voorhees, Gmelin and Walker Handle Interior Decoration." *American Architect*. 140 (December 1931), 44–46, 76.

Clute, Eugene. "Modern Decorative Light Sources." *Architecture*. 64 (August 1931), 71–76.

Clute, Eugene. "Modern Veneer Construction." *American Architect*. 140 (September 1931), 36–41, 90–91.

Gray, Christopher. "A Bank's Art Deco Signature." *New York Times*. 1 August 1999, sec. 11, p. 5.

"The Head of Wall Street in 1930." Irving Trust Company, 1930. The Bank of New York Archives.

The Irving's New Headquarters. New York: Irving Trust Company, 1931. Building guide. The Bank of New York Archives.

"Irving Trust Company." *Architecture and Urbanism*. 291 (December 1994), 176–183.

"Irving Trust Company, A New Neighbor for Trinity Church." *Architecture and Building*. 63 (March 1931), 70–72.

"The Irving Trust Company New York: History, Book X." Newspaper scrapbook. The Bank of New York Archives.

Lee, Anne. "Hildreth Meiere: Mural Painter." *Architectural Record*. 62 (August 1927), 103–112.

Meeks, Everett V. "Return to Functional Architecture." *Yale Review*. 23 (December 1933), 284–300.

Meiere, Hildreth. "The Question of Decoration." *Architectural Forum*. 57 (July 1932), 1–8.

Meiere, Hildreth. "Symbolism of Lobby Ceiling. Number One Wall Street." Draft #1. The Bank of New York Archives

"Number One Wall Street, An Address of Distinction." *Through the Ages*. 9 (October 1931), 19–25.

One Wall Street. New York: Cruikshank Company, 1931. Rental brochure. The Bank of New York Archives.

One Wall Street construction drawings, HLW International, New York.

Pierson, Lewis B. "Address at Luncheon Prior to the Laying of the Corner Stone of One Wall Street." 14 January 1930. Typescript. The Bank of New York Archives.

Shapley, John. "Architecture in New York." *Parnassus*. 1 (May 1929), 3–8.

Sparling, Earl. "Architect Designed the Irving Trust on Basis of Its 'Biological Appeal.'" *New York World-Telegram*. 11 November 1931.

OTHER FINANCIAL DISTRICT BUILDINGS

"Bank of Lee, Higginson & Company." *Architecture*. 60 (October 1929), 187–199.

"Bank of New York and Trust Company." *The Architect*. 11 (March 1929), 622, 637–661.

Bolton, Reginald Pelham. *From Sheep Pasture to Skyscraper*. New York: Equitable Trust Company, 1926.

Boyd, John Taylor, Jr. "The New York Zoning Regulation and Its Influence Upon Design." *Architectural Record*. 48 (September 1920), 192–217.

Chambers, Ralph W. "The New Standard Oil Building." *American Architect*. 122 (27 September 1922), 282–292.

Chappell, Sally A. Kitt. "A Reconsideration of the Equitable Building in New York." *Journal of the Society of Architectural Historians*. 49 (March 1990), 90–95.

Cortissoz, Royal. "The Cunard Building." *Architectural Forum*. 35 (July 1921), 1–8.

"The Equitable Trust Company's Building, New York." *Architecture and Building*. 60 (April 1928), 105–113.

"Insurance Company of North America, New York City Branch Building." *Architectural Record*. 74 (August 1933), 91–104.

Michalis, Clarence G. *Seamen's Bank*. New York: Newcomen Society, 1954.

Miller, S. O. "Structural Features of the Cunard Building, New York." *Architectural Forum*. 35 (July 1921), 17–20.

Morris, B. W. "The Cunard Building, New York." *Architectural Forum*. 33 (July 1920), 1–6.

Place, Clyde R. "Plumbing in the Cunard Building." *Architectural Forum*. 35 (July 1921), 24.

Proctor, Carlton S. "Special Problems in Foundations of the Cunard Building." *Architectural Forum*. 35 (July 1921), 21–22.

Seamen's Bank for Savings. *One Hundred Fifteen Years of Service, 1829–1944*. New York: Seamen's Bank for Savings, 1944.

"Seamen's Bank for Savings." *The Architect*. 8 (April 1927), 55–65.

The Seamen's Bank for Savings in the City of New York, 1829–1926. New York: Seamen's Bank, 1926.

"29 Broadway Building." *Architectural Forum*. 55 (November 1931), 572–578.

Winter, Ezra. "Mural Decorations of the Cunard Building." *Architectural Forum*. 35 (July 1921), 9–16.

GENERAL SKYSCRAPERS AND ARCHITECTURE

Bossom, Alfred C. *Building to the Skies: The Romance of the Skyscraper*. New York: Studio Publications, 1934.

Bragdon, Claude. *The Frozen Fountain*. New York: Alfred A. Knopf, 1932.

Bruegmann, Robert. *The Architects and the City: Holabird & Roche of Chicago, 1880–1918*. Chicago: University of Chicago Press, 1997.

Chase, W. Parker. *New York: The Wonder City*. New York: Wonder City Publishing, 1931.

Cheney, Sheldon. *The New World Architecture*. New York: Tudor Publishing Company, 1935.

Domosh, Mona. "The Symbolism of the Skyscraper: Case Studies of New York's First Tall Buildings." In *Re-reading Cultural Geography*, ed. Kenneth E. Foote et al. Austin: University of Texas, 1994.

Doumato, Lamia. *American Skyscrapers*. Monticello, Ill.: Vance Bibliographies, n. d.

Fenske, Gail, and Deryck Holdsworth. "Corporate Identity and the New York Office Building: 1895–1915." In *The Landscape of Modernity: New York City, 1900–1940*, ed. David Ward and Olivier Zunz. Baltimore: Johns Hopkins University Press, 1992.

Ferriss, Hugh. *The Metropolis of Tomorrow*. New York: Ives Washburn, 1929. Reprinted by Princeton: Princeton Architectural Press, 1986.

Gebhard, David. *The National Trust Guide to Art Deco in America*. New York: John Wiley & Sons, 1996.

Gibbs, Kenneth Turney. *Business Architectural Imagery in America, 1870–1930*. Ann Arbor: UMI Research Press, 1984.

Goldberger, Paul. *The Skyscraper*. New York: Alfred A. Knopf, 1985.

Haskell, Douglas. "Building or Sculpture? The Architecture of 'Mass.'" *Architectural Record*. 67 (April 1930), 366–368.

Hastings, Thomas. "The City of Dreadful Heights." *Forum*. 77 (April 1927), 571–575.

Koolhaas, Rem. *Delirious New York: A Retroactive Manifesto for Manhattan*. New ed. New York: Monacelli Press, 1994.

Le Corbusier. *When the Cathedrals Were White: A Journey to the Country of Timid People*. First published in French, 1938–39. New York: Reynal and Hitchcock, 1947.

Mujica, Francisco. *History of the Skyscraper*. Paris: Archaeology and Architecture Press, 1929.

Mumford, Lewis. *Sidewalk Critic: Lewis Mumford's Writings on New York*, ed. Robert Wojtowicz. New York: Princeton Architectural Press, 1998.

Nash, Eric P. *Manhattan Skyscrapers*. New York: Princeton Architectural Press, 1999.

Robinson, Cervin, and Rosemarie Haag Bletter. *Skyscraper Style: Art Deco New York*. New York: Oxford University Press, 1975.

Sexton, R. W. *American Commercial Buildings of Today*. New York Architectural Book Publishing, 1928.

Shultz, Earle, and Walter Simmons. *Offices in the Sky*. Indianapolis: Bobbs-Merrill, 1959.

Starrett, William A. *Skyscrapers and the Men Who Build Them*. New York: Charles Scribner's Sons, 1928.

Stern, Robert A. M., Gregory Gilmartin, and Thomas Mellins. *New York 1930: Architecture and Urbanism Between the Two World Wars*. New York: Rizzoli, 1994.

Striner, Richard. "Art Deco: Polemics and Synthesis." *Winterthur Portfolio*. 25/1 (Spring 1990), 21–34.

Tafuri, Manfredo. "The Disenchanted Mountain: The Skyscraper and the City." In *The American City: From the Civil War to the New Deal*, trans. Barbara Liuggia La Penta. London: Granada, 1980.

Tafuri, Manfredo. "The New Babylon: The 'Yellow Giants' and the Myth of Americanism." In *The Sphere and the Labyrinth: Avant-Gardes and Architecture from Piranesi to the 1970s*, trans. Pellegrino d'Acierno and Robert Connolly. Cambridge: MIT Press, 1990.

Tauranac, John. *The Empire State Building: The Making of a Landmark*. New York: Scribner, 1995.

Upton, Dell. *Architecture in the United States*. New York: Oxford University Press, 1998.

Van Leeuwen, Thomas A. P. *The Skyward Trend of Thought: The Metaphysics of the American Skyscraper*. Cambridge: MIT Press, 1988.

Willensky, Elliot, and Norval White. *AIA Guide to New York City*. 3rd ed. New York: Harcourt Brace Jovanovich, 1988.

Willis, Carol. *Form Follows Finance: Skyscrapers and Skylines in New York and Chicago*. New York: Princeton Architectural Press, 1995

Willis, Carol. "Light, Height, and Site: The Skyscraper in Chicago." In *Chicago Architecture and Design, 1923–1993: Reconfiguration of an American Metropolis*, ed. John Zukowsky. Munich: Prestel-Verlag, 1993.

Willis, Carol. "Zoning and *Zeitgeist*: The Skyscraper City in the 1920s." *Journal of the Society of Architectural Historian*. 45 (March 1986), 47–59.

Zukowsky, John, ed. *Chicago Architecture, 1872–1922: Birth of a Metropolis*. Munich: Prestel-Verlag, 1987.

Zukowsky, John, ed. *Chicago Architecture and Design, 1923–1993: Reconfiguration of an American Metropolis*. Munich: Prestel-Verlag, 1993.

CHAPTER ONE: INTRODUCTION

Bletter, Rosemarie Haag. "The Invention of the Skyscraper: Notes on Its Diverse Histories." *Assemblage*. 2 (February 1987), 110–117.

Landau, Sarah Bradford, and Carl W. Condit. *Rise of the New York Skyscraper, 1865–1913*. New Haven: Yale University Press, 1996.

Revell, Keith D. "Regulating the Landscape: Real Estate Values, City Planning and the 1916 Zoning Ordinance." In *The Landscape of Modernity: New York City, 1900–1940*, ed. David Ward and Olivier Zunz. Baltimore: Johns Hopkins University Press, 1992.

Severini, Lois. *The Architecture of Finance: Early Wall Street*. Ann Arbor: UMI Research Press, 1983.

Stern, Robert A. M., Gregory Gilmartin, and John Montague Massengale. *New York 1900: Metropolitan Architecture and Urbanism 1890–1915*. New York: Rizzoli, 1983.

Weiss, Marc A. "Density and Intervention: New York's Planning Traditions." In *The Landscape of Modernity: New York City, 1900–1940*, ed. David Ward and Olivier Zunz. Baltimore: Johns Hopkins University Press, 1992.

CHAPTER TWO: THE CLIENTS

WALL STREET FINANCIAL DISTRICT

Atlas of the Borough of Manhattan. Philadelphia: G. W. Bromley & Company, 1921.

Berle, Adolf A., and Gardiner Means. *The Modern Corporation and Private Property*. New York: Macmillan Company, 1936.

Bierman, Harold, Jr. *The Causes of the 1929 Stock Market Crash*. Westport, Conn.: Greenwood Press, 1998.

"Big Boom on Wall Street." *Inside U.S. Trust*. April–May 1975.

Brooks, John. *Once in Golconda: A True Drama of Wall Street, 1920–1938*. New York: Harper & Row, 1969.

Cleveland, Harold Van B., and Thomas F. Huertas. *Citibank, 1812–1970*. Cambridge: Harvard University Press, 1985.

Collins, Frederick. *Money Town*. New York: G. P. Putnam, 1946.

Duffus, R. L. "The Principality We Call Wall Street." *New York Times Magazine*. 22 May 1932, 7, 18.

Encyclopedia of American Business History and Biography: Banking and Finance, 1913–1989, ed. Larry Schweikart. New York: Facts on File, 1990.

Geisst, Charles R. *Wall Street: A History*. New York: Oxford University Press, 1997.

Huertas, Thomas F., and Joan L. Silverman. "Charles E. Mitchell: Scapegoat of the Crash?" *Business History Review*. 60 (Spring 1986), 81–103.

International Directory of Company Histories. 27 vols. Chicago: St. James Press, 1988–99.

Lawrence, David. "American Business and Business Men." *Saturday Evening Post*. 26 July 1930, 34.

Levinson, Leonard Louis. *Wall Street: A Pictorial History*. New York: Ziff & Davis, 1961.

Manhattan Land Book. New York: G. W. Bromley, 1934.

Mayer, Martin. *Wall Street: Men and Money*. New York: Harper & Brothers, 1955.

Peterson, Jaffray. *Sixty-Five Years of Progress and A Record of New York City Banks*. New York: privately printed, 1935.

Rochester, Anna. *Wall Street*. New York: International Pamphlets, 1932.

Sanborn Map Company. *Manhattan Land Book of the City of New York: 1955*. Pelham, N. Y.: Sanborn Map Company, 1955.

Sobel, Robert. *The Age of Giant Corporations: A Microeconomic History of American Business, 1914–1970*. Westport, Conn.: Greenwood Press, 1972.

Weissman, Rudolph. *The New Wall Street*. New York: Harper & Brothers, 1939.

Wilson, John Donald. *The Chase: The Chase Manhattan Bank, N.A., 1945–1985*. Boston: Harvard Business School Press, 1986.

CITIES SERVICE COMPANY AND HENRY L. DOHERTY

Cities Service Company. *Annual Reports*. 1929–34. CSCC, Box 18, Folder 2.

"Doherty: Drops High-Power Sales of Cities Service Stock." *Newsweek*. 5 August 1933, 22–23.

"Doherty: Federal Inquiry Discloses His Huge Profits." *Newsweek*. 6 May 1923, 23–24.

"Doherty: A Locomotive Drive and a Memory Like an Elephant." *Newsweek*. 26 October 1935, 26–27.

Doherty, Henry L. *Principles and Ideas for Doherty Men: Papers, Addresses and Letters by Henry L. Doherty*, comp. Glenn Marston. 6 vols. New York: Henry L. Doherty & Company, 1923.

Doherty News. CSCC, Boxes 9, 14 , 17.

Ellis, William Donahue. *On the Oil Lands with Cities Service*. Tulsa: Cities Service Company, 1983.

Gibbons, Henry. "Cadet Schools of Business." *The Forum*. 8 (December 1917), 741–748.

Jones, W. Alton. *The Cities Service Story*. New York: Newcomen Society, 1955.

"'Ned the Newsboy' in Real Life." *Literary Digest*. 2 June 1923, 56, 58.

"Other People's Money." *New Republic*. 6 June 1934, 100–101.

Parsons, Floyd W. "A Skyscraper Home." *World's Work*. 43 (March 1922), 505–512.

Serving a Nation. New York: Henry L. Doherty & Company, 1923. CSCC, Box 26, Folder 1.

"This Millionaire Makes Science a Hobby." *Current Opinion*. 73 (December 1922), 737–738.

Who's Who in the Doherty Organization. 1930. CSCC, Box 43.

REAL ESTATE ECONOMICS

Ballard, Robert F. *Directory of Manhattan Office Buildings*. New York: McGraw-Hill, 1978.

Clark, W. C., and J. L. Kingston. *The Skyscraper: A Study in the Economic Height of Modern Office Buildings*. New York: American Institute of Steel Construction, 1930.

Keast, W. R. Morton, and A. B. Randall. "The Minimum Building for Varying Land Values." *Architectural Record*. 67 (April 1930), 375–395.

MacDonald, Gordon D. *Office Building Construction Manhattan 1901–1953*. New York: The Real Estate Board of New York, 1952.

"Obsolescence of Modern Skyscrapers." *The Architect and Engineer*. 104 (January 1931), 125–126.

Palmer, C. F. "Office Buildings From an Investments Standpoint." *Architectural Forum*. 52 (June 1930), 891–896.

"Reveals No Overproduction in Office Buildings." *Real Estate Record and Guide*. 24 August 1929, 7–8.

Robertson, Paul. "The Skyscraper Office Building." *Architectural Forum*. 52 (June 1930), 879–880.

Shachtman, Tom. *Skyscraper Dreams: The Great Real Estate Dynasties of New York*. Boston: Little, Brown & Company, 1991.

Shultz, Earle. "Build for Profit." *Skyscraper Management*. 16 (March 1931), 19–20.

Shultz, Earle. "The Office Building and the City." *Architectural Forum*. 41 (September 1924), 141.

"Skyscrapers: Pyramids in Steel and Stock." *Fortune*. August 1930, 60–61, 72–75.

Taylor, C. Stanley. "Financing the Office Building." *Architectural Forum*. 41 (September 1924), 137–139.

CHAPTER THREE: THE ARCHITECTS

Placzek, Adolf K, ed. *Macmillan Encyclopedia of Architects.* 4 vols. New York: Free Press, 1982.

Withey, Henry F., and Elsie Rathburn Withey. *Biographical Dictionary of American Architects (Deceased).* Los Angeles: Hennessey & Ingalls, 1970.

PROFESSIONAL PRACTICE

"Architects' Fee in Getting Business." *Architectural Record.* 69 (May 1931), 423–425.

Coley, Clarence T. "Office Buildings, Past, Present and Future." *Architectural Forum.* 41 (September 1924), 113–114.

Dalmas, Priscilla Ogden. "Simplified Practice for Drafting Room Efficiency." *Architectural Forum.* 56 (May 1932), 515–518.

Ellis, William Marshall. "The Architect and the Building Manager." *Architectural Forum.* 41 (September 1924), 135–136.

Francis, Dennis Steadman. *Architects in Practice New York City 1840–1900.* New York: Committee for the Preservation of Architectural Records, 1970.

Oliver, Richard, ed. *The Making of an Architect, 1881–1981: Columbia University in the City of New York.* New York: Rizzoli, 1981.

Taylor, Howell. "Organization in the Architect's Office." *Architectural Forum.* 39 (August 1923), 55–58.

Ward, James. *Architects in Practice: New York City, 1900–1940.* Union, N. J.: J. & D. Associates, 1989.

CLINTON & RUSSELL, HOLTON & GEORGE

"Architects of Today: Clinton & Russell." *Architecture.* 16 (15 July 1907), 102–125.

Clinton & Russell. *The Architects and Their Works.* 1 (14 November 1908).

Clinton & Russell, Holton & George. New York: Architectural Catalog Company, 192–.

L. R. E. P. "A Suggestion for Utilizing Blackwell's Island, New York, as a Site for Municipal Buildings." *House and Garden.* 6 (July 1904), 21–23.

ELY JACQUES KAHN

Kahn, E. J. "American Office Practice." *Journal of the Royal Institute of British Architects.* 64 (September 1957), 443–451.

Kahn, Ely J. "Economics of the Skyscraper." *Architectural Record.* 63 (April 1928), 298–301.

Kahn, Ely Jacques. *Ely Jacques Kahn, New York Architect.* Reprint with intro. and list of works by Françoise Bollack and Tom Killian. New York: Acanthus Press, 1995.

Kahn, Ely Jacques. "Sources of Inspiration." *Architecture.* 60 (November 1929), 249–256.

RALPH WALKER

Bzdak, Meredith Arms. "The Architecture of Ralph Thomas Walker: 1919–1939." Ph. D. dissertation. Rutgers, The State University of New Jersey, 1995.

Walker, Ralph. "Architecture." *North American Review.* 231 (June 1931), 528–531.

Walker, Ralph. "Architecture of To-Day." *Creative Art.* 5 (July 1929), 460–465.

Walker, Ralph. "Color in Architecture." *Architectural Record.* 63 (January 1928), 80.

Walker, Ralph. "Paper, Romance, and the Humble Architect." *American Architect.* 139 (April 1931), 28–29, 84, 86.

Walker, Ralph. *Ralph Walker, Architect.* New York: Henahan House, 1957.

Walker, Ralph. "The Relation of Skyscrapers to Our Life." *Architectural Forum.* 52 (May 1930), 687–695.

OTHER ARCHITECTS

"Arbiter of the Arts [Everett V. Meeks]." *Architectural Forum.* 86 (June 1947), 74–76, 152, 154.

Goldstone, Aline Lewis, and Harmon H. Goldstone. *Lafayette A. Goldstone: A Career in Architecture.* New York: privately printed,1964.

Gray, David. "Thomas Hastings: Memoir." In *Thomas Hastings, Architect: Collected Writings.* Boston: Houghton Mifflin, 1933.

H. Craig Severance, Architect. New York: Architectural Catalog Company, 1928.

Schwartz & Gross, Architects. New York: Architectural Catalog Company, 1927.

CHAPTER FOUR: PLANNING

Bailey, George R. "Analyzing Alternative Floor Plans." *Bulletin of the National Association of Building Owners and Managers.* 15 (March 1930), 183–184.

Bruner, Warren D. "Office Layouts for Tenants." *Architectural Forum.* 52 (June 1930), 905–908.

Corbett, Harvey Wiley. "The Planning of Office Buildings." *Architectural Forum.* 41 (September 1924), 89–93.

Fitzpatrick, F. W. "The 'Stepped Back' Building." *The Western Architect.* 30 (October 1921), 108.

Harmon, Arthur Loomis. "The Design of Office Buildings." *Architectural Forum.* 52 (June 1930), 819–820.

Kahn, Albert. "Designing Modern Office Building." *Architectural Forum.* 52 (June 1930), 775–777.

Kilham, Walter H., Jr. "Tower Floor Plans of New York Skyscrapers Compared." *American Architect.* 138 (October 1930), 30–31, 76, 78.

Kocher, A. Lawrence, and Albert Frey. "Planning Offices for Economy." *Architectural Record.* 72 (September 1932), 197–202.

Newman, James B. "Factors in Office Building Planning." *Architectural Forum.* 52 (June 1930), 881–890.

Shreve, R. H. "The Economic Design of Office Buildings." *Architectural Record.* 67 (April 1930), 340–359.

CHAPTER FIVE: CONSTRUCTION

Horowitz, Louis J., and Boyden Sparkes. *The Towers of New York: The Memoir of a Master Builder.* New York: Simon & Schuster, 1937.

Shreve, R. H. "The Empire State Building Organization." *Architectural Forum.* 52 (June 1930), 771–774.

"Skyscrapers: Builders and Their Tools." *Fortune.* October 1930, 85–94.

Starrett, Paul. *Changing the Skyline: An Autobiography.* New York: McGraw-Hill, 1938.

Willis, Carol, and Donald Friedman. *Building the Empire State.* New York: W. W. Norton, 1998.

CHAPTER SIX: TECHNOLOGY

Bahnam, Reyner. *The Architecture of the Well-Tempered Environment.* 2nd ed. Chicago: University of Chicago Press, 1984.

Belknap, B. H. "Modern Office Building Appliances." *Architectural Forum.* 41 (September 1924), 155–157.

Gray, G. W. "Every Modern Convenience." *World's Work.* 61 (February 1932), 34–38.

Lampugnani, Vittoria Magnago et al., eds. *Vertical: Lift Escalator Paternoster: A Cultural History of Vertical Transport,* trans. Robin Benson and Catherine Kerkhoff-Saxon. Berlin: Ernst & Sohn, 1994.

Meyer, Henry C. "Electrical, Heating and Ventilating Equipment of the Cunard Building." *Architectural Forum.* 35 (July 1921), 22–23.

Place, Clyde R. "The Mechanical Equipment of Office Buildings." *Architectural Forum.* 41 (September 1924), 147–152.

Ralston, Louis T. M. "The Engineer's Problem in Tall Buildings." *Architectural Forum.* 52 (June 1930), 909–920.

"Skyscrapers: Life on the Vertical." *Fortune.* November 1930, 77–80, 105.

CHAPTER SEVEN: EXTERIOR EXPRESSION

See "General Skyscrapers and Architecture" *above.*

CHAPTER EIGHT: INTERIOR DISTINCTION

"American Board Rooms: Directors and Decorations." *Fortune.* October 1931, 96–100.

"Architecture and Decoration in the Modern Office." *American Architect.* 128 (1 July 1925), 15–20.

Boyd, John Taylor, Jr. "Office Interiors." *Architectural Forum.* 41 (September 1924), 143–145.

Clute, Eugene. "Easy Fabricating." *American Architect.* 140 (November 1931), 42–47, 59.

De Brie, Sydney. "Decorating the Eight-Hour House." *Country Life.* 48 (October 1925), 116–120.

Dreyfuss, Henry. "The Modern Business Address." *Skyscraper Management.* 17 (August 1932), 9–10, 18.

"The Executive and His Office." *Fortune.* July 1930, 38–39.

Harmon, Arthur Loomis. "The Interior Architecture of Offices." *Architectural Forum.* 52 (June 1930), 862–865.

Lamb, William F. "Office Building Vestibules." *Architectural Forum.* 41 (September 1924), 105–108.

Van Vleck, Edward. "Materials and Maintenance." *Architectural Forum.* 41 (September 1924), 119–120.

CHAPTER NINE: SKYSCRAPER LIVES

Collins, William. "Our Queerest Building Custom." *Pencil Points.* 12 (March 1931), 179–182.

Harris, Neil. *Building Lives: Constructing Rites and Passages.* New Haven: Yale University Press, 1999.

Manhattan Address Telephone Directory. New York: New York Telephone Company, 1933.

OFFICE WORK

Cavan, Ruth Shonle. "The Girl Who Writes Your Letters." *Survey.* 15 July 1929, 438–439.

Coyle, Grace L. "The Clerical Worker and Her Job." *Survey.* 15 December 1928, 361.

Davies, Margery W. *Woman's Place Is at the Typewriter: Office Work and Office Workers, 1870–1930.* Philadelphia: Temple University Press, 1982.

Forty, Adrian. *Objects of Desire.* New York: Pantheon Books, 1986.

Heywood, Johnson. "Taking the Starch Out of White-Collar Workers." *World's Work.* 60 (September 1931), 58–59, 74.

Kwolek-Folland, Angel. *Engendering Business: Men and Women in the Corporate Office, 1870–1930.* Baltimore: Johns Hopkins University Press, 1994.

"Modernizing the Office." *Review of Reviews.* 83 (February 1931), 84–87.

"New Office Machines Change Clerking." *New York Times.* 29 April 1928, sec. 10, p. 3.

"The Plight of the White-Collar Army." *Literary Digest.* 7 June 1930, 69–70.

Rotella, Elyce J. "The Transformation of the American Office: Changes in Employment and Technology." *Journal of Economic History.* 41 (March 1981), 51–57.

"Salaries of Clerical Workers in New York City." *Monthly Labor Review.* 35 (July 1932), 171–172.

Strom, Sharon Hartman. *Beyond the Typewriter: Gender, Class, and the Origins of Modern American Office Work, 1900–1930.* Urbana: University of Illinois Press, 1992.

Urry, John. "The Growth of Scientific Management: Transformation in Class Structure and Class Struggle." In *Class and Space: The Making of Urban Society,* ed. Nigel Thrift and Peter Williams. London: Routledge & Kegan Paul, 1987.

"When Wall Street Calls Out the Reserves." *Business Week.* 11 December 1929, 36 , 38.

Zunz, Olivier. *Making America Corporate, 1870–1920.* Chicago: University of Chicago Press, 1990.

IN ART

Abbott, Berenice. *A Guide to Better Photography.* New York: Crown Publishers, 1945.

Abbott, Berenice, and Elizabeth McCausland. *Changing New York.* New York: E. P. Dutton & Company, 1939.

Anton Schutz: Etchings of New York City. Intro. by Barry Walker. New York: Harbor Gallery, 1985.

Bailey, Vernon Howe. *Skyscrapers of New York.* New York: William Edwin Rudge, 1928.

Bailey, Vernon Howe, and Arthur Bartlett Maurice. *Magical City: Intimate Sketches of New York.* New York: Charles Scribner's Sons, 1935.

Chave, Anna C. "'Who Will Paint New York?' 'The World's New Art Center' and the Skyscraper Paintings of Georgia O'Keeffe." *American Art.* 5 (Winter/Spring 1991), 86–107.

City Life: New York in the 1930s. New York: Whitney Museum of American Art, 1986.

Duffy, Betty, Douglas Duffy, and Janet A. Flint. *The Graphic Work of Howard Cook.* Bethesda, Md.: Bethesda Art Gallery, 1984.

Fine, Ruth E. *John Marin.* New York: Abbeville, 1990.

Flint, Janet. *The Prints of Louis Lozowick, A Catalogue Raisonné.* New York: Hudson Hills Press, 1982.

Hirshler, Erica E. "The New New York and the Park Row Building: American Artists View an Icon of the Modern Age." *American Art Journal.* 21/4 (1989), 26–45.

John Marin's New York. New York: Kennedy Galleries, 1981.

Levin, Gail. "The Office Image in the Visual Arts." *Arts Magazine.* 59 (September 1984), 98–103.

Lozowick, Louis. *Survivor From a Dead Age: The Memoirs of Louis Lozowick,* ed. Virginia Hagelstein Marquardt. Washington: Smithsonian Institution Press, 1997.

Oltar-Jevsky, W. K. *Contemporary Babylon.* New York: Architectural Book Publishing Company, 1933.

O'Neal, Hank. *Berenice Abbott: American Photographer.* New York: McGraw-Hill Book Company, 1982.

Ramirez, Jan Seidler, ed. *Painting the Town: Cityscapes of New York.* New York: Museum of the City of New York, 2000.

Ricciotti, Dominic. "Skyscrapers and Monuments: Images of the Skyscraper in American Art." *Landscape.* 25/2 (1981), 22–29.

Rub, Timothy. "American Architectural Prints." *Print Review.* 18 (1983), 6–19.

Schleier, Merrill. *The Skyscraper in American Art, 1890–1931.* New York: Da Capo, 1986.

Sussman, Elisabeth. *City of Ambition: Artists and New York, 1900–1960.* New York: Whitney Museum of American Art, 1996.

Taylor, Joshua C. *America as Art.* Washington: Smithsonian Institution, 1976.

Troyen, Carol, and Erica E. Hirshler. *Charles Sheeler: Paintings and Drawings.* Boston: Little, Brown & Company, 1987.

Walkowitz, Abraham. *Improvisations of New York: A Symphony in Lines.* Girard, Kansas: Haldeman-Julius Publications, 1948.

Weegee [Arthur Fellig]. *Weegee.* Intro. by André Laude. New York: Pantheon Books, 1986.

Weegee. *Weegee's People.* New York: Duell, Sloan & Pearce, 1946.

Yochelson, Bonnie. *Berenice Abbott: Changing New York.* New York: New Press, 1997.

Zabel, Barbara. "Louis Lozowick and Urban Optimism of the 1920s." *Archives of American Art Journal.* 14/2 (1974), 17–21.

NEW YORK CITY

Douglas, Ann. *Terrible Honesty: Mongrel Manhattan in the 1920s.* New York: Farrar, Straus & Giroux, 1995.

Jackson, Kenneth T. "The Capital of Capitalism: The New York Metropolitan Region, 1890–1940." In *Metropolis, 1890–1940,* ed. Anthony Sutcliffe. Chicago: University of Chicago Press, 1984.

Jackson, Kenneth T. *The Encyclopedia of New York City.* New Haven: Yale University Press, 1995.

Taylor, William R. *In Pursuit of Gotham: Culture and Commerce in New York.* New York: Oxford University Press, 1992.

Tobier, Emanuel. "Manhattan's Business District in the Industrial Age." In *Power, Culture & Place: Essays on New York City,* ed. John Hull Mollenkopf. New York: Russell Sage Foundation, 1988.

Ward, David, and Olivier Zunz, eds. *The Landscape of Modernity: New York City, 1900–1940.* Baltimore: Johns Hopkins University Press, 1992.

Cities Service (now AIG) Building at night.
Norman McGrath